Martyr of the American Revolution

Last Words of Captain Nathan Hale, Hero-Martyr of the American Revolution.
Alexander Hay Ritchie's 1858 engraving after the painting by Felix O. C. Darley.
Courtesy of the Yale University Art Gallery, New Haven, Conn.
Reproduced with permission.

Martyr *of the* American Revolution

The Execution *of*
Isaac Hayne, South Carolinian

C. L. Bragg

The University of South Carolina Press

© 2016 University of South Carolina

Published by the University of South Carolina Press
Columbia, South Carolina 29208

www.sc.edu/uscpress

Manufactured in the United States of America

25 24 23 22 21 20 19 18 17 16
10 9 8 7 6 5 4 3 2 1

Library of Congress Cataloging-in-Publication Data
can be found at http://catalog.loc.gov/.

ISBN: 978-1-61117-718-3 (cloth)
ISBN: 978-1-61117-719-0 (ebook)

This book was printed on recycled paper with
30 percent postconsumer waste content.

"Had the enemy wit enough to play a generous game, we should be ruined; but with *them* humanity is out of the question. They will treat the people with severity, rouse opposition in every quarter, and send recruits to our standard, till they accomplish their own destruction."

Attributed to Gen. Francis Marion in Alexander Garden,
Anecdotes of the Revolutionary War in America, 1822

Contents

Part III

Illustrations

Preface

On August 4, 1781, Col. Isaac Hayne was hanged by the British in Charleston, South Carolina. This book is not a biography of Isaac Hayne per se; neither is it a strict chronological retelling of the events that occurred in Charleston during the second summer of the thirty-two-month British occupation of that city, from May 1780 to December 1782. It is rather a consideration of factors that were independently set in motion and that culminated in the demise of a loving father and devout patriot. The death of a patriot in the cause of liberty is not a unique occurrence, but the unusually well-documented events surrounding the execution of Colonel Hayne and the involvement of his friends and family make his situation compelling and poignant. Unlike young Capt. Nathan Hale, who suffered a similar fate in 1776, Hayne did not become a folk hero but remained a rather tragic figure trapped by cruel choices while trying to cope with factors beyond his control.[1]

Writing of Isaac Hayne in his war memoir first published in 1812, Lt. Col. Henry "Light Horse Harry" Lee succinctly and accurately characterized the premise on which this book is predicated. "In a civil war," began Lee, "no citizen should expect or desire neutrality. Whoever attempts to place himself in that condition misunderstands human nature, and becomes entangled in toils always dangerous—often fatal. By endeavoring to acquire, with the most virtuous motive, a temporary neutrality, Hayne was unwisely led into a compact which terminated in his ruin." Lee was commenting about a man and an event that were well known to his contemporaries, not just in South Carolina but throughout North America and in England; Hayne's execution sparked perhaps the most notable controversy of the Revolutionary War. Yet his name today is as obscure as the little country cemetery in which he is buried.[2]

A modern historian rightly noted that "the American Revolutionary War is popularly remembered as a war fought in the northern states. The imagery of New England minuteman facing redcoats at Concord Bridge and the stories of Washington's frostbitten soldiers suffering through the frigid winter of 1777–1778 at Valley Forge are seared into Americans' collective historical subconscious." Notwithstanding, of equal importance are the oft-neglected events that transpired in the southern theater, and these also warrant close attention.[3]

Accepting the proposition that the Revolutionary War is popularly remembered as a war fought in the northern states, now say the words "martyr of the Revolutionary War." Who comes to mind? Nathan Hale, most likely, unless one lives in Charleston, South Carolina, and then Nathan Hale may still come to mind. But what if there was another martyr? From the South? And if so, then why has this patriot-martyr been relegated to obscurity beyond the borders of his home state? The answer to these questions, particularly the last one, is partly rooted in the intractable sectional ideology and pride that existed on both sides of the Mason-Dixon Line before and after the American Civil War.

A review of the historiography of the Revolutionary War reveals bitter regional disagreement over the importance of the roles played by the people of the North and South, a rift that developed among historians during the decades preceding the Civil War. Parallel to the political arguments over slavery and states' rights, historical authors and orators of that era developed regional biases and differed with one another, sometimes bitterly, over who fought harder, sacrificed more, died better, or made the greatest contribution to securing our liberty.[4]

This contention came to full fruition after Appomattox, when the North truly gained the upper hand through control of the publishing houses and our nation's historical narrative. The history of the Revolutionary War in the South became what one latter-day historian characterized as "historical terra incognita," at least for a time. Fortunately, interest in the South seemed to revive during the Bicentennial and has been on the upswing in the decades since.[5]

With sectional rhetoric put aside, let us now stipulate that there was indeed a patriot-martyr in the South. That being accomplished, comparisons are inevitable between the heroic and well-commemorated Captain Hale of Connecticut, who was hanged by the British as a spy in 1776, and the relatively obscure Colonel Hayne of South Carolina, who faced the hangman in 1781. One was a young, naive, eager-to-impress, patriotic idealist who volunteered for what many believed was a suicide mission. After being captured, he confessed, perhaps uttered the statement (or something like it)[6] that catapulted him into the pantheon of our nation's history, and swung from a scaffold before anyone on the American side knew what had happened to him. Denied a Bible and the comfort of a minister, Hale made no excuses and did not plead for his life.

The other gentleman was the most prominent American executed by the British for treason. Approaching his thirty-sixth birthday, Isaac Hayne was a member of South Carolina's lowcountry planter aristocracy. He certainly loved his country but was also a devoted husband and father who bore the heavy burdens that husbands and fathers bear. Presented with terribly difficult choices on two occasions, Hayne ultimately found himself irresistibly swept into the vortex of an unfortunate chain of events and circumstances that were not entirely of his own making. Requests for mercy fell on deaf ears. After the noose was placed around his neck, he was given the opportunity to say his last words. Instead of giving a stirring patriotic speech, he remanded his children to the care of friends before signaling that he was ready to meet his doom.[7]

Aside from their similar endings, Hale and Hayne shared another commonality— they were used to prove just how serious the British were about enforcing policy. Hale's quick summary execution demonstrated to one and all that the British would deal harshly with captured spies. Hayne's hanging perfectly illustrated, in a broad sense, that treason would not be tolerated, though in a narrow sense it can be argued that anger and frustration on the part of two British officers, Lt. Col. Nisbet Balfour and Lt. Col. Francis Lord Rawdon, helped Hayne earn his sentence.[8]

"Had British authorities executed Isaac Hayne early in the Revolution rather than on August 4, 1781, he might now be remembered as a patriot martyr of Nathan Hale stature," observed David K. Bowden in the preface of his 1977 monograph, *The Execution of Isaac Hayne,* published during the Bicentennial. Hayne's great-grandson Franklin B. Hayne would have agreed with Bowden. He pointedly stated in 1905 that if his ancestor had been executed in Boston instead of Charleston, "a monument would have been erected to him quite as high as the Bunker Hill monument, while in South Carolina no one even knows where he is buried." The descendant Hayne was bothered that both Hale's home state of Connecticut and the nation had furnished monuments in his honor, yet in South Carolina nothing had been done for his great-grandfather, who he thought was at least equally deserving. Not until 1929 was Isaac Hayne honored with a memorial.[9]

Returning momentarily to historiography, the British historian Mark Urban notes that biases exist because of Britons' and Americans' different perspectives on the Revolutionary War. As victors, Americans have controlled the narrative (much the same as did the North after the American Civil War), the Hayne story in particular, painting his British antagonists in the worst possible light. I concur with Urban that Americans "tend to overestimate British military efficiency at the beginning of the war, and underestimate it at the end. Inventive leadership, enthusiasm, and bravery are virtues that many American writers expect to find only in the ranks of Washington's army." Americans therefore stereotype the redcoat[10] as a brutalized robot.[11]

I have been guilty of that predisposition in the past and have attempted to be evenhanded in the treatment of Balfour and Rawdon. Though linked by and vilified for a single heinous act, they were not dishonorable men and gave their king and country good service. But while I find myself in general agreement with Bowden's thesis that Hayne's execution was ultimately a result of misguided

British policy, a perception of meanness and unrepentant vindictiveness born of desperation on the part of Balfour and Rawdon is inescapable. There is a rational explanation for this perception.

One factor is that reports of unwarranted harshness attributed to Balfour and Rawdon may accurately reflect the reality of the circumstances. However, the reader should be aware that both intentional and unintentional pro-American and anti-British biases are found in the primary and early secondary sources and are difficult to keep out of the narrative. The earliest published accounts of the Isaac Hayne story were probably contaminated by hearsay, and only one of these accounts was an eyewitness report. The other versions originated with men who either knew Hayne personally or were temporally if not geographically so close to his execution that their emotional reaction clouded their objectivity. Nor can British accounts be considered completely reliable. Whatever British records were kept concerning the Hayne affair disappeared soon after the event, and the recollections of Rawdon, set to paper more than three decades later, are remarkably self-serving if not suspect for their uncommon clarity. It is fair to say that men on both sides of the argument engaged in hypocrisy, and it is for The reader to decide to whom belongs the greater guilt.[12]

To understand the tragedy and the repercussions of the death of Isaac Hayne at the hands of his two antagonists, Nisbet Balfour and Francis Rawdon, the first chapter of this book examines the series of events that set Hayne on a collision course with Balfour and Rawdon. The next two chapters are devoted to the lives of Balfour and Rawdon in an attempt to shed light on why these two professional soldiers were driven to commit a seemingly wrongheaded and rather arbitrary deed that halted prisoner exchange and nearly brought disastrous consequences to captive British officers. The fourth through sixth chapters address the life of Isaac Hayne, his capture, and the legal wrangling that preceded his hanging.

The story does not end with the demise of our protagonist. If the British used Hayne to make a point and to serve as a deterrent to would-be traitors, the plan backfired, and his death became an effective instrument of propaganda for the Americans. The final chapters address the consequences of Hayne's death and how an obscure militia officer became a topic of discussion among the upper echelons of the military command and in the legislative halls of the opposing sides. While the story of Isaac Hayne naturally became a part of America's early historical narrative, his life and dramatic execution were also integrated into early American compositional art and literature. A survey of the Hayne story as rendered in drawing, painting, poetry, drama, and prose is found in the final chapter of this book.

Acknowledgments

To South Carolina's historians of the past and present I am indebted beyond measure: David Ramsay, William Moultrie, Alexander Garden, William Gilmore Simms, Edward McCrady, David K. Bowden, Carl P. Borick, and Walter B. Edgar. Their collective writings laid the groundwork for my study of the events surrounding the execution of Isaac Hayne. In addition, the work of Mark Urban and Paul David Nelson provided the basis for the material about this book's two antagonists.

My friends Charles B. Baxley, of Lugoff, S.C.; R. Douglas MacIntyre, of Charleston; and William R. Raiford, of Thomasville, Ga., provided invaluable editorial guidance, and I am also particularly obliged to Alexander Moore, acquisitions editor at the University of South Carolina Press in Columbia, who shepherded me through the publication process with wisdom and compassion.

Along the way I received the enthusiastic assistance of a number of individuals: Daniel J. Bell, historic resource coordinator of the South Carolina State Park Service in Charleston; Carl P. Borick, director of the Charleston Museum in Charleston; Vicki C. Brown, reference librarian at the Colleton County Memorial Library in Walterboro, S.C.; Michael D. Coker, operations assistant at the Old Exchange Building and Provost Dungeon in Charleston; Wade H. Dorsey, reference archivist at the South Carolina Department of Archives and History in Columbia; Graham Duncan, manuscript specialist at the South Caroliniana Library, University of South Carolina, in Columbia; Virginia L. Ellison, archivist, and Mary Jo Fairchild, director of archives and research at the South Carolina Historical Society in Charleston; Tyler Gilmore, of the research and instructional services staff at the Louis Round Wilson Special Collections Library at the University of North Carolina in Chapel Hill, N.C.; James N. Green, librarian, and Nicole Joniec, print department assistant and digital collections manager, both at the Library Company of Philadelphia in Philadelphia, Pa.; Jane E. Hamilton of Charleston; Rachel Jirka, research services librarian at the Society of the Cincinnati in Washington, D.C.; Angela B. McGuire, at the Thomas County Public Library in Thomasville, Ga.; Anna Smith, special collections librarian at the

Charleston Library Society in Charleston; Sarah Sturtevant, operations specialist at the South Carolina Department of Parks, Recreation and Tourism in Columbia; and Walter and Helen Taylor of Columbia.

Finally, a special thank you goes to my wife, Kim, and to my three sons, Chris, Taylor, and Thomas. They have always wholeheartedly supported my compulsion to write about the people and events that shaped our nation's historical narrative.

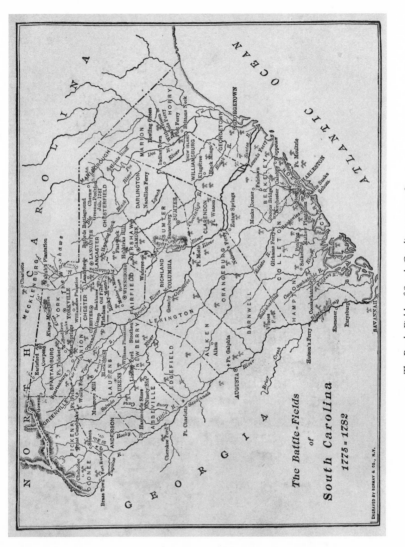

The Battle-Fields of South Carolina, 1775–1780.

Edward McCrady, *The History of South Carolina in the Revolution, 1780–1783* (New York: Macmillan, 1902), ii.

Prologue

The appointed hour had finally arrived. Colonel Hayne walked to the place of his execution, preferring to travel by foot rather than endure the degradation of riding in a cart. Even so, he bore the indignity of having his arms pinioned. The cart that followed was empty, except for the driver and one other thing: the coffin that had been thrust into his cell the night before in a wanton act of cruelty. Along the way he was accompanied by a friend who carried an umbrella to shade his hatless head from the searing August sun. A clergyman and a few of Hayne's other friends trod behind.[1]

Hayne regarded the familiar streets of Charleston as he purposefully strode toward his destiny. The streets were crowded with thousands of anxious spectators, yet the morning was dolefully silent aside from the rattle and tramp of Hayne's military escort. A few bystanders quietly offered words of encouragement or a "God bless and keep you, Colonel." Many wept.[2]

The dreaded destination was just beyond the city lines at a place within a stone's throw of where the Orphan House would later be built. Upon reaching the outskirts, the soldiers formed a hollow square around the scaffold, the British troops occupying the front and rear and the Hessians forming on the right and left. The hangman, masked and muffled to conceal his identity, patiently waited to perform his grim duty.[3]

To the British, Hayne was a traitor. To Americans, he would be a martyr.

"Let the prisoner prepare himself."[4]

Part I

Sir Henry Clinton.
Engraving by Alexander H. Ritchie after a painting by John Smart. Author's collection.

Chapter 1

The British Violate Their Terms and Rule by Edict

Lt. Gen. Sir Henry Clinton should have kept his word. Instead, after concluding a successful campaign to capture Charleston, South Carolina, in May
1780 he initiated a cascade of events that not only climaxed with the hanging of
a patriot but also vastly altered the tone and course of the Revolutionary War in
the South. Born about 1730 in Newfoundland, he was the only son of George
Clinton, an admiral in the Royal Navy who also served as governor of colonial
Newfoundland in 1731 and as governor of New York from 1743 to 1753. Little is
known of Henry's early life. His wife, Harriet, bore him five children in five years
of marriage until her death in 1772, a loss that left him emotionally devastated. He
was an able soldier but known to be prickly and quarrelsome, often aloof, insensi-
tive, and at times petulant. After studying his voluminous writings and consulting
with his biographer, a psychologist inferred that Clinton was compulsive, neurotic,
blame-shifting, self-defeating, and guilt-ridden. In reality he was a paradox; he
resented authority while under it, was greedy for it, yet was uncomfortable when
wielding it. During his career he proved himself to be a troublesome subordinate,
a trying colleague, and a vexing superior.[1]

Clinton became a provincial army officer in New York in 1745 and a regular British army officer in 1751. Because of his distinguished service in Germany
during the Seven Years' War, he ascended through the ranks of the officer corps
so that by the time he landed in Boston in 1775 he had attained the rank of major
general. He exhibited coolness and initiative under fire at Bunker Hill on June
17, 1775. The following year he failed to capture Sullivan's Island, South Carolina, in his first independent army command, yet in recognition of his conspicuous gallantry during the capture of New York he was promoted to lieutenant
general and knighted by George III. In 1778 he succeeded Lt. Gen. Sir William
Howe as commander in chief of British forces in North America. It was while
moving his army from Philadelphia to New York that he fought Washington
to a stalemate in a pitched battle at Monmouth Courthouse on June 28, 1778.[2]

"I put out my proclamation."[3] When the usually verbose Sir Henry penned his journal entry for May 25, 1780, this terse statement was all he said about what was arguably his greatest error of generalship in the war. Clinton had only weeks before presided over the surrender of besieged Charleston. If he indeed erred, and it will be subsequently shown that he did, then what predisposed him to make such a gross miscalculation? The deposed royal governors of North and South Carolina and Virginia had convinced British authorities that most of the inhabitants of the South remained loyal British subjects, lacking only arms and support to restore order. This long-held assumption dated as far back as the 1775–1776 southern campaign that ended abruptly at Sullivan's Island on June 28, 1776. Now, four years later, the American secretary, Lord George Germain, and Sir Henry still believed that this assessment was accurate—that the inhabitants were disenchanted with the patriot government and tired of the devastation and privation of war. These suppositions turned out to be horribly wrong, and instead of capitalizing on their ascendancy, the British would inadvertently galvanize their opposition's determination to resist.[4]

Charleston, South Carolina, is located on a peninsula formed by the confluence of the Ashley River, from the northwest, and the Cooper River, from the northeast. At the time of the Revolutionary War, Charleston was the economic, social, and political epicenter of colonial South Carolina and the most important city in the South. As such, the British viewed the seaport as a prime target as early as 1776. The capture of Charleston would conceivably launch a restoration of royal government in the region. Two attempts to accomplish this goal were frustrated, first by the defeat of Commodore Sir Peter Parker's naval squadron by Col. William Moultrie and his resolute South Carolinians, who defended an unfinished fort of palmetto logs and sand on Sullivan's Island on June 28, 1776. Moultrie again repulsed the British from the landward side of Charleston in May 1779.

It was Henry Clinton, still a major general and General Howe's second-in-command, who had developed the strategy for the first southern campaign in 1776, but he and Commodore Parker failed to come up with a cogent plan for a cooperative overland and naval assault on Fort Sullivan. Due to poor reconnaissance of an inlet that turned out to be too deep to ford, Clinton and his troops were consigned to the role of tactical spectators on Long Island (present-day Isle of Palms), across Breach Inlet from the north end of Sullivan's Island. Meanwhile, Parker's attempt to batter into submission the heavily outgunned South Carolinians holding Fort Sullivan was a bloody disaster for the Royal Navy.[5]

Charleston barely survived a second British challenge in 1779, but in March 1780 Clinton, now a lieutenant general, was back with a third superior army.

Employing formal siege operations, by the end of April he had invested the town. Never before had an American general allowed a Continental army to be trapped in a besieged town, but that is exactly what happened. Maj. Gen. Benjamin Lincoln, commanding the Southern Department, believed that Charleston was defensible or could be held at least long enough for reinforcements to lift a siege. He refused to evacuate his troops before Clinton's redcoats severed all avenues of escape. And so Charleston became the greatest disaster to befall an American army during the war. Lincoln surrendered his 5,600 Continentals and militiamen to the British on May 12, 1780.[6]

Under the terms of the articles of capitulation agreed upon by Generals Clinton and Lincoln, the Continental troops and sailors would remain prisoners of war until they were exchanged, whereas "the militia now in garrison shall be permitted to return to their respective homes as prisoners upon parole, which parole, as long as they observe, shall secure them from being molested in their property by the British troops." The signed parole read, "I do hereby acknowledge myself to be a prisoner of war, upon my parole, to his Excellency, Sir Henry Clinton, and that I am thereby engaged, until I shall be exchanged, or otherwise released therefrom, to remain in the town of Charleston, unless when permitted to go out by the commandant; and that I shall not, in the meantime, do, or cause any thing to be done, prejudicial to the success of his majesty's arms, or have intercourse or hold correspondence with his enemies; and that upon a summons from his Excellency, or other person having authority thereto, that I will surrender myself to him or them at such time and place, as I shall hereafter be required."[7]

So much for the Continental soldiers and militiamen in Charleston. What about militiamen who were not members of Charleston's garrison? Brig. Gen. Thomas Sumter's militia was active in the faraway backcountry, but the militia units that would later operate in the lowcountry under the commands of Brig. Gen. Francis Marion and Col. William Harden were yet to organize. It appears that after Charleston surrendered, the militiamen who were not part of the garrison reasonably believed that the articles of capitulation also applied to them. They disbanded and went home to quietly await the outcome of the war.[8]

Clinton was fully confident of continued British success in South Carolina. Before departing for New York and leaving Lt. Gen. Charles Earl Cornwallis in command of British forces, he inaugurated a new policy, first advertised in the form of a handbill (Appendix A), that he supposed would ensure the reestablishment of peace and good government for the rest of the province. To this end he called for a revitalized force of loyalists who would be expected, if necessary to maintain good order, to take up arms against their neighbors, their friends, and, in many instances, their kinsmen. In this scheme there would be no neutrals, "but that every man, who did not avow himself an enemy to the British government, should take an active part in its support."[9]

Clinton then issued a series of three proclamations (Appendix A) over the next twelve days to expand, clarify, and reinforce his nonneutrality policy. The first two proclamations, issued on May 22 and June 1,[10] assured the king's faithful and peaceful subjects that they would meet with effectual countenance (appropriate oversight), protection, and support. Once civil government and peace were restored, they would receive "full possession of that liberty in their persons and property which they had before experienced under the British government." Clinton also promised mercy and forgiveness to those deluded subjects who had been "perverted from their duty by the factious arts of self-interested and ambitious men," but only if they would "immediately return to their allegiance, and a due obedience to those laws and that government which they formerly boasted was their best birthright and noblest inheritance." Once they had proved their sincerity, they would be granted a full and free pardon for the treasonable offenses that they had committed.[11]

Persistent transgressors "who, notwithstanding their present hopeless situation . . . are nevertheless still so hardened in their guilt, as to endeavour to keep alive the flame of rebellion in this province" were to be excluded. Clinton emphatically stated "that if any person hereafter appear in arms, in order to prevent the establishment of his majesty's government in this country . . . or who shall hinder or intimidate . . . the King's faithful and loyal subjects from joining his forces . . . such person or persons so offending shall be treated with that severity so criminal and hardened an obstinacy will deserve, and his or their estates will be immediately seized in order to be confiscated." Allegiance and protection versus punishment and confiscation were the choices, but there were additional expectations. To root out rebellion and readily restore peace and prosperity to what he called a "desolated and distracted country," Clinton commanded all persons to assist the British army whenever and however possible.[12]

About this time word reached Charleston that a force of 150 loyalists and British cavalry led by Lt. Col. Banastre Tarleton had overtaken and soundly defeated more than 400 retreating Virginia Continentals under Col. Abraham Buford on May 29, 1780, killing 113, wounding 150, and taking 53 prisoners. News of the Battle of Waxhaws, or the so-called Waxhaws Massacre because the British refused quarter to Americans who had thrown down their arms, cast a deep pall on the already disheartened people of Charleston.

A third proclamation, posted on June 3, had a more direct affect on the militiamen who had been captured in Charleston or who had voluntarily surrendered themselves as prisoners and then afterward been dismissed on their paroles. The recent surrender of Charleston and the defeat and dispersion of the rebel forces had, in Clinton's view, rendered paroles unnecessary. Therefore, he instructed that all persons, militiamen and civilians alike, "should take an active part in settling and securing His Majesty's government, and delivering the country from that anarchy which for some time hath prevailed." Clinton thus declared that all of the inhabitants of South Carolina who were prisoners on parole and who were not part of the Continental garrison of Charleston at the time of capitulation and surrender or who at the time of surrender were already confined as prisoners would be from June 20 on released from their paroles and restored to all the rights of loyal subjects. And as loyal subjects they had an expressed duty to serve in the loyal militia.[13]

But there was a catch! All persons meeting his description who failed to sign an oath of allegiance and to swear fealty to His Majesty's government would be considered enemies and rebels and treated accordingly. Over time, those who previously had been on parole with an expectation of being protected in their persons and property were subjected to depredations at the hands of the British army and loyalist militia unless they committed to the British. The estates of the holdouts were indiscriminately plundered and devastated, their slaves were carried off, their livestock confiscated, their houses put to the torch, and their crops destroyed. They were frequently insulted and threatened, often cruelly beaten, and occasionally butchered. There was little if any distinction between those actively engaged in rebellion and those who hoped to sit out the war in peace. Since there was no parole for American militiamen and no neutrality for anyone, the citizens were forced to commit to one side or the other. The harsh treatment suffered at the hands of the British pushed many of those who would have preferred to remain quietly at home back to the American side.[14]

Charles Cornwallis, second Earl and first Marquess Cornwallis, is the best remembered of the British officers who served on the North American continent during the Revolutionary War. He was born into an aristocratic family in 1738 and schooled at Eton, later studying strategy and tactics at the military academy in Turin, Italy, an unusual step for a young nobleman with a purchased commission (secured in 1756, when he was not quite eighteen years of age). The Seven Years' War brought ample opportunities for him to acquire battlefield experience; he served with distinction and rose through the ranks accordingly. Cornwallis had everything going for him when he came to America in 1776 as a major general: noble birth, a solid education, proven talent and ability, close ties to the monarch, and political experience from having served in both houses of Parliament. Yet his would be the name most closely associated with British defeat.[15]

For most of the war Cornwallis served as second in command to Clinton, first on the abortive attempt to take Charleston and then during the battles that led to the capture of New York in 1776. Alongside Clinton he gave a rather good account of himself in New Jersey at the Battle of Brandywine on September 11, 1777, and again at Monmouth Courthouse on June 28, 1778. Cornwallis had come to America against the entreaties of his wife, Jemima, and he returned home for a time when she became dangerously ill. After her death in 1779, he again offered his services to the king and rejoined Clinton's army in New York. As was the case with everyone in similar circumstances, it seems, the longer Cornwallis served under Sir Henry the worse their relationship became, though their relations improved somewhat when Clinton left him with independent command of South Carolina after the capitulation of Charleston in 1780.[16]

Out in the field, General Cornwallis was surprised and startled to read a copy of Clinton's June 1 proclamation. Writing from the British outpost at Camden to Charleston's commandant Brig. Gen. James Patterson on June 10, he expressed grave doubts about Clinton's "idea of granting indiscriminate protections, by which means some of the most violent rebels and persecutors of the whole province are declared faithful subjects, and are promised to be protected in their persons and properties." In the view of Cornwallis, only those men who joined the loyalist militia could be trusted. All others should be obliged to give up their protection, given paroles as prisoners of war, and exiled to the islands on the coast.[17]

The prominent Charleston physician and historian Dr. David Ramsay noted in *The History of the Revolution in South Carolina* that "while some of the inhabitants were felicitating themselves in having a respite from the calamities of war, they were no less astonished than confounded by the proclamation by which they were called to take arms in support of royal government." This forcing of the issue—compelling men to declare for one side or the other—virtually ensured that war in South Carolina would continue. In his memoirs William Moultrie observed that "this violation of all faith, this ill-grounded policy, enrolled into the American service, thousands of their citizens, who had indulged themselves with the pleasing hopes of remaining neuter until the end of the war; but they said, 'if we must fight let it be on the side of America, our friends and countrymen.'" The British thus unwittingly dug themselves into a hole from which there would be no extrication.[18]

What Clinton had accomplished by issuing these proclamations, the last one in particular, was multifold. First, he unilaterally altered the terms that he had granted to the American combatants at Charleston, terms that had been accepted in good faith by the Americans while they still had arms in their hands. "[T]he surrender had been upon terms," wrote Edward McCrady, "—terms, it is true, dictated by the conquerors, but still upon terms. . . . Sir Henry Clinton had obtained the surrender of the garrison of Charlestown upon a contract and pledge that the militia and citizens should be treated as prisoners of war on parole, and the same terms had been held out and granted to others who would come in and surrender." Clinton was concerned by reports that a French fleet had set sail for North America, raising the possibility of a forthcoming attack for the relief of Charleston or perhaps New York. Therefore it was vital for him to ensure the capitulation of Charleston as expeditiously as possible without the losses that would result from a direct assault on the rebel defensive works.[19]

Second, by forcing a difficult choice upon the inhabitants, he subdivided them into three groups. There were true loyalists who had always borne allegiance to the Crown, even before British occupation. Next were those on parole who believed they now had an absolute right to rejoin the rebels after the June 3 proclamation, which stated that after June 20 "they were released from every engagement to their conquerors." Finally, in between were the many who had accepted their paroles with an expectation that they would be allowed to reside unmolested on their estates at full liberty to carry on their private business. They were motivated by fear or convenience to submit to protection, but, according to David Ramsay, they still "retained an affection for their American brethren in the other states, and shuddered at the thought of taking arms against them."[20]

On the basis of their subsequent conduct, said Ramsay, it is fair to assume that many of the third group gave allegiance to the Crown "with a secret reservation of breaking the compulsory tie when a proper opportunity would present itself. Had this severe alternative never been offered, and had the people been indulged in the quiet possession of their property and their domestick [sic] ease," American forces might not have been able to ultimately wrestle the state out of the hands of the British.[21]

General Clinton would rationalize this last proclamation as a means to expel rebels who were unwilling to swear allegiance to the Crown: "This I looked upon as a most prudent measure, because under the sanction of those paroles a great number of inveterate rebels might remain in the country, and by their underhand and secret counsel and other machinations prevent the return of many well disposed persons to their allegiance, or [in] other ways retard the restoration of tranquillity and order. But by thus obliging every man to declare and evince his principles I gave the loyalists an opportunity of detecting and chasing from among them such dangerous neighbors, which they could not with any propriety have attempted as long as those paroles continued in force and the persons sanctioned by them were not guilty of an open breach of their promise."[22]

It is no small irony that in his first proclamation Clinton reviled the "deluded subjects . . . [the] wicked and desperate men, who, regardless of the ruin and misery in which the country will be involved, are still endeavouring to support the flame of rebellion, and, under pretense of authority derived from the late usurped legislatures, are attempting, by enormous fines, grievous imprisonments, and sanguinary punishments, to compel his majesty's faithful and unwilling subjects to take up arms against his authority and government." These are exactly the same measures that the British would themselves adopt in order to compel cooperation with their policies. In time this abuse of power would be an integral part of their own undoing because droves of would-be noncombatants, infuriated rather than cowed, would return to American arms.[23]

The last royal governor of North Carolina, Josiah Martin, attributed Clinton's policy to misguided leniency that was utterly abortive and prejudicial to British affairs: "It was clearly seen by every man of the commonest reflection in this army and was accordingly lamented and I may truly add generally reprobated." Clinton later attempted to distance himself from the bad effects of his third proclamation and to shift the blame to others. "But, as I did not remain there myself to watch its progress and assist its operation," he wrote rather defensively, "I shall not take upon me to disprove the evil consequences ascribed to it since, as from the powers I gave Lord Cornwallis I cannot think myself responsible for them. I may, however, venture to avow the goodness of my intention and the strong probability there was at the time of its success."[24]

Moultrie had quite a bit to say about those persons who took British protection under duress. "A great many exchanged their paroles for protections . . . many at first refused, some were persuaded, and others threatened that if they did not sign, they would be informed against." And in some cases he thought it not an unpardonable sin: "The taking protection, and remaining quiet was no great offence; it was unavoidable with many. I advised several of my friends, after the fall of Charleston (who were not in the Continental Army) to take that step, and to stay with their families, till we could come in force to release them." Moultrie implied by this statement that if American forces were to regain control of a region, the forsworn allegiances would become null and void.[25]

Left in command of the southern theater when Clinton returned to New York in June 1780, Cornwallis was more explicit about how the rebels should be treated. Soon after he routed Maj. Gen. Horatio Gates's Continental army at Camden, on August 16, 1780, he wrote to Lt. Col. John Harris Cruger, the loyalist officer commanding the British fort at the settlement of Ninety Six: "I have given orders that all the inhabitants of this province, who have subscribed and taken part in this revolt, should be punished with the greatest rigor; also, that those who will not turn out [for militia duty], may be imprisoned, and their whole property taken from them, and destroyed. I have also ordered that satisfaction should be made for their estates, to those who have been injured and oppressed by them. I have ordered, in the most positive manner, that *every militia man who has borne arms with us and afterwards joined the enemy, shall be immediately hanged* [emphasis added]. I desire you will take the most vigorous measure to punish the rebels in the district in which you command, and that you will obey, in the strictest manner, the directions I have given in this letter, relative to the inhabitants of this country."[26]

Cornwallis was not making idle threats, and a number of men were hanged at Camden and elsewhere. This is the only instance in which Cornwallis's public orders directed capital punishment, and it prompted a terse exchange between George Washington and Henry Clinton in October 1780 over the implementation of harsh measures to enforce British edicts that were contrary to the terms of the Charleston articles of capitulation. But when Cornwallis wrote these words the British still had the upper hand. Charleston had fallen, crushing victories had been won in the backcountry, and the province of South Carolina appeared to have been subdued. True, the Continental Army had ceased to exist, but the war was far from over.[27]

"The revolutionary struggle in Carolina was of a sort utterly unknown in any other part of the Union," wrote William Gilmore Simms in his 1844 biography of Francis Marion. After the surrender of Charleston and the devastating Continental defeats at Waxhaws and at Camden, the Revolutionary War in the South devolved into a vicious and bitter civil conflict between the friends of liberty and the adherents of the Crown. Heavyhanded tactics employed by both patriots and loyalists alike combined to convert former friends, neighbors, and brothers into determined and deadly foes. "Motives of private anger and personal revenge embittered and increased the usual ferocities of civil war," Simms said, and, indeed, the entire population of the colony seemed to divide itself into opposing armed camps. The ensuing warfare war laid waste to the countryside.[28]

At a time when the Continental army in the South was impotent, the partisan militias rose to the task of challenging their loyalist counterparts and British regulars. Notwithstanding a reputation in other parts of the country for being badly equipped, poorly led, and generally unreliable, the South Carolina militiamen and partisans harassed and distracted a superior enemy, threatened its supply lines, and inspirited their oppressed countrymen. Simms, a great admirer of the partisans, insisted that, "but for this militia, and the great spirit and conduct manifested by the partisan leaders in Carolina, no regular force which Congress would or could have sent into the field, would have sufficed for the recovery of the two almost isolated States of South Carolina and Georgia."[29]

In time the tide of the war began to shift, and British primacy was put to the test. First were the stunning American victories at Kings Mountain on October 7, 1780, and at Cowpens on January 17, 1781. The series of British setbacks in the South provoked an increasing sense of desperation. Lt. Col. Nisbet Balfour, whom Cornwallis assigned to the post of commandant at Charleston in mid-August 1780, informed Clinton in New York on May 6, 1781, that, notwithstanding Lt. Col. Francis Lord Rawdon's brilliant success at Hobkirk's Hill, near Camden, on April 25, he feared for the safety of Charleston. "The general state of the country is most distressing," wrote Balfour, adding that enemy parties were everywhere. He was cut off from Savannah, Augusta was invested, the village of Ninety Six, in backcountry South Carolina, was in a most crucial situation, and "the defection of this province [is] so universal that I know no mode short of depopulation to retain it."[30]

Rawdon was obliged to evacuate Camden later that very month. An American army recaptured Augusta, Georgia, from the British on June 6 and very nearly captured the fort at Ninety Six a couple of weeks later. Ninety Six was finally abandoned by the British in July. All the while, patriot militias in South Carolina, their ranks swelled by Clinton's third proclamation, enjoyed a resurgence and varying degrees of success under Gens. Francis Marion, Andrew Pickens, and Thomas Sumter, taking Orangeburg and other British-held outposts.

The concluding paragraph in Balfour's May 6, 1781, dispatch to Clinton deserves particular attention. Referring to those who had taken protection but had subsequently found occasion to take up arms and rise against the British, Balfour determined that it was advisable "to make the most striking examples of such." He closed the letter without further amplification, but subsequent events show that he had something particular in mind.[31]

The most Noble Marquis Cornwallis, K.G.
Daniel Orme's 1794 engraving after the 1786 painting by John Smart.
From the Anne S. K. Brown Military Collection, John Hay Library,
Brown University, Providence, Rhode Island. Reproduced with permission.

Chapter 2

A Proud and Haughty Scot
Takes Command of Charleston

Nisbet Balfour was born at Dunbog parish in the Scottish shire of Fife on January 20, 1743. Contrary to assertions in some quarters that he was the son of a small Edinburgh bookseller, he came from a noble if not wealthy family that possessed a strong military heritage. He may have attended the University of St. Andrews for a term or two but did not complete his studies there. Instead, at the age of eighteen he purchased a commission in the British army and joined the Fourth (The King's Own) Regiment of Foot as an ensign in 1761.[1]

Balfour was promoted to lieutenant in 1765 and rose to the rank of captain in 1770. The regiment embarked for America in May 1774 and camped on the Boston Common in June of that year. Elements of the Fourth Regiment were involved in the Battle of Lexington, on April 19, 1775, though Balfour is not thought to have been on the march that day. He did, however, take his light company into the bloody maelstrom of Bunker Hill on the horrendously hot day of June 17. In the face of withering musketry poured down on them from the entrenchments above, the King's Own carried the heights at bayonet point, driving off three times their number. Balfour went into battle with a full company but came out with only five men, himself slightly wounded in the abdomen during the fighting when a musket ball struck his cartridge box. He again fought with his regiment during the rout of Washington's army at the Battle of Brooklyn Heights, on August 27, 1776.[2]

For his conspicuous service Balfour was promoted to brevet major and assigned to the staff of General Howe as aide-de-camp. Howe honored Balfour by sending him home to England bearing dispatches detailing British successes in New York. Formal promotion to major came the following November. He developed a very close personal and professional relationship with Howe, so much so that other officers believed that Balfour held undue sway over the general and suspected that he pushed Howe to adopt brutal measures meant to bring the rebellion to a more rapid end.[3]

After defeating Washington's Continental army at Brandywine on September 11, 1777, Howe's redcoats captured the American capital, Philadelphia. Part of his army occupied the city, and the rest camped at Germantown. Taking advantage of Howe's divided force, Washington launched a well-planned but poorly coordinated assault on Germantown in the predawn hours of October 4. The Americans were encouraged by success early in the battle, but a British rally took advantage of American confusion and the redcoats retained possession of the field at the end of the day.

While the British occupied Philadelphia, Balfour was involved in matters of intelligence. A rumor circulated that the British had been surprised at Germantown because of Balfour's ineptitude or laziness—that he had refused to get out of bed to question an American deserter who had brought word of the attack. It is more likely that the British were not warned by the locals. Balfour was infuriated and threatened to retaliate by torching houses for miles around.[4]

Balfour's correspondence during this period indicates that he developed a disdain for his American opponents on the battlefield. As a result of political moves that worked against Howe, he also became contemptuous both of Britain's American secretary, Lord George Germain, and of Parliament, which he referred to as "a nest of faction and disingenuity." He was, however, on good terms, even friends, with many of his brother officers, including Francis Rawdon, who considered Balfour one of his most intimate associates. Balfour also earned the admiration and respect of the enlisted men who served under him.[5]

He possessed a fearsome temper, but that was only one attribute of this imposing character. He was ambitious, brave to a fault and politically astute, tireless to duty, possessed of an eye for detail, and meticulous in his correspondence. He was perhaps an ideal aide-de-camp for Howe, to whom he was intensely loyal. Balfour was an advocate of merit, but he also fully realized the value of patronage and of being well connected. Interestingly, he was unconcerned for those over whom he climbed on the way up. "The friend you like, and the woman you love, are the only objects worth giving oneself a moment's trouble about" was his personal philosophy. He never married but sired at least one daughter.[6]

What Balfour lacked were money and political connections. Commissions through the rank of colonel were generally obtained in the British army by purchase through a system that ensured that, because of expense and with few exceptions, the officer corps remained populated with men of fortune, typically landed aristocrats. Under this system a less experienced or incompetent junior officer with financial means could purchase a higher rank over the head of an officer who deserved an elevation in rank due to meritorious service. An officer desiring a higher rank had only to pay the difference between his current rank and the rank he wished to attain, provided a vacancy was available in the regiment in which he sought to serve. The value of a rank depended upon the prestige of the regiment. The successive acquisition of higher rank enabled an officer to build equity, and if he left the service the sale of his commission would provide him with a lump sum. Unfortunately, if an officer died in service, his commission reverted to the Crown with no compensation to his survivors.[7]

The Balfours were Scottish gentry with familial ties to the aristocracy of Galloway, in southwestern Scotland, but they had become nearly impoverished, having sunk unrecoverable thousands of pounds into army commissions—Nisbet's father and two of his three brothers had been officers, and all three had died in service. His mother lived on the brink of financial ruin, and Nisbet applied to Lord Germain to provide her a pension. Germain ignored the request, which further fueled Balfour's contempt for the American secretary. To obtain the rank of major, which he deserved on the basis of merit, he was forced to borrow at usurious rates. His indebtedness quickened his return to America to evade his creditors.[8]

Howe promoted the thirty-five-year-old Balfour to lieutenant colonel and command of the Twenty-third Regiment of Foot, the Royal Welch Fusiliers, in January 1778. The Twenty-third was a storied unit that would fight in nearly every campaign from Lexington to Yorktown. Howe tried to soften the financial blow by allowing Balfour to purchase the rank at a discount, but, discount or not, Balfour was still monstrously in debt. Ten days into the march from Philadelphia to New York, when the British evacuated the former seat of the Continental Congress, he was at the head of the Fusiliers at the Battle of Monmouth Courthouse, on June 28, 1778. While Gen. Henry Clinton turned on the attacking Americans, Balfour and the Fusiliers were part of a division ordered by Clinton to continue in the direction of New York. Balfour saw no action against a rejuvenated Continental Army—the one that had wintered at Valley Forge under the tutelage of Maj. Gen. Friedrich Wilhelm Augustin von Steuben.[9]

In the face of British failures in North America, Howe resigned as the commander in chief, placing Balfour in a politically awkward situation. For one thing, Balfour despised Clinton, who replaced Howe in the spring of 1778. At the same time, he enjoyed warm relations with Clinton's second-in-command, General Cornwallis, who considered Balfour a zealous, intelligent, and deserving officer. Clinton and Cornwallis distrusted each other, and they would later engage in a bitter war of words. Aware that Balfour favored Cornwallis, on at least one occasion Clinton schemed against the subordinate Balfour, and he was certainly critical of Balfour in his postwar writing. Balfour took advantage of an opportunity to get away from his commanding officer in August and September 1778 when he volunteered the Royal Welch Fusiliers for sea duty as marines aboard the larger ships of the fleet commanded by Adm. Lord Richard Howe, William Howe's brother. Balfour himself went to Howe's flagship, the sixty-four-gun *Eagle*.[10]

An interesting episode occurred when Balfour came ashore from his stint at sea. Catching up on the local New York news by perusing the *Royal Gazette,* he became increasingly aware that blame for the British defeat at Saratoga was being ascribed to General Howe. Balfour blamed the newspaper's owner, the commissioned "Printer to the King's Most Excellent Majesty," James Rivington, for what he perceived to be a grave injustice. It was November, and Balfour was just a few days away from boarding a ship bound for England, where he expected to visit friends and family, but his primary motive for the voyage to assist Howe in defending himself at a Parliamentary inquiry into his conduct in North America. Before departing, Balfour confronted Rivington at his home and demanded an explanation. Rivington, who had once been burned in effigy by the Sons of Liberty, refused to back down, and a heated argument ensued that mercifully stopped short of blows, though Balfour did his best to intimidate his adversary.[11]

Rivington sent an account of the confrontation to Richard Cumberland, an associate of Lord Germain, warning that the American secretary could expect more such behavior from Balfour when he arrived in England. Fortunately for Balfour's career, this turned out not to be the case. One curious element to the story is that, unbeknownst to the British, at some point Rivington became a very important spy for George Washington. Exactly when he changed sides is uncertain, but if the notorious public Tory had already become a clandestine patriot, it is conceivable that he relished an opportunity to stir the pot and sow seeds of contention among British officers and politicians.[12]

From the end of 1778 until early 1780 Balfour was in London with William Howe. He was physically ill with scurvy, his misery compounded by news of the loss of a brother at sea. A high point was a brief audience with King George III at St. James's Palace on January 4, 1779. Other than seeing to the welfare of new recruits raised to augment the ranks of the Twenty-third Regiment, he stagnated and was never called to testify on behalf of his mentor. Meanwhile, in New York, General Clinton reformulated a southern strategy.[13]

Two previous abortive attempts to capture Charleston notwithstanding, Clinton remained convinced that southern port was an attainable prize. His strategic goals in 1780 were no different from those of his 1776 campaign—to capture Charleston, rally southern loyalists, and reestablish royal government in the southern colonies. To accomplish this mission, a fleet of warships and transports commanded by Vice Adm. Mariot Arbuthnot sailed from New York on December 26, 1779, carrying more than 8,700 British, provincial, and Hessian soldiers—the flower of the British army in North America, including the Royal Welch Fusiliers—with more to come.[14]

Clinton's troops landed without incident below Charleston on the night of February 11. The British encountered little resistance until after they crossed the Ashley River to begin a descent on Charleston on March 29. On April 1 the redcoats broke ground on the excavation of formal siege works, and for the third time in course of the war Charleston was under serious threat of attack. This time the ranks of the American defenders consisted of approximately 5,600 defenders, and when Clinton first viewed the earthworks, redans, batteries, and other obstacles behind which they were stationed, he grudgingly conceded that the American defenses were "by no means contemptible."[15]

Lieutenant Colonel Balfour had been absent from the Twenty-third Regiment for about sixteen months. When he finally rejoined his regiment on March 10, 1780, the Royal Welch Fusiliers were not in the siege lines on the outskirts of Charleston but were performing outpost duty about forty miles up the Cooper River. From that position they remained on alert for any American reinforcements that might arrive from that direction, but all was quiet. "No laurels can I boast of, they grow not near here," Balfour wrote to a friend.[16]

Charleston's garrison surrendered on May 12. Soon afterward, Clinton embarked for New York, but not before he issued a series of proclamations that altered the status of his American prisoners. Clinton left behind Cornwallis and a small army with which to maintain order and support the loyal civilian populace, a force that included Balfour and the Royal Welch Fusiliers. Given this, Clinton had a plan in mind for Balfour. He would send the lieutenant colonel of the Twenty-third Regiment on a mission to subdue the lawless backcountry. Aware of Balfour's partisanship in favor of Cornwallis and sensing the lieutenant colonel's pessimism about restoring royal government ("I think he means to throw cold water on our past endeavours to re-establish the province," Clinton wrote of Balfour in his journal), he may have deliberately assigned Balfour a task that he thought had little likelihood of success. On May 22 Clinton ordered Balfour inland with a detachment of the Fusiliers, some light infantry, and loyalist militia, all totaling 580 troops. Balfour was to destroy the remaining rebel militia and seize the village of Ninety Six.[17]

Clinton assigned Maj. Patrick Ferguson to Balfour's command as inspector of militia tasked to raise regiments of Tories in the backcountry. Like Balfour, Ferguson was from Scotland; he was known for designing the first breech-loading rifle used in the British army. Despite a severe wound to his right arm at the Battle of the Brandywine in 1777, he was an able commander who had gravitated from service in regular army regiments to the command of loyalist forces. The innovative

Scotsman was a versatile if not brilliant leader in guerrilla warfare and was considered by many to be the finest marksman in the British army.[18]

Balfour disliked and mistrusted Ferguson immensely, felt strangely hampered by his presence, and even described him to Cornwallis as capricious and violent. Accordingly, he vigorously protested Ferguson's appointment to Clinton and Cornwallis, but to no avail. Ferguson would achieve some success raising militia, but for the duration of his association with Balfour a simmering antipathy existed between them. Balfour rarely passed up an opportunity to disparage Ferguson in his dispatches to Cornwallis.[19]

David Ramsay, M.D.
James Barton Longacre's engraving from a drawing by Charles
Fraser after a painting by Charles Willson Peale (New York: Herman
Bancroft, 1836). From the collections of the Society of the Cincinnati,
Washington, D.C. Reproduced with permission.

Balfour reached Ninety Six by mid-June. There he and Ferguson recruited seven loyalist regiments consisting of more than four thousand men, but he was doubtful of their value. Keeping Cornwallis fully apprised of his situation, he suggested that the best way to dominate the backcountry would be to march to disaffected villages and then to disarm and punish the disloyal people or make the leading men answerable for their misconduct. A posting that might have been meant to be a trap set by Clinton won for Balfour the approbation of Cornwallis, who was learning to trust and value his subordinate's opinions. Cornwallis gave him high praise for his attention and diligence in letters to Germain.[20]

While at Ninety Six, Balfour had several conversations with Brig. Gen. Andrew Williamson of the South Carolina militia, who was the highest-ranking patriot officer in South Carolina not a prisoner. These discussions would later have far-reaching implications for Williamson, Balfour, and a South Carolina militia colonel named Hayne. The Scottish-born Williamson (c.1730–1786) was a prosperous planter and trader from Ninety Six who had earned renown as an Indian fighter. He received a promotion to brigadier general in 1778 and faithfully commanded South Carolina militia in the backcountry and in Georgia until the fall of Charleston. Now, with the backcountry under British control, Williamson took protection and swore allegiance to the Crown in order to preserve his property and fortune. To Cornwallis, Balfour wrote that Williamson had "a strong sound understanding, and, if I am not much deceived indeed, will be infinitely useful here if properly treated." Williamson would not actively fight, but he was willing to help the British in other ways, and Balfour volunteered to serve as his fellow Scotsman's handler.[21]

David Ramsay noted that the British administration of the district of Ninety Six was at first moderate in tone. Unfortunately, many local loyalists who had acted like "banditti, to whom rapine and violence were familiar" were put in positions of power by the conquerors. When these base men gratified their private resentments for plunder, many of the newly made subjects were so distressed that they broke their commitment to British allegiance. Their revolt cast suspicion and prejudice upon even those who had no intention to rejoin the Americans, and severe measures instituted by Balfour only worsened the jealousies and distrust. Ramsay, who knew and disliked Balfour immensely, described him as "an haughty and imperious officer," whose command in that district "was more calculated, by his insolence and overbearing conduct, to alienate the inhabitants from a government already beloved, than to reconcile them to one which was generally disliked."[22]

"By an unwarrantable stretch of his authority," noted Ramsay, Balfour issued a proclamation declaring "that every man who was not in his house by a certain day, should be subject to military execution," and complaints to Balfour were peremptorily or summarily ignored. According to Ramsay, during the thirteen months that the British held the district, "there was not a single instance wherein punishment was inflicted either on the soldiery or tories [sic]. The people soon found that there was no security for their lives, liberties, or property."[23]

Balfour had been at Ninety Six for only a month when he received orders from Cornwallis to replace the sickly Brig. Gen. James Patterson as commandant at Charleston. Cornwallis knew that Balfour would have preferred to remain with the Fusiliers, but the good of the service demanded that he become commandant of the town. "I insist on having no excuses," Cornwallis wrote to Balfour on July 17, 1780. Always obedient, Balfour traveled immediately to Charleston. On August 6 he settled into his new office on King Street, located in a beautiful Georgian Palladian home built by Miles Brewton, a successful Charleston merchant who had been lost at sea with his family in 1775.[24]

To Balfour's deep chagrin, however, when Cornwallis marched north out of South Carolina, the new commandant did not get the elevation he thought he deserved—command of South Carolina. Cornwallis instead bestowed that position on Lieutenant Colonel Rawdon, whom the older Balfour outranked. Cornwallis's preference for Rawdon caused resentment on Balfour's part and an estrangement between the two colonels, but there was little Balfour could do but serve faithfully. Cornwallis sought to mollify any hurt feelings on Balfour's part, and he praised his subordinate, adding a personal touch by commending him for having done "what few officers in our service are capable of doing—voluntarily taken responsibility on yourself to serve your country and your friend."[25]

Ramsay was outspoken in his criticism of the new commandant's character and conduct, maintaining that Balfour "displayed, in the exercise of this new office, all the frivolous self-importance, and all the disgusting insolence, which are natural to little minds when puffed up by sudden elevation, and employed in functions to which their abilities are not equal." Balfour assumed and exercised legislative, judicial, and executive powers over citizens, jailing them without trial for committing slight offenses or for being the subject of accusations based on sketchy evidence.[26]

Ramsey had an axe to grind when writing his history, as he was among the more than thirty Charleston patriots whom Balfour, acting on orders from Cornwallis, had rousted from their beds early one morning in August 1780 and escorted under armed guard to the ship *Lord Sandwich* under suspicion of plotting insurrection. From there they were subsequently exiled to St. Augustine in East Florida to await exchange. In June 1781 Balfour added insult to injury when he issued orders banishing the wives and children of exchanged prisoners from the town and the province, allowing them little more than a month to leave. Deliberately or not, he made their departure more difficult by issuing a proclamation forbidding them to raise funds by leasing their houses (which were subsequently confiscated), thereby forcing more than a thousand of them to rely on charity from strangers.[27]

British victories in the field brought additional American prisoners to Charleston. When guarding and feeding them became increasingly problematic, Balfour resorted to the expediency of putting them aboard prison ships in the harbor. Later, when he became furious over the brutal killing of loyalists by Gen. Francis Marion's South Carolina militia, Balfour used the prison ships as a deterrent by sending 130 American militiamen to the hulks as hostages. The mortality aboard the prison ships was so great at one point that he confided to Rawdon that "the rebell [*sic*] Prisoners die faster even than they used to desert." This practice, protested vehemently by Brig. Gen. William Moultrie, who was Charleston's ranking American prisoner of war, freed redcoat regiments for service in the countryside and lightened the duties of the garrison.[28]

That was not the end of Balfour's misuse and exploitation of his captives in Charleston. In the spring of 1781, on the advice of Cornwallis, he made a public display of threatening to ship Continental and militia prisoners to the West Indies. This was a ploy on the part of Cornwallis to force Maj. Gen. Nathanael Greene to consent to a prisoner exchange. The collusion went so far that Balfour intentionally misled Royal Navy officers into believing that he was acting in earnest. Moultrie protested, of course, and sent letters to General Greene and the Continental Congress informing them of what was about to transpire, unwittingly playing into Balfour's and Cornwallis's hands.[29]

As Charleston's commandant, Balfour was charged with establishing supply and communication lines to Cornwallis and his troops in the backcountry, a task that became increasingly difficult and dangerous as a result of the widespread and pervasive resistance from the king's enemies. Food and forage had to be obtained locally, and currency was in short supply. Balfour responded to the exigency by confiscating provisions from wealthy patriots. Uniforms, camp gear, arms, and ammunition, however, came from supply ships that had to brave bad weather, privateers, and the French navy.[30]

General Moultrie had gotten along well with the new commandant's predecessor, General Patterson, but Moultrie and Balfour contended with each other from the very beginning of Balfour's administration. William Moultrie was a congenial man and slow to anger or take offense, but there was an almost immediate clash of personality between the American general and his jailor, whom he described as "a proud, haughty Scot, [who] carried his authority with a very high hand."[31]

Moultrie bristled at what he considered arbitrary and capricious British violations of the articles of capitulation, and he blamed Balfour for allowing, even instigating, the infractions. When Moultrie protested the seizure of prominent civil and militia officers (David Ramsay among them), all prisoners on parole, and their placement aboard the *Lord Sandwich* prior to their transportation to St. Augustine, the prickly Balfour responded that he would "not return any answer to a letter wrote in such exceptionable and unwarrantable terms as that to him from Gen. Moultrie . . . nor will he receive any further application from him upon the subject of it." Moultrie once objected to Balfour's refusal to allow a doctor to attend sick soldiers, and when he appealed to Balfour's humanity, asking him, "for

God's sake, to permit Dr. Oliphant to attend the hospital whenever he shall judge it necessary," Balfour called Moultrie's plea pathetic. On another occasion he sent word that he "would do as he pleased with the prisoners . . . and not as General Moultrie pleases."[32]

In an effort to end Moultrie's incessant objections, protests, and complaints, Balfour attempted to silence him. First he made an overture to Moultrie's son William in January 1781, playing on the son's interest in the family estate since he was his father's only heir. If General Moultrie were to resign his commission, suggested Balfour, as British officers could at any time and place, he promised that the estate would be restored, all damages paid, and that William Jr. would never be asked to bear arms against his father. That failing, Balfour tried to squelch Moultrie's advocacy through the power of intimidation by insinuating that Moultrie might have breached his parole. This also failed, and Moultrie remained a thorn in Balfour's side until Moultrie departed Charleston on parole, bound for Philadelphia in July 1781 to await formal exchange.[33]

Balfour had been at his new post for less than a fortnight when Cornwallis routed a Continental army commanded by Maj. Gen. Horatio Gates at Camden on August 16, 1780. This British victory seemed to renew his optimism, at least in his reports to General Clinton. In private, however, he was less sanguine, confessing to a friend that "the rebels . . . have managed to collect again and make many very serious incursions into this province." When loyalist militiamen under Ferguson's command were decimated and Ferguson himself killed at Kings Mountain on October 7, his doubts redoubled.[34]

Cornwallis had marched his army into North Carolina after whipping Gates at Camden, only to return to South Carolina in the aftermath of Kings Mountain. Overcoming his reluctance to give what might be unwelcome advice from a subordinate, Balfour warned Cornwallis that leaving South Carolina under the protection of loyalist militia and a few regulars while attempting to gain North Carolina ran a risk of losing both provinces. Balfour's concerns were heightened when Cornwallis did exactly that; after a British detachment led by Lieutenant Colonel Tarleton was decisively beaten by Brig. Gen. Daniel Morgan's force of Continentals and militia at Cowpens on January 17, 1781, Cornwallis chased Greene's Continental army into North Carolina. Cornwallis beat Greene at Guilford Courthouse on March 15, 1782, but took causalities he could ill afford to lose. He subsequently marched his army further away from South Carolina and toward its eventual fate in Virginia as Greene's army slowly advanced toward Charleston. To Balfour's dismay and despite Cornwallis's contrary reassurances, Balfour's fears of losing the province were becoming reality as British forces became increasingly impotent in the face of rebel opposition.[35]

By July 1781 the British situation in Charleston had become increasingly precarious. A pervasive sense of abandonment and confinement added to the stultifying summer heat. Camden and Ninety Six had been forsaken, Greene's Continental army and rebel militias were active outside Charleston, and reports were coming in that loyalists beyond the limits of British control were suffering inhumane treatment, summary execution, and even simple murder. A Continental officer commented that "the two opposite principles of whiggism and toryism have set the people of this country to cutting each other's throats, and scarce a day passes but some poor deluded tory is put to death at his door . . . the [American] people, by copying the manners of the British, have become perfectly savage." Pushing the power shift were Americans who had once taken British protection but were now rejoining the American ranks in droves, sending loyalists from all parts of the province into Charleston.[36]

Balfour had already taken paroled American militiamen and confined them in Charleston harbor on the prison ships *Torbay* and *Pack Horse* to encourage fair treatment of captive loyal militiamen. But something more severe was needed to discourage the continuing acts of terror committed by the patriots who had overtaken the countryside. Balfour was entirely exasperated because he had been prevented by his superiors from administering the capital penalty to deserving offenders tried by court-martial in Charleston. Nonetheless, he still sought a way to make a striking example of an American officer who had taken protection and subsequently rejoined the patriot side. He would, if he had his way, convincingly demonstrate to both friend and foe that there was no weakening of British resolve.[37]

Francis Lord Rawdon.
Engraving by Thomas Cook, from the *Westminster Magazine*
([London]: J. Walker, July 31, 1781). Reproduced by permission of the
Society of the Cincinnati, Washington, D.C.

Chapter 3

A Fierce and Unrelenting
Soldier Comes in from the Field

Another British officer of the same rank and merit as Lieutenant Colonel Balfour arrived in Charleston in July 1781. Balfour's friend and colleague Lt. Col. Francis Lord Rawdon was nominally in command of British forces in South Carolina beyond the environs of Charleston, and he shared Balfour's condescending attitude and unconcealed disdain for his American opponents. Rawdon was described as tall, dark, with "long curly hair, of firm forehead, and large widely spaced eyes. His mouth was rather small, and his upper lip was prominent." He was considered by some the ugliest man in England, but his portraits do not support this characterization. His friends found him to be polished but occasionally pompous and stuffy, a sincere Christian, benign but somewhat loquacious, and financially extravagant though beneficent. With his soldiers he could be a martinet. Against his enemies on the battlefield he had earned a well-deserved reputation as a fierce and unrelenting soldier with good instincts for strategy and tactics.[1]

Francis Rawdon, first Marquess of Hastings and later second Earl of Moira, was born into the Anglo-Irish aristocracy on December 9, 1754, at Moira in County Down, Ireland. He was the eldest son of John, Baron Rawdon, later first Earl of Moira, and his second wife, Lady Elizabeth Hastings. Francis received his education at Harrow before matriculating at Oxford, but he did not complete a degree and left there in 1773. It was at Oxford that Rawdon developed a lasting friendship with his schoolmate Banastre Tarleton. It is an interesting paradox that in his youth Rawdon expressed immature opinions in favor of colonial resistance and liberty; of course, his thinking became more hawkish once he joined the army and realized that the battlefield was the pathway to promotion and glory.[2]

The Rawdon family's military heritage was said to derive from one Paulyn de Rawdon, who commanded archers at the Battle of Hastings in 1066. Whether or not this was a factor, with the encouragement of his maternal uncle Francis Hastings, Earl of Huntingdon, young Rawdon decided to pursue a military career. His

uncle purchased for him an army commission, and the seventeen-year-old was ga-
zetted an ensign in the Fifteenth Regiment of Foot on August 7, 1771. Prior to joining his regiment, in the company of his brother John and his Uncle Huntingdon,
he embarked on a grand tour of Europe in 1773. This trip was considered necessary
in those days to give a finishing touch to the education of a "young gentleman
of quality."[3]

On October 20, 1773, while touring the continent, Rawdon was promoted
to lieutenant of the Fifth Regiment of Foot, the Northumberland Fusiliers. Once
again the purchase price was provided by his uncle. He joined the regiment in late
1773 and immersed himself in the process of learning his chosen profession. The
Fifth Regiment was subsequently sent to North America to help suppress the ever-
growing rebellion in the colonies and embarked from Ireland for an eight-week
voyage to Boston on May 7, 1774. The regiment was ashore by the first week in
July, and so began the nineteen-year-old Rawdon's eight-year sojourn in America.[4]

The Fifth Regiment was part of the disastrous British expedition to destroy
ordnance stores in Lexington and Concord on April 19, 1775, but Rawdon remained behind in Boston on that particularly momentous day. The redcoats were
badly mauled by the New England militiamen as they marched cross-country in
the springtime heat, and in the battle's aftermath Rawdon was chosen to replace
a wounded lieutenant who was second in command of the Fifth Regiment's company of grenadiers. Like Nisbet Balfour, Rawdon faced his first trial by fire at Bunker Hill on June 17. About noontime a force of 2,400 men, Rawdon's grenadiers
among them, landed unopposed on the Charlestown peninsula under the covering
fire of British naval guns. When the British approached Breed's Hill, instead of
finding an unprepared disorganized rabble, they were confronted by 1,200 well-
entrenched rebels with quite a number more waiting behind them on Bunker Hill.[5]

The first and second assaults on the defensive works on Breed's Hill failed
miserably, but a third attempt to move up the hill did not falter. With bayonets
fixed, Rawdon's grenadiers reached the enemy entrenchments. Along the way, Capt.
George Harris was grazed in the head by American musketry and fell into the arms
of Rawdon, exclaiming, "For God's sake, let me die in peace!" Harris survived the
wound, but Rawdon assumed company command for the rest of the day. During
this battle, of which Maj. Gen. John Burgoyne would write, "the Fifth has behaved
the best, and suffered the most," two balls passed through Rawdon's cap but he
was otherwise unscathed as his men drove the rebels from their position. It was a
sanguinary victory, but Rawdon's steadfastness under the thickest fire gained him
the notice of his superiors, a July 12 promotion to captain (paid for by his patron
uncle), and command of a company of the Sixty-third Regiment. Of the young
captain General Burgoyne noted, "Lord Rowdon [sic] behaved to a charm; his

name is established for life." Perhaps from a British standpoint his name was established for life, but not yet from an American point of view. That would come later.[6]

Rawdon was unimpressed and even dismayed by the performance of the British army at Bunker Hill, bemoaning that some troops had shown infinite courage but others had behaved rather miserably. If a British defeat had occurred, he wrote, "it would have been over with the British Empire in America, and I can assure you that one time the chance was against us." His general displeasure with the state of affairs in America improved considerably when General Howe took command of British forces in North America. Despite the miserable conditions suffered by the British in Boston, Rawdon's own prospects began to improved, for he learned that both Howe and Maj. Gen. Henry Clinton desired his service as their aide-de-camp.[7]

Eager for active service, Captain Rawdon accepted Clinton's offer to join his staff as aide-de-camp and deputy adjutant general. In February 1776 he joined Clinton on the first southern expedition, the one that ended badly for the British in South Carolina at Sullivan's Island on June 28, 1776. Nonetheless he was completely absorbed by his duties and considered working under Clinton a highly valuable experience. "I have I think improved myself a good deal this campaign," he wrote Huntington. "One picks up hints of knowledge everywhere." During the operation he became intimately acquainted with Lord Cornwallis, whom he liked and respected immensely. Despite the overall British failure, Rawdon saw the campaign as a great adventure, and his letter to his uncle in part reads almost like an account of a holiday—healthful climate, sun and sand, physical exercise, and camping on the beach.[8]

It is interesting and a bit ironic to note that Rawdon's name was familiar to the inhabitants of lowcountry South Carolina at that early time, probably from what they had read in the newspapers. The Charleston lawyer Richard Hutson wrote to his brother-in-law Isaac Hayne a few days before the British attack on Sullivan's Island: "One day the week before last, a hat was taken up off of Simmons Island [present-day Seabrook Island, about twenty miles southwest of Charleston] by some persons going in a boat to town, and carried to the President [John Rutledge]. It was cocked Jockey fashion, laced with gold, had a cockade and feather in it, and on the inside of the crown Lord Rawden's [sic] name in Capitals. This is the villain that was coming out a volunteer against America."[9]

Postulating that Rawdon had lost the cap when he drowned in a shipwreck, Hutson told Hayne "that in all probability Lord Rawden [sic] has met with a fate which I think he merited for voluntarily engaging in such nefarious service." Alexander Garden[10] explained that by "coming out a volunteer against America," Rawdon was trying to build his reputation, and to do so he had "quitted the free enjoyment of every blessing that rank and fortune could bestow, to bear arms against a people who had never injured or offended him, and to whom it appears, that he had previously declared himself much attached . . . aiming at military distinction, so to gain the smiles of his king." It would prove unfortunate for Hayne that rumors of Rawdon's death were unfounded.[11]

After returning north, Rawdon remained under Clinton's tutelage as the British evicted Gen. George Washington's Continental army from Long Island on August 27, 1776, and occupied New York City on September 15. During this interval he deepened the acquaintance made with Cornwallis during the southern expedition, and by this time he and Capt. Nisbet Balfour had an established relationship. Balfour was General Howe's aide-de-camp, and Rawdon had entrusted him with letters for home when Balfour carried Howe's dispatches to England.[12]

Rawdon certainly came from an more affluent background than Nisbet Balfour, yet their military careers ran roughly parallel, at least while they were on the continent of North America. In due course they became acquaintances, then friends, but also occasional competitors. They shared a contempt for their American enemies, but Rawdon's was more strident. He detested the rebels, whom he referred to as infamous scoundrels and "[deluded] ignorant bigots of this country," and he clearly felt little if any sympathy for the plight of American women who suffered indignities, assaults, and rape at the hands of British occupiers. "The fair nymphs of this isle are in wonderful tribulation, as the fresh meat our men have got here has made them as riotous as satyrs," he wrote to his uncle from Staten Island in August 1776. "A girl cannot step into the bushes to pluck a rose without running the most imminent risk of being ravished, and they are so little accustomed to these vigorous methods that they don't bear them with the proper resignation, and of consequence we have most entertaining courts-martial every day."[13]

This mindset informed how Rawdon thought the war should be waged. Pillage and plunder were acceptable tools alongside the bayonet and the torch so that "these infatuated creatures may feel what a calamity war is." Rawdon became a hardliner, more of a "draw the sword and throw away the scabbard" type of warrior who would be a relentless foe to his adversaries. His harsh attitude is remarkable because often the views of subordinates were greatly influenced by the attitudes of their commanding officers. Rawdon's military mentor Henry Clinton sincerely espoused winning over the hearts and minds of the disaffected inhabitants and a restoration of the status quo, and Howe and Clinton both tried to minimize the ill usage of civilians and punished soldiers who engaged in plundering.[14]

Likewise, William Howe was moderate and restrained, opposed to coercion, and willing to negotiate with the rebellious Americans. When given command of the British army and navy in North America in 1776, he and his brother Adm. Lord Richard Howe were also granted limited powers to act as peace commissioners.

The Howe brothers proceeded in good faith though their attempt at diplomacy was doomed from the start—they were authorized merely to grant pardons and propose the unacceptable: full American submission. Only after that precondition was fulfilled would political reform be considered. The American commissioners who met with Lord Howe at Staten Island on September 11, 1776, were John Adams, Benjamin Franklin, and Edward Rutledge. Upon hearing the British terms, they summarily dismissed the offer of peace and pledged to continue the struggle for independence.[15]

In January 1777 Lord Rawdon was pleased to accompany Clinton home to England, where he reunited with family, friends, and his uncle Lord Huntingdon. Aside from the enjoyment of being away from the army, he found the trip not dull but generally unremarkable except for a happenstance introduction to the Marquis de Lafayette at a ball given by the American secretary, Lord George Germain. By July 5 he and Clinton had again traversed the Atlantic and landed in New York. Not long afterward Clinton ascended to the command of British forces in North America, superseding General Howe, and he reaffirmed Rawdon's appointment as his aide-de-camp. Clinton and his entourage moved to Philadelphia on May 1, 1777.[16]

Clinton championed the raising of a provincial Irish regiment, which he designated the Volunteers of Ireland. In Rawdon he had "the person of that nation in this army whose situation pointed him out the most strongly for the command." Rawdon relished the opportunity to lead troops in the field and win battlefield laurels for himself. Clinton announced Rawdon's appointment to the temporary rank of colonel of provincial troops on May 25, 1778, and before long 380 American deserters were enrolled. Rawdon bore the burdensome expense of clothing, arming, and equipping his corps, and he was highly pleased with the result.[17]

Clinton rewarded Rawdon's administrative ability on June 19, 1778, when he named him to fill the post of adjutant general of the army. With the job came a promotion to the permanent rank of lieutenant colonel in the regular army, a higher rank than his colonelcy of provincials. But it was also time for the British to evacuate Philadelphia. The French had entered the war on the American side in early 1778, and Clinton needed to move his army to New York to strengthen the city against the possibility of a joint Franco-American attack. He retained Rawdon as aide-de-camp on the march, and it was in this capacity that Rawdon served alongside Clinton on June 28, 1778, during the Battle of Monmouth sourthouse when Washington's Continental army attacked the rear of the redcoat column.[18]

Rawdon was pleased and honored by Clinton's approbation, and over the next eighteen months he devoted himself to the varied and unending tasks of administering an army. His heart, though, was with his Irish volunteers, and by the summer of 1779 he had grown weary of both the exhausting duty and Clinton's quarrelsome personality—in fact, tension had been building in their relationship for some time. On September 30 he tendered his resignation as adjutant general, a move that was widely lamented in the army. Clinton accepted Rawdon's resignation without argument. It was personality differences that ended their relationship as commander in chief and adjutant general, but they still managed to part without acrimony. Clinton would later be instrumental as an intercessor on Rawdon's behalf with Lord Germain and the king when, through no fault of Rawdon's, the young lieutenant colonel's standing in the army was threatened. In Rawdon's place Clinton appointed Maj. John André, whom Rawdon helped settle into the job.[19]

When General Clinton sailed for Charleston on December 26, 1779, Lieutenant Colonel Rawdon was disappointed to learn that he and his Volunteers of Ireland were not a part of the first wave of the expedition. But when Clinton called for reinforcements as the British settled in for what looked to be a protracted siege of Charleston, Rawdon's regiment was transported south. The *Royal Gazette* reported that prior to sailing from New York, on March 17 in honor of St. Patrick, he "munificently entertained" his regiment quartered at Jamaica, Long Island. On reaching South Carolina, the Irishmen were not placed in the siege lines but instead were sent to the north side of the Cooper River to augment the troops under the command of Cornwallis. There they remained until the Americans surrendered Charleston on May 12.[20]

After Charleston fell, Clinton put into action a plan to subdue and protect the interior of South Carolina. He fanned British forces across the province, posting contingents in a defensive screen from east to west at Cheraw, Camden, Rocky Mount (in South Carolina near Hanging Rock), Ninety Six, and Augusta, which was just across the Savannah River in Georgia. On the coast he maintained garrisons at Georgetown, Charleston, Beaufort, and Savannah. Balfour commanded at Ninety Six while Cornwallis and Rawdon occupied Camden. Clinton left Cornwallis with four thousand troops when he departed Charleston for New York on June 8, and Cornwallis subsequently returned to Charleston, leaving Rawdon in command at Camden. Cornwallis considered Rawdon his next-in-command in South Carolina as he contemplated offensive movement into North Carolina.[21]

When Lt. Col. Banastre Tarleton's mounted troopers shattered Col. Abraham Buford's 350 Virginia Continentals at Waxhaws on May 29, South Carolina seemed to be firmly in the grip of the British. The illusion did not last long; loyalist support in the backcountry never came together as hoped or expected, in part because Clinton's proclamations had galvanized rebel opposition. On June 22 Rawdon sent his first report as an independent commander to Cornwallis. In this dispatch he informed his chief of the defeat and dispersion of a large loyalist force by rebels who might have otherwise been disinclined to mobilize, organize, and bear arms: "The proclamation [of June 3] strikes home at us now, for these frontier districts, who were before secured under the bond of paroles, are now at liberty to take any steps which a turn of fortune might advise."[22]

"That unfortunate proclamation . . . has had very unfavorable consequences," Rawdon wrote to Cornwallis from Camden on July 7. "The majority of the inhabitants in the frontier districts, tho' ill disposed to us, from circumstances were not actually in arms against us. They were therefore freed from the paroles . . . and nine out of ten of them are now embodied on the part of the rebels." In light of Tarleton's alleged brutality at Waxhaws, Rawdon was also rightly concerned about a backlash against loyalists taken captive in what was shaping into a ferocious civil war in the backcountry: "Yet here again the proclamation wounds us, for should any person in this predicament fall into our hands . . . the punishment due to his crime may by misrepresentation furnish a pretext to the rebels for exercising inhumanity upon some friend of ours in their hands. Perhaps I ought not to question the expediency of that proclamation, but I so immediately feel the effects of it that I may fairly be excused."[23]

But if Rawdon was angered by what he considered duplicitous actions on the part of the inhabitants who, having sworn their allegiance under duress and coercion, afterwards did their best to undermine the royal interests, he was absolutely enraged when desertion from the Volunteers of Ireland became rampant. He was convinced that the inhabitants of the countryside had conspired to facilitate their escape. To put a stop to the desertion, he called upon the local populace to detain stragglers and to sound an alarm to call for help when necessary. If loyalty to their sovereign would not move them to check this crime, he would urge them to do their duty as good subjects by employing "invariable severity." Anyone found giving shelter or aid to deserters "may assure themselves of rigorous punishment either by whipping, imprisonment, or by being sent to serve his majesty in the West-Indies." He also promised an inducement of "ten guineas for the head of any deserter belonging to the Volunteers of Ireland, and five guineas only if they bring him in alive." When the letter containing these threats came into possession of George Washington it caused quite a stir, though Rawdon confessed to Cornwallis that the letter contained only empty threats contrived for the purpose of intimidation. Nevertheless, word got out of Rawdon's supposed ruthlessness.[24]

Of more immediate concern to Rawdon was that on June 27 the "Hero of Saratoga," Maj. Gen. Horatio Gates, advanced from North Carolina toward Camden with 3,700 troops consisting of Continentals from Virginia, Maryland, Delaware, and North Carolina, a force that was augmented by assorted militia and state troops. Rawdon's command of 1,100 regulars, provincials, and loyalist militia included the Royal Welch Fusiliers, the Volunteers of Ireland, and companies of infantry and cavalry of Tarleton's Legion. Rawdon had closely monitored American movements and, judging Camden indefensible, had shifted troops twenty miles north to strongholds at Hanging Rock and Rocky Mount. But when Brig. Gen. Thomas Sumter's South Carolina militia attacked his forward positions twice during the first week of August, he pulled back to a defensive position near Camden and awaited reinforcement. Cornwallis hurried to the scene, arriving on August 13 and bringing the total British force to 2,200 men. Rawdon quickly apprised him of all that had happened, and Cornwallis in turn decided to implement a plan formulated by Rawdon for moving ahead and attacking Gates the next day.[25]

In the darkness of early morning on August 16, the two opposing forces collided on a narrow neck of land between two swamps six miles north of Camden. A thorough discussion of the tactical evolution of the battle is beyond the scope of this narrative, but suffice it to say that the arrangement of troops pitted hardened British veterans of the Royal Welch Fusiliers against green Virginia militiamen on the American left. The British advance ended with disastrous results for the Americans. The rebels were decimated by the redcoat onslaught, and a panicked retreat ensued during which Tarleton's cavalry pursued the Americans northward for twenty-two miles to Hanging Rock. General Gates himself rode nonstop to cover the sixty miles to Charlotte with Tarleton's cavalrymen chasing him much of the way.[26]

As commanding general Cornwallis received credit for achieving a crushing victory at Camden over a numerically superior foe. In truth, however, Rawdon deserves the lion's share of the laurels for his skillful delay of Gates until Cornwallis brought reinforcements, for his knowledge of the terrain and troop dispositions, and for conducting much of the day's battle. Cornwallis gave him somewhat cursory praise in his report to George Germain, remarking on his "capacity and zeal for the service." Rawdon was annoyed that he did not receive more notice: "I did not think myself equitably treated in his recital of the event," he wrote to a friend. Nevertheless, Rawdon was gracious and did not allow his disappointment to spoil the deepening feelings of friendship and respect that he had for his general, sentiments that were reciprocated by Cornwallis.[27]

Emboldened by success, Cornwallis pressed forward into North Carolina, taking Charlotte on September 25. An elated Rawdon and Cornwallis grew increasingly optimistic that the spectacular victory at Camden would quell whatever American resistance remained, but their optimism proved to be unfounded. They were soon stunned to learn that Maj. Patrick Ferguson and his 1,100 loyalist militia were cornered and routed at Kings Mountain on October 7. The failure of loyalist support required to reestablish royal dominance combined with the debacle at

Kings Mountain forced Cornwallis to pull back into South Carolina. Along the way he became so completely incapacitated by a fever that Rawdon had to assume command of the retreat to Winnsboro, South Carolina.[28]

From Winnsboro Rawdon resumed his post at Camden, a position he disliked immensely. When Cornwallis marched into North Carolina on January 1 to face Nathanael Greene, who had superseded Gates, Rawdon found himself the military authority over all British forces in South Carolina outside the environs of Charleston. It was lonely and frustrating work, devoid of any military glory whatsoever. A detached contingent of Continentals and patriot militia from Greene's army soundly whipped Tarleton's Legion ninety miles to the northwest at the Battle of Cowpens on January 17, and Cornwallis won a pyrrhic victory over Greene at Guilford Courthouse in North Carolina on March 15, but all the while Rawdon was occupied trying to fend off the militias of Marion, Sumter, and Pickens. The insurgents were resurgent—continually disrupting supply lines and generally creating havoc for the strung-out British occupiers. On March 7 Rawdon complained to Cornwallis of "the savage cruelty of the enemy, who commit the most wanton murders in cold blood upon the friends of the Government that fall into their hands."[29]

Cornwallis subsequently took his army into Virginia, where he met his destiny at Yorktown on October 19, 1781. His departure left the Carolinas virtually unprotected, and the path was open wide for an advance by Greene. The American commander turned south and headed to Camden, where he positioned 1,500 troops on a ridge called Hobkirk's Hill. Greene's army would compel the British to pull out of Camden—but not without a fight. On April 25 the outnumbered and desperate but determined Rawdon, who had armed his musicians, drummers, and anyone who could carry a musket, took his men along a circuitous route close to a swamp and through the woods to launch an audacious morning assault on Greene's left flank. After a brisk engagement with relatively heavy losses on both sides, the motley British force overpowered the Americans, pushing them off the summit of the ridge. A three-mile pursuit ended with the British returning to their own lines and Greene eventually reoccupying the hill.[30]

Hobkirk's Hill was Rawdon's personal military high-water mark in America, and he received praise from Cornwallis, who termed the victory "glorious" and "by far the most splendid of the war." By checking Greene, Rawdon allowed his army to retire from Camden unmolested on May 10, and the British crossed the Santee River at Nelson's Ferry with minimal American interference on May 14. Balfour, who had come up from Charleston, was waiting for him south of the Santee, and they established a camp at Moncks Corner.[31]

Balfour informed Cornwallis of "the most horrid accounts of the cruelty of the enemy [militia] and the numberless murders committed by them." In a letter dated May 20 Cornwallis urged Rawdon to "put a stop to them by retaliation or such means as may appear most efficacious." Cornwallis had always encouraged Rawdon and Balfour to work in support of each other, and from Moncks Corner on May 24 they issued a joint proclamation exhorting the king's friends to stand firm in their duty and principles despite the loss of the upper parts of the province. They invited loyalists who had been forced to join the rebels out of self-preservation but who remained unshaken in their fidelity to escape and to come into the British lines with their arms. "We desire all such to be confident, that they run no risk of suffering from us, through indiscriminate vengeance; reminding them, that the British Government never extends its hand to blood, without the most convincing proofs of intentional guilt."[32]

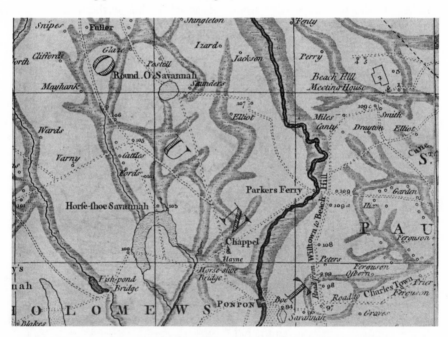

A section of St. Bartholomew's Parish, Colleton County, from *A Map of South Carolina and a Part of Georgia* by William Faden. The river depicted is the Edisto River. Jacksonboro is called Ponpon, and Hayne Hall is marked approximately four miles to the northwest. Courtesy of the Library of Congress Geography and Map Division, Washington, D.C.

The activity of the previous months had exacted a heavy toll; Rawdon was exhausted to the point of near-incapacitation and prostrated by a fever, his health almost entirely broken by campaigning in the backcountry. He reluctantly left his command at Moncks Corner and retired to Charleston for recuperation. Unfortunately, by late May the last two British outposts in the backcountry, at Ninety Six and Augusta, were under siege. Augusta surrendered on June 5, but the star-shaped earthen fort at Ninety Six yet withstood Greene's efforts to breach its walls. Despite his precarious and debilitated physical condition, Rawdon mounted a foray in the beastly summer weather to relieve loyalist Lt. Col. John Harris Cruger's besieged garrison at Ninety Six. The operation to and from the little village consumed most of the month of June. The march in the oppressive heat and humidity claimed the lives of a number of newly arrived and poorly acclimated wool-clad redcoat reinforcements, but at Rawdon's approach Greene gave up his siege.[33]

Rawdon's timely arrival notwithstanding, the British subsequently abandoned Ninety Six, and Rawdon withdrew his small force toward Orangeburg. Greene's army shadowed him but did not attempt to engage. While at Orangeburg, Rawdon received word from Balfour apprising him of the sharply increasing rebel activity ongoing between Rawdon's column and Charleston. Rawdon would later explain "that an insurrection had taken place in the rear of my army, but had luckily been crushed. [Balfour] stated the imperious necessity of repressing the disposition to similar plots of treachery, by making an example of the individual who had planned, as well as headed the revolt, and who had fallen into [his] hands." Balfour sought Rawdon's concurrence, and Rawdon replied "that there could be no doubt as to the necessity for making the example, to which I would readily give the sanction of my name."[34]

On returning from what would be his last military campaign in North America, Rawdon remained in Charleston from mid-July on, resting to recover his health enough to sustain a voyage home to England. His only encouragement came from learning that Clinton had recommended his promotion to brigadier general of provincial troops. Otherwise, he was as sick, disillusioned, and as full of loathing for the Americans as ever.[35]

Part II

Isaac Hayne, Carolina Patriot.
Unknown artist. The style of dress is consistent with that of the 1790s or later, increasing
the likelihood that the image is of Dr. Isaac Hayne (1766–1802), eldest son of Col. Isaac Hayne.
Margaret Hayne Harrison, *A Charleston Album* (Rindge, N.H.: Richard R. Smith, 1953),
plate facing page 48. Courtesy of Bauhan Publishing, Peterborough, N.H.

Chapter 4

"I do not mean to desert the cause of America"

One came from titled Irish nobility, wealth, and privilege. The second arose from Scottish gentry but lacked money and political connections. The third was a member of the South Carolina lowcountry planter aristocracy. Their ages spanned a period of more than a decade. Lieutenant Colonel Balfour, the oldest, was thirty-eight years old. Colonel Hayne would soon be thirty-six. Lieutenant Colonel Rawdon was only twenty-six.

The Irishman and the Scotsman, professional soldiers far away from home, were single men. The first was ill, and both were exhausted. With each passing day their rancor increased in proportion to their shrinking sphere of influence as they were obliged by the hated rebels to relinquish territory they had fought hard to conquer.

The American lived close by with his family, or what remained of it. All he had really wanted was to go home and to be left alone. But he had been pushed to make irresoluble choices, first to take protection from a king to whom he was supposed to pledge his allegiance and then to take up the sword again, against that same king and his armies.

Isaac Hayne was born September 23, 1745, in St. Bartholomew's Parish, Colleton County, South Carolina, the second child and only son of Isaac Hayne and his third wife, Sarah Williamson. He was the only one of five siblings to survive into the 1770s and was in fact the second son to be named Isaac—a half-brother of the same name who preceded him by five years had survived only thirteen months. Our Isaac was of the third generation of his family born on American soil; his great-grandfather John Hayne, the progenitor of the Hayne family in America, had come to this continent from Shropshire, England, in 1700.[1]

Practically nothing is known of Hayne's formative years. By the time he was six years old, he and his older sister Mary were orphans and were likely being raised by relatives. From his father he inherited the nine-hundred-acre

Hayne Hall at Pon Pon (Jacksonboro)* complete with twenty-three slaves. Over time, he increased his holdings considerably, both in land and in chattel. At the time of his death he owned the Sycamore plantation with its 650 acres, the 700-acre Pear Hill plantation, five lots in Beaufort, two lots in Charleston, 6,500 acres scattered about South Carolina, mostly in the backcountry, and a thousand acres on the Turtle River in Georgia.[2]

Just where Isaac Hayne received his education is uncertain, but that he was well educated is made clear by the fact that he was an avid correspondent and meticulous record-keeper. Like so many scions of the lowcountry planter aristocracy, he may have studied in England. More likely, because of the deaths of his parents, he received his earliest lessons from private tutors, or perhaps he attended one of the several schools that were operated in the vicinity of Charleston. As an adult Hayne was a member of the Charleston Library Society, founded in 1748 as the third subscription library established in the colonies. The Charleston Library Society contained more than five thousand books when it was engulfed by fire in 1778, and Hayne obviously valued his membership—his will specified that it be transferred to his eldest son, Isaac, in the event of his death.[3]

Hayne's life was generally placid before revolution and war came to the South Carolina lowcountry: "He was a planter, eminently domestic, a country gentleman, whose pride and pleasure it was to maintain that character par excellence." Indeed, the blue-eyed, ruddy-complexioned Hayne was reputedly handsome and amiable, benevolent and conciliating in his disposition and possessed of an irreproachable character. He was also a renowned horseman and horse breeder. Like so many of the lowcountry gentry, Hayne was known to be somewhat averse to politics, and he seemingly possessed no military ambition, but once the Revolution was in motion he warmly espoused the Whig cause.[4]

Hayne Hall in Colleton County, a few miles from Jacksonboro and a little more than thirty miles west of Charleston, consisted of a center three-story wooden building with a cupola flanked by two wings. The manor was altogether "a very large and elegant residence, with accommodations and grounds fitted up after the English style," and always the center of profuse, genial, and elegant hospitality. The flower garden was adorned with an artificial fishpond.[5]

The cultivation of rice and indigo necessitated a huge labor force of slaves. In addition to field hands, plantations required a large number of other workmen, household servants, and personal attendants. Hayne also employed the occasional

---

*"Pon Pon" is an Indian name given to the last twenty miles of the Edisto River. An Indian settlement by that name preceded the establishment of the town of Jacksonboro. "Pon Pon" was also used at the time to refer to the environs of Jacksonboro.

indentured servant. The only glimpse into Hayne's treatment of his slaves is found in a 1767 letter in which he is chided for not whipping a young slave woman who had committed an offense that warranted corporal punishment. "I am almost sorry you did not order the Wench another flogging," wrote his correspondent, who added that it was not too late to do it.[6]

As a member of the lowcountry elite, Hayne moved in prominent circles. He counted among his intimate friends Dr. David Ramsay (1748–1815), a transplanted physician from Pennsylvania who became an ardent patriot. After the war Ramsay was one of the new republic's first and most prolific historians. Hayne's oldest and dearest friend, however, was Richard Hutson (1747–1795), a College of New Jersey (now Princeton University) classmate of Ramsay. Hutson was both a planter and a lawyer who served as a delegate to the Continental Congress from South Carolina and signed the Articles of Confederation. He would be elected South Carolina's lieutenant governor in 1782 and became the first intendant (mayor) of Charleston when the city incorporated in 1783. In 1788 Hutson served as a delegate to the state convention that adopted the U.S. Constitution.[7]

Richard Hutson, Member of the Continental Congress.
Etching by Max Rosenthal (n.d.). From the Thomas Addis Emmet, Collection of
Illustrations Relating to the American Revolution and Early United States History.
Courtesy of the New York Public Library.

The Hutsons became more than friends to Isaac Hayne. They became his extended family on July 18, 1765, when twenty-year-old Isaac married Richard Hutson's older sister Elizabeth (born 1746) at the Independent or Congregational

Church[8] in Charleston. Their decade of marriage before the war produced eight children, six of whom were still living in 1780. When Isaac's sister Mary died in 1769, leaving him without a sibling, Elizabeth's widowed older sister Mary (Mrs. Arthur Peronneau) and her brother Richard certainly helped to fill the void.[9]

The close relationship that existed between Isaac Hayne and his in-laws was evident in the spring and summer of 1776, when the South Carolina lowcountry was preparing for the anticipated attack of a combined British expeditionary force commanded by Cdre. Peter Parker and Maj. Gen. Henry Clinton. Elizabeth Hayne, prone to bouts of melancholy, was in precarious health and pregnant with twins at Hayne Hall. Isaac would soon be reporting to Charleston to assist in the town's defense. Richard Hutson earnestly sought Isaac's permission to move Elizabeth and the rest of the Hayne family, first to his house in town, then later to the safety of his well-guarded Montpelier plantation on James Island, which was closer than Hayne Hall to Charleston. Mary Peronneau was there, and Elizabeth would receive the best of care. Hutson was well prepared in case the British appeared off Charleston Harbor, which they eventually did, in June 1776. He kept his large boat at his front landing, ready at all times to evacuate the family to Pon Pon (Jacksonboro) if the British took Fort Johnson on James Island and moved in their direction. Isaac was not persuaded and offered the Hutsons the protection of Hayne Hall instead.[10]

Under South Carolina's royal rule, the Commons House of Assembly was popularly elected from the parishes. It generally followed the procedures and customs of the British House of Commons to enact public and private statutory legislation. In a special 1769 election held to replace a deceased member, the twenty-four-year-old Hayne was elected to represent the parish of St. Bartholomew in the Twenty-ninth Royal Assembly. He qualified for his seat on February 2, 1770, and during the course of the remainder of the 1769–1771 session he was appointed a commissioner to stamp and issue bonds to defray the expense of building courthouses and jails in several districts.[11]

Transitioning from royal government to constitutional self-government, with a Provincial Congress (1775–1776) as an intermediate step, South Carolina adopted a new constitution on March 26, 1776. The legislative body under this new constitution consisted of a general assembly. Without his knowledge Hayne was elected to the Second General Assembly (1776–1778) from the parish of St. Paul. "I think it will be extraordinary if I should give you the first intelligence of your election as a Representative in Assembly for the Parish of St. Paul, Stono," wrote Richard Hutson to his brother-in-law on January 18, 1777, adding, "It will indeed convince me that you are a recluse."[12]

Of the balloting Hutson wrote, "the return was made to the House on Wednesday last. It is said that you had but four votes, and it has been thrown out by some of the high churchmen [Anglicans] that were they in your situation they would not serve, but I hope you will make it a point at this juncture, as we stand in need of your assistance." Hutson's interest in Hayne's election extended beyond the familial, as the issue of disestablishment of the Church of England as the officially sanctioned Church of the state was being debated on the assembly floor. The dissenters' petition for disestablishment had come before the legislature during the previous week, and Hutson was garnering support for the measure. Hayne, a devout and prominent member of the Bethel Presbyterian Church and Congregation of Pon Pon and therefore a dissenter, did in fact decline his election, but Hutson need not have worried. A second constitution adopted on March 19, 1778, disestablished the Church of England. The constitution also divided the legislature into a senate and a house of representatives. At the next election Hayne consented to represent St. Bartholomew in the senate for the term of the Third General Assembly (1779–1780).[13]

Hayne was called to other duties as well. For example, after the inhabitants of South Carolina were shocked to learn that British troops had fired on and been fired upon by American militiamen in Massachusetts at Lexington and Concord on April 19, 1775, the Provisional Congress determined, among other things, to reaffirm its stance on nonimportation and nonconsumption of British goods. This was accomplished by instituting a three-month moratorium on the export of rice from the province and by purchasing quantities of rice and flour for stockpiling in public granaries that would be set up at Charleston, Jacksonboro, Beaufort, Dorchester, Georgetown, Orangeburg, Ninety Six, and other strategic locations. Isaac Hayne was appointed one of three commissioners to receive and inspect the rice and flour in Jacksonboro.[14]

Hayne served as a captain of the Pon Pon company in the Colleton County militia and was posted for a time in late 1775 at Dorchester. On January 14, 1776, he brought 150 privates and 13 officers for service in Charleston. When the Council of Safety requested that Col. William Moultrie submit a plan for the town's defense in preparation for a British attack, Moultrie posted Captain Hayne's detachment at the northwest corner of Broad and Meeting Streets in front of the State House, fronting to the east in the direction of the Royal Exchange and Customs House. Hayne's early biographers maintain that sometime later he was nominated colonel of the regiment but that when, "owing to some intrigues believed to be practiced in favor of his competitor," a less meritorious junior officer was unjustly elected over him, Hayne resigned in disgust and served in the ranks instead. True or not, the story goes that "by his exemplary zeal and obedience he very much advanced the discipline of his regiment, and highly contributed to its subsequent utility."[15]

In 1778 Hayne's entrepreneurial spirit intersected with patriotism when he entered into a joint venture with Col. William Hill, giving him half-ownership of an ironworks and foundry in York District, located in the north-central part of the state close to the North Carolina line. The iron ore in that region of the country was by contemporary accounts plentiful and produced on average half its weight in pure iron. John Rutledge, South Carolina's president (governor), foresaw the difficulty of procuring sufficient quantities of cannon shot with which to make a defense in case of invasion; encouraged by Rutledge, the Provincial Congress of South Carolina had, in March 1776, granted Hill a premium of £1,000 currency as an inducement to begin construction of an ironworks and funded an additional £7,000 currency two years later.[16]

Under his agreement with Hayne, Hill was managing partner of the facility, named the Aera Furnace. He was responsible for procuring iron ore and hardwood for fuel and for hiring an overseer, a clerk, and skilled laborers. An unskilled work-force was needed; that is where Hayne came in. Joining with Hill in March 1778, Hayne provided additional funding and at least thirty slaves by the end of the year (more than half were women). Together the partners fed, clothed, and equipped the workers, and the company ran a farm to grow their food.[17]

The Aera Furnace was situated on Allison Creek two miles from the Catawba River. According to John Drayton it was by far the most complete and extensive ironworks in the upcountry. The manufactory consisted of a forge of four fires and two hammers, a furnace for melting iron ore and making castings, a sheet-iron rolling mill, a nail manufactory, and several outbuildings. The aim of the Provincial Congress in subsidizing this private enterprise was to encourage the casting of cannonballs, shells, kettles, utensils, and other implements for use by the army. In this the Aera Furnace was very successful, producing a variety of items for camp such as kettles, Dutch ovens, and stoves but also anvils, hammers, andirons, fire-backs (carrying the slogan "Liberty or Death"), and parts for wagons and carts. According to a notice placed by Hayne in the Charleston newspapers, the firm would cast to order "Swivel Guns and Cohorns [mortars], of any size, 2, 3, or 4 Pounders, with Balls to suit, with any fixed Cannon Ball or any other casting in Iron."[18]

Hill later argued that while it was in operation, the Aera Furnace almost wholly supplied the garrison of Charleston with cannonballs and other iron articles "without which, they could not have made the glorious and gallant defence which they did against the Enemy." It was only natural that a legitimate military target like the ironworks would eventually attract the attention of the British. The site was raided on June 18, 1780, by Capt. Christian Huck, who led a detachment of Tarleton's dragoons and loyalist militia. Hill wrote that Huck's men "destroyed all the property they could not carry away. Burned the forge furnace, grist and saw mills together with all other buildings even to the negro huts, & bore away about 90 negroes." The marauders absconded with all of the wagons, cattle, and horses. As a consequence of the raid, Hill's wife and children were reduced to living in a little log hut. General Cornwallis considered the destruction of the Aera Furnace vital to ending resistance in South Carolina.[19]

By the time of the 1780 siege of Charleston, Hayne was senior captain of the Round O[20] company of the Colleton County regiment, which evidence suggests was a mounted corps. The company was stationed at an outpost somewhere behind the British lines from whence Hayne and his men could engage in quick hit-and-run sorties; surprise and ambush were their forte. Accordingly, they were not trapped inside the Charleston siege lines at the time of capitulation on May 12, 1780. After Charleston surrendered, Hayne and his comrades assumed that even though they were not part of the garrison, the articles of capitulation applied to them. They disbanded and went home.[21]

What happened next is somewhat murky. General Greene in his report to the Continental Congress stated that Hayne "left the place of his residence . . . and retired about two hundred miles into the back Country, intending to remain there, as he conceived he might with safety, until the Troops under Major General Baron de Kalb, who were daily expected, should arrive, and, whom on their coming into the State, he intended to join." Instead he was taken prisoner by a party of the enemy, carried to Charleston, and given a choice of either taking protection or being sent to St. Augustine aboard a prison ship." Where Greene got his information is unknown, but he was not in full possession of the facts.[22]

Dr. Ramsay, whose account carries the weight of an eyewitness, has Hayne going home first and then to Charleston voluntarily: "After the capitulation, there being no American army in the state, and the prospect of one being both distant and uncertain, no alternative was left but either to abandon his family and property, or to surrender to the conquerors. This hard dilemma, together with well-founded information, that others in similar circumstances had been paroled to their plantations, weighed with colonel Hayne so far as to induce a conclusion, that, instead of waiting to be captured, it would be both more safe and more honourable to come within the British lines, and surrender himself a voluntary prisoner. He therefore repaired to Charleston, and offered to bind himself by the honour of an American officer, to do nothing prejudicial to the British interest till he should be exchanged."[23]

Lt. Col. Henry "Light Horse Harry" Lee (1756–1818), who commanded a legion under Greene in the Carolinas in 1781, offered more details and a different slant in his memoirs, first published in 1812. In Lee's account, Hayne headed home presuming he was under the protection of the fourth article of the capitulation, which said: "The militia now in garrison shall be permitted to return to their respective homes, as prisoners upon parole, which, so long as they observe it, shall secure them from being molested in their property by the British troops." Sometime between mid-June and mid-July 1780, Col. Robert Ballingall, a prominent St. Bartholomew planter appointed by Cornwallis to command the Colleton County loyal militia, visited Hayne's residence out of personal respect and communicated the intent of "the extraordinary proclamation of Sir Henry Clinton, which ordered all our militia prisoners on parole, not taken by capitulation, or in confinement, at the surrendering of Lincoln, to become British subjects, or return instantly to the commandant of Charleston."[24]

Whatever the military factors weighing on Hayne as he decided to report to Charleston or was coerced into going, there was another matter over which he was practically distraught. Smallpox was ravaging the district, and the dreaded disease was raging through his own family. His eighteen-month-old daughter Eliza had already died, his wife was nigh unto death herself, and most if not all of his children were perilously sick. William Edward, age four, was so gravely ill and the expectation of his recovery was so slight that a coffin had been made for him. He survived, but his twin sister, Mary, was not so fortunate.[25]

When Hayne's argument of inviolability—that he was covered by the articles of capitulation—seemed to fall on deaf ears, he declared to the loyalist officer that "no human force should remove him from the side of his dying wife." Following a protracted discussion with Ballingall, Hayne finally agreed to go to Charleston, but not before he and Ballingall agreed in writing that Hayne would "demean himself as a British subject so long as that country should be covered by the British army."[26]

So Hayne set off for town, primarily to obtain a physician, medicines, and other necessaries for his desperately ill wife and children. While there, naively hoping to remain neutral under the covenant that predated Clinton's proclamation, he intended to reaffirm, on his honor as an American officer, his intention to do nothing prejudicial to British interests until he was properly exchanged. If all went according to plan, he would return home straightaway. With grave misgivings he took leave of his wife, anticipating a homecoming on the morrow.[27]

It did not go well for Hayne at all. To his astonishment and great mortification, when he presented himself to Charleston commandant Brig. Gen. James Patterson, showing the commandant his agreement with Ballingall and asking permission to return to his family forthwith, Patterson peremptorily refused. He had been told of Hayne's military ability and influence. Instead, he informed Hayne that he must take the king's protection, swear allegiance, and become a loyal British subject or else face imprisonment. For the sake of his honor Hayne would have gladly submitted to close confinement, but what of his family? He felt an overwhelming compulsion to get home as soon as possible—they needed him. To abandon his family "was too much for a tender husband and a fond parent. To acknowledge himself the subject of a king whose government he had from principle renounced, was repugnant to his feelings; but without this he was cut off from every prospect of a return to his family."[28]

Hayne immediately sought the advice of his friend David Ramsay (not yet an exiled captive of the British). He bared his soul: "If the British would grant me the indulgence which we, in the day of our power gave to their adherents, of removing my family and property, I would seek an asylum in the remotest corner of the United States rather than submit to their government; but as they allow no other alternative than submission or confinement in the capital, at a distance from my wife and family, at a time when they are in the most pressing need of my presence and support, I will for the present yield to the demands of the conquerors."[29]

Hayne was aware of how his actions might appear to others and asked Ramsey to be his witness: "I request you to bear in mind, that, previous to my taking this step, I declare, that it is contrary to my inclination, and forced on me by hard necessity. I never will bear arms against my country. My new masters can require no service of me but what is enjoined by the old militia-law of the province, which substitutes a fine in lieu of personal service. That I will pay as the price of my protection. If my conduct should be censured by my countrymen, I beg that you would remember this conversation, and bear witness for me, that I do not mean to desert the cause of America."[30]

Calmed by Ramsey, Hayne returned to Patterson and signed a declaration of allegiance to King George III, albeit under tremendous duress. It was a moral necessity—a conscious choice of a husband and father making peace with the British government on the only terms the British would allow. In doing so he expressly objected to the clause that required him to take active part in efforts to support the royal government, under arms if necessary. According to Ramsay, General Patterson and intendant of the British police James Simpson assured him that this would not be an issue, telling Hayne that "when the regular forces could not defend the country without the aid of its inhabitants, it would be high time for the royal army to quit it." The terms of Hayne's reluctant submission were well known to the patriots in Charleston. With the permission of the British, he then journeyed home to his family. Not long after his return to Hayne Hall, his wife succumbed to her illness.[31]

The grave of Elizabeth Hutson Hayne (1746–1780).
Author's collection.

Chapter 5

The Captor Becomes the Captive

A representation of Hayne's motivations and actions was offered to the British reading public in Lt. Roderick MacKenzie's 1787 rebuttal of Lt. Col. Banastre Tarleton's *A History of the Campaigns of 1780 and 1781, in the Southern Provinces of North America,* first published in 1781. MacKenzie was contemporaneously credited with accurately pointing out the errors in Tarleton's self-aggrandizing work, but when it came to Isaac Hayne he was writing fiction. "Upon the entrance of General Greene into South Carolina," MacKenzie began his outlandish account, "Mr. Hayne accepted a commission in the American service in a secret manner, soon after which he came to Charlestown, renewed his oath of allegiance to the King, and at his own request was appointed to the command of a corps of militia. When he had remained long enough in that garrison to obtain every possible intelligence, partly by persuasion, partly by force, he occasioned the revolt of the whole body which he commanded to the Americans. The first advice which our commanders received of this treachery, was the account of an expedition in which Mr. Hayne surprised a number of sick and wounded British soldiers, within two miles of Charlestown, where he was charged with committing some extraordinary acts of barbarity."[1]

In truth Hayne tried to keep his end of the bargain with the British, and he managed to do so for about ten months even though his friends and neighbors sought to have him put in command of their local militia regiment. One who tried to influence Hayne was Col. William Harden, an exceedingly popular militia leader from Prince William's Parish who himself had submitted to the British after the fall of Charleston and for a while had followed the rules of his parole at his estate. Inspired by the successes of Generals Marion and Sumter, Harden eventually began to gather partisan fighters to serve with him under the command of the "Swamp Fox," Marion. By April 1781 Harden's men had wrested control of the Jacksonboro area from Ballingall's loyalist militia and set up camp at the Horse Shoe, a section of high land between Horse Shoe Creek and Chessey

Creek near the Ashepoo River and three miles north by northwest of Hayne Hall. Expecting Hayne to take the field, Harden had brought him a colonel's commission from Marion.[2]

Hayne's young friend Paul Hamilton, who would survive the war to serve as governor of South Carolina and secretary of the U.S. Navy, delivered the commission, which Hayne summarily refused. Nor would he allow Hamilton to appropriate any of his horses for use by the Americans. In fact, Hayne told Hamilton that as soon as he learned of Harden's approach he ordered all his horses spirited away lest he give the appearance of assisting Harden and thus be perceived by the British as violating his oath of allegiance. Harden's impatience and frustration at Hayne's refusal to waver is evident in his letter to Marion on April 7, 1781: "You will receive a letter from Col. Hayne with the commission. You will hear his reasons for not accepting it. This gentleman has kept many from joining me on his staying on too much formality."By adhering to his pledge to the British, Hayne not only kept himself out of the fight but, by his restraint, also prevented others who vacillated over the same choice.[3]

For a time the region of Hayne's domicile alternated in possession by the two opposing sides. The British would not leave him alone, plundering his property yet repeatedly calling him to join the loyalist militia and threatening close confinement if he didn't. Hayne steadfastly refused to be intimidated or to give in to what he considered violation of the stipulation he had given Patterson and Simpson when he took protection (such as it was), even though his profession of allegiance to the British king had been an act of necessity given under duress. Moreover, General Greene's reestablishment of American control over most of South Carolina made it impossible for him to receive the promised British protection unless he went into their camps, which he would not do.[4]

But once the Americans retained firm possession of the country well below where Hayne resided, his patriot neighbors again pressed him to accept a colonel's commission and assume command of the Colleton County Regiment of Militia. It soon became clear that if he refused to bear arms with his countrymen he would be putting himself at risk of being taken prisoner and subjected to harsh treatment by those whom he considered friends and comrades-in arms. Neutrality was out of the question. He would have to declare for one side or the other. "If for Us," wrote Rutledge, it was important "that he shd. shew he was in Earnest—If against Us, his Person & Property were at our Mercy, & he could not, in that Case, have expected any Favour." If Isaac Hayne truly intended to remain out of the war and if what Rutledge said is true, then the burden of responsibility for what happened to Hayne consequent to his decision to rejoin the fight on the rebel side belongs in part to the Americans rather than wholly to the British.[5]

His change of heart seems to have come about not long after his initial refusal to accept a commission. On April 18 Harden reported to Marion that Hayne was nearly ready to commit and that if he did, two hundred men would follow him. Only after the British were driven below the Edisto River and the area secured did Hayne finally return to active duty, though precisely when is unclear. Except for assertions that he "entered the field with boldness, enterprise, and vigor" and that he was elected colonel of a regiment of his own, little is known of his service until he embarked on the raid in July that would carry him to his destiny. Nor is it known whether Hayne had given due consideration to the fact that by returning to active service he risked not only the enemy's guns but the gallows as well, that, as McCrady aptly put it, he was fighting "truly, if figuratively, with a halter around his neck."[6]

It is only fair to say that patriot militiamen had been guilty of behavior disgraceful to the American cause, and lawless acts against loyalists cannot be denied. But, said Maj. Alexander Garden who served under Henry Lee and as aide-de-camp to General Greene, "no man lamented them with greater sincerity than Colonel Hayne, for none more anxiously wished the American character to be free from reproach." When Hayne's friends and neighbors urged him to resume a hostile position and to become their leader, he made an honorable and open declaration "that he could only be induced to comply with their wishes, by obtaining a solemn promise from all who were to serve under him, that an immediate stop should be put to every unnecessary severity; a desideratum [prerequisite] the more to be insisted upon, as he was resolved that exemplary punishment should be indicted on every individual who should indulge in pillage, or commit any act of inhumanity against the foe." A written copy of this declaration was alleged to have been found on his person when he was captured.[7]

Hayne's return to duty along with the others who were willing to follow his example swelled the ranks of the patriot militia and posed a real hazard for the British. Now the patriot militias patrolled between Lord Rawdon's army and Charleston, actively interfering with British lines of supply and communication between the main army and Charleston. Lieutenant Colonel Balfour in Charleston purportedly first became aware of Hayne in late June while Rawdon was making his way back toward Charleston from his expedition to break the siege at Ninety Six. Hayne was also active enough to attract the notice of former royal lieutenant governor William Bull II who mentioned him in a letter to Lord George Germain on July 2, 1781.[8]

Hayne found it difficult to navigate between Scylla and Charybdis before recommitting to the patriot cause, but such was not the case for Brig. Gen. Andrew

Williamson from Ninety Six. In June 1780 Williamson took protection and swore allegiance to the Crown in order to preserve his property and fortune. Soon afterward he began to cooperate with the British by giving military information and supplying provisions, actions for which he was decried as a traitor to the patriot cause.* Rebel militia captured him at his home, White Hall, near Ninety Six, in December 1780, perhaps hoping to convince him to reconsider his defection. He escaped forthwith and retired to the supposed safety of Horse Savannah plantation, located inside the British lines of Charleston on the road to Dorchester near the Quarter House tavern, about five miles north of town.[9]

Colonel Hayne set out from camp at the Horse Shoe with a party of Colleton County mounted militia during the night of Thursday, July 5, to see if he could capture Williamson. His party penetrated the Charleston neck into enemy territory undetected and quietly deployed in a circle around Williamson's plantation. Catching him completely by surprise ("in a situation not creditable to him as a man of family" by one exaggerated account), they took him from his bed without even allowing him time to properly dress and rode hard back to the Horse Shoe with him in close custody. What great fortune! The Americans had badly wanted Williamson back, presumably to carry him to Greene's camp, where he would be tried on charges of treason and, presupposing a guilty verdict, hanged by the neck until he was dead.[10]

The British were livid over Williamson's capture, concerned for his life, and embarrassed by their apparent inability to safeguard a loyal citizen. Charleston commandant Nisbet Balfour feared that Williamson's defection to the British side might cause the rebels to subject him to the harshest of measures, and he immediately mobilized ninety dragoons of Maj. Thomas Fraser's mounted South Carolina Loyalist Rangers to pursue and retake Williamson. By avoiding main roads and acting with utmost secrecy, Fraser and his men covered seventy circuitous miles through the woods to Harden's camp at the Horse Shoe. On the morning of Saturday, July 8, Fraser launched a surprise attack that caught the Americans completely by surprise.[11]

The accounts of what happened that morning are rather sketchy and to a degree speculative, but it appears that Hayne and his second-in-command, Lt. Col. Thomas McLaughlin, accompanied by Maj. Charles Glover and a few of their men, were not at the Horse Shoe when the British column assaulted the main camp. Instead, they were a mile and a half or so to the northwest at Woodford

---

*Brig. Gen. Andrew Williamson's sobriquet "Benedict Arnold of South Carolina" may not be deserved. Evidence suggests that while behind British lines he supplied information to Maj. Gen. Nathanael Greene. This subject is addressed in Chapter 9.

plantation, home of the widow Mary Ford. Woodford, where Hayne had made his temporary quarters, was more than eight miles south-southwest of the Edisto crossing at Parker's Ferry, and Hayne may have stopped over on the way back to the Horse Shoe—his fine mount, King Herod, had grown too heavy for great exertion during his period of inactivity and had foundered during the raid. Another story is that Hayne either called or was summoned to a meeting at Woodford that morning but that it was all a pretense and a trap and that Mrs. Ford signaled to the British by waving her handkerchief from an upstairs window. Or perhaps he and McLaughlin and Glover were merely having breakfast with friends at the wrong place at the wrong time.[12]

Capture of Hayne and Death of M'Laughlin.
A woodcut illustration from Horatio Newton Moore, *The Life and Times of Gen. Francis Marion* (Philadelphia: Leary, Getz, 1845), 141. Courtesy of the Special Collections and Archives Division, Robert M. Strozier Library, Florida State University, Tallahassee, Fla.

At no time do the accounts of Hayne's capture specifically mention General Williamson's whereabouts or the details of his liberation except for the *Royal Gazette*'s statement that he was in confinement "at a house in the neighbourhood," which could have been the Ford house. John Rutledge later maintained that Hayne "used him like a Gentleman, & immediately gave him his Parol to Charles-Town," but this doesn't stand up to reason—why go to the trouble to capture Williamson only to release him? Had Hayne done this, the British sortie to rescue Williamson would have been unnecessary.[13]

As noted earlier, the British attacked the Horse Shoe camp first. Harden was there and withstood the enemy despite taking heavy losses, but he had insufficient numbers to mount a pursuit. At some point the British learned Hayne's location. Onward went the dragoons to the Ford house, thundering down a tree-lined road. Hayne was oblivious to their approach until they were too close—a hungry but negligent guard had supposedly left his post in search of fruit or some other food. The Americans attempted a quick escape across a rice field toward a causeway that led to the safety of a swamp. Coming to a fence, King Herod gave out and balked, forcing Hayne to dismount to take down the fence, thus losing precious time. Pressing on, he tried to leap a ditch, but the bank caved and both horse and rider fell. Captain Archibald "Mad Archy" Campbell's South Carolina Light Dragoons of Fraser's corps had been steadily gaining on Hayne, and Campbell himself rode up to capture his bruised and semiconscious quarry. In the short but vicious melee, McLaughlin was killed while trying to fend off Fraser's dragoons with his sword.[14]

The Royal Exchange and Customs House where Isaac Hayne was held prisoner. Photograph by Rick Rhodes, Charleston, S.C. Reproduced with permission.

His captors immediately conveyed Hayne to Charleston, where he was incarcerated in the city jail or provost, located in the cellar under the Royal Exchange and Custom House. The massive stone building on the waterfront of the Cooper River at the foot of Broad Street had served as the center of Charleston's import-export trade. It had also housed meetings of South Carolina's nascent revolutionary government—the state's delegates to the First Continental Congress were elected in the Great Hall upstairs. During the siege of Charleston, just days before capitulation, General Moultrie had ordered gunpowder moved from the town's old powder magazine to a hidden compartment in the cellar (adjacent to the provost), where confiscated British tea had once been stored before the war. The powder went undiscovered by the redcoats and was recovered in 1783. The U.S. Constitution would be ratified there in 1788, and in 1791 President George Washington on his southern tour would address a cheering crowd from a platform raised behind the grand balustrade in front.[15]

But these were dark days in Charleston generally and at the Exchange in particular, and the most shameful chapter in the history of the building began when Hayne entered the dark and dank confines of the cellar's brick barrel-vaulted walls and ceiling. There he languished for almost three weeks. The record is silent concerning his treatment. If he was allowed visits from friends and family there is no record; whether he was spitefully abused or treated with respect is unknown. Perhaps the silence bears its own evidence, for if he had been abused during his period of confinement certainly some mention of his maltreatment would be found in the documentation that begins on July 26.

The delay in the disposition of Hayne's case was conceivably a matter of inattention on the part of Charleston's commandant, Lieutenant Colonel Balfour. Perhaps Balfour was too distracted by his duties to give due time and attention to Hayne's case. He had issued proclamations for the governance of the citizens under his power and seen to the exchange of American prisoners held captive under his charge. He had banished the families of the patriot exiles in St. Augustine and harassed them in their departure by burdening them with onerous economic restrictions. Or perhaps he was holding Hayne in reserve, as McCrady suggested, "as a choice morsel on which the cruel vindictiveness of his nature should have full leisure to expend itself."[16]

There are in fact more compelling motives to explain the delay. Recall that Balfour's relationship with Henry Clinton was rather fragile—he got along much better with Lord Cornwallis, who commanded the southern theater. Rawdon on the other hand was favored by both senior officers. Complicating matters was the fact that the relationship between Balfour and Rawdon had been strained by questions of rank and command. Cornwallis's clear preference for Rawdon as the de facto commander of British forces in South Carolina beyond Balfour's Charleston domain irked Balfour, who held a regular army rank of lieutenant colonel, higher than Rawdon's provincial rank of full colonel. Whatever the case, while Rawdon made his way back from relieving Cruger's garrison at Ninety Six, Balfour made him aware of his intention to use a captured rebel officer (Hayne) as an example. If Rawdon would agree, and it turned out that he did, then Balfour would be insulated from censure by Clinton.[17]

Representatives of Generals Greene and Cornwallis had already agreed upon and signed articles of a Southern Department prisoner exchange cartel on May 3, 1781. The cartel stipulated that regular troops were to be exchanged for regulars and militia for militia and that officers who could not be exchanged for want of a captured opponent of similar rank were to be paroled to their homes to await exchange. Technically, because the date of his capture by the British was July 8, Hayne was not covered by the exchange cartel, which affected captives taken between the onset of hostilities and June 15, 1781. He was taken prisoner three weeks beyond the deadline.[18]

In June 1781, Greene's deputy commissary general of prisoners, Maj. Edmund M. Hyrne, traveled to Charleston under the terms of the cartel to finalize the exchange of prisoners. While there he discovered that Balfour had refused to release according to the terms of the cartel six American captives because of certain alleged infractions. Two of the six were accused of having taken up arms against the British after declaring allegiance, and one man was being held for violating his parole. Hyrne was unable to negotiate their release, and in his correspondence with Greene he named five of the six. The only prisoner not specifically named could have been Hayne unless Balfour kept Hayne deliberately out of Major Hyrne's sight. Hyrne and the British were unable to satisfactorily resolve the status and fate of these prisoners, but it is clear that at no time in the negotiations did the British declare their intention to impose the death penalty.[19]

On Thursday morning, July 26, Hayne received a short note from Maj. Charles Fraser[20] stating that he (Fraser) was "directed by the Commandant to acquaint you, that a Board of Field officers will assemble tomorrow at ten o'clock for your trial." Later in the day he received another communiqué from Fraser informing him "that instead of a Board of Field Officers, as is mentioned in my letter of this morning, a Court of Enquiry, consisting of four field officers, and five captains, will assemble to-morrow at 10 o'clock, at the State House, for the purpose of ascertaining, in what point of view you are to be looked upon." He would be allowed paper, pen, and ink; for legal representation, "any person you may name will be permitted to attend you as your Counsel, at the above place and hour."[21]

The court of inquiry seems to have been an invention of Lieutenant Colonel Balfour, but there was a legal precedent, at least in Balfour's mind. The rebels had convened just such a tribunal for the purpose of examining Maj. John André, who was captured and hanged as a spy in October 1780 after Maj. Gen. Benedict Arnold's infamous defection to the British. Balfour did not dare subject Hayne to a civilian trial for fear that his popular prisoner might be acquitted. Nor did he have the power to convene a general court-martial as Hayne was not a British soldier.

He sought the advice of Lord Rawdon, who, after looking into the facts, was finally convinced that "by all the recognized laws of war, nothing was requisite in the case of Hayne, but to identify his person previous to hanging him on the next tree." It is worth noting that while operating in the field Rawdon had imposed capital punishment but Balfour had not.[22]

The Unfortunate Death of Major André.
John Goldar's engraving after the painting by William Hamilton; an illustration from
Edward Barnard, *The New, Comprehensive and Complete History of England* (London: Alexander
Hoag, 1783), plate following page 694. National Archives and Records Administration, Washington, D.C.

The hearing took place on Friday and Saturday, July 27 and 28, and what exactly occurred is unknown as no minutes are extant. An unnamed American staff officer, a prisoner on parole said to have been present, described the proceedings as the most summary imaginable, the agenda confined to establishing conclusively that Hayne had taken protection and then resumed his arms. The lieutenant marshal of the provost had been unable to locate John Colcock, the person whom Hayne had named as his counsel. Having no idea that he was attending anything but a court of inquiry that would determine in what point of view he was to be looked upon, Hayne did not summon any witnesses, though doing so was within his rights. No matter, Hayne thought—witnesses and legal representation could wait for a full court-martial or other tribunal that would more intensively examine the facts. Under these circumstances he appeared before the court without any legal assistance whatsoever, and the proceedings convinced him that his supposition of the purpose of the court of inquiry was correct: the members of the court were not sworn and witnesses were not examined under oath.[23]

According to Alexander Garden, it was during Hayne's appearance before the tribunal that a copy of the address found on his person at the time of his capture declaring his honorable intentions was presented to a Major McKenzie,[24] who was acting as president of the court. McKenzie, "with great expression of sensibility, requested the prisoner 'to retain it till he should be brought before the Court-Martial that was to determine his fate,' assuring him, 'that the present Court were only directed to inquire, whether or not he acknowledged himself to be the individual who had taken protection.'"[25]

Imagine Hayne's astonishment and dismay on July 29 when he received notice that "in consequence of the Court of Enquiry held on him, yesterday, and the preceding day, Lord Rawdon, and the Commandant have come to a resolution that he shall be executed on Tuesday, the 31st inst., at 6 o'clock in the morning, for being found in arms, and levying a Regiment to oppose the British Government, notwithstanding he had become a subject, and had accepted the protection under that government, after the reduction of Charles Town."[26]

No lawyer present! No witnesses called, though he could have called many! No defense at all mounted by the accused! A capital sentence to be carried out on such short notice! Writing to Balfour and Rawdon, Hayne protested, albeit humbly, that it must have been obvious to everyone present—the members of the court, the witnesses—from the questions he asked and the tenor of his conduct throughout that Hayne had not the least notion that his life depended on the outcome of the proceedings and the findings of the court. Hayne declared that he did not believe that the members of the court themselves or any person present conceived that the stakes were so high. He could understand the brevity and the abrupt verdict were he a spy—"because the single fact, whether a spy or not, is all that is inquired into; and his entering the lines of the Enemy's Encampment or garrison, subjects him to military execution." But such was not the case. That accusation had not been, nor could it be, made against Hayne; the only question was whether he should be considered a British or an American subject: "if the former, to be intitled [sic] to a fair and legal trial; if the latter, to be admitted to Parole."[27]

Immediately on receiving what amounted to his death warrant, Hayne again sent for Colcock, a Charleston attorney whom he had known for years. Colcock had lost his post as justice of the peace for Berkeley County in 1770 for being a "Son of Liberty" and had served St. Mark's Parish in South Carolina's Provincial

Congress. Now Colcock and Hayne feverishly went to work. Later that day (July 29) they sent Rawdon and Balfour a packet containing a letter from Hayne and Colcock's legal brief outlining the reasons that that the proceedings against Hayne had deprived his client of due process and were thus unlawful. In the letter Hayne asked, for the sake of justice and equity, that he be granted the favor of a regular trial—he had much to say in his defense. But, if not granted a trial, "I have to request, as I earnestly do, that the time of my execution be extended, that I may take a last farewell of my Children, and prepare for the awfull [*sic*] change."[28]

Colcock's legal brief (Appendix C) answered with four arguments a rhetorical question posed by Hayne: "whether the proceedings had are warranted by any Law and the Sentence thereupon Legal?" First Colcock pointed out that when Hayne was notified of his impending arraignment he was not informed of the specific accusations to be considered by the court of inquiry or the charges against him to which he would be required to furnish a defense. Second, the lawyer maintained that "no Enemy is liable to suffer Death by the Articles of War or any other Military rule of Law . . . without Trial, except Spies, who are by the Articles of War, are expressly deprived of that right."[29]

Third was the argument that "no subject is liable or can be deprived" of his "Life, Liberty or prosperity but by the Judgment of his Peers or the Law of the Land." There was no law, at least none that Colcock knew, that merited the type of trial and summary condemnation that Hayne had received. Furthermore, "it is an afixed [*sic*] rule of Law that a Man is to be presumed innocent 'till found Guilty," and "even being found or taken in Arms is not such a proof of Guilt as prevents a defense." Colcock's fourth and final argument was this: no matter which way the British considered Hayne, whether as an enemy combatant (not a spy) or as a British subject, the proceedings against him had been unwarranted and unlawful.[30]

Colcock's legal opinion of Hayne's situation did not sway Rawdon and Balfour to reverse their verdict, and they wasted no time responding to Hayne's plea for a trial. Major Fraser delivered this message at one o'clock on the following day (Monday, July 30): "I am to inform that you [were] not ordered for Execution in consequence of any sentence from the Court of enquiry, but by their Authority which is invested in them as Commander in Chief of the Army in South Carolina, & Commandant of Charlestown—therefore their resolution remains unalterable." Seemingly resigned to his fate, Hayne begged Fraser to intervene on his behalf so that he would have time to send for his children for a last farewell. Rawdon and Balfour at first seemed indisposed to show mercy of any kind and denied his request. At one o'clock in the morning of July 31—the date appointed for his execution—he was informed by the deputy provost that it was time for him to prepare for death. An escort would arrive to take him from his room at the provost at five o'clock.[31]

Isaac Hayne Being Led from the Exchange to the Scaffold. Painting by Carroll N. Jones Jr., 1973. Courtesy of the South Carolina Historical Society, Charleston, S.C.

Chapter 6

"The imminent and shocking doom of the most unfortunate Mr. Hayne"

Whether one believes that the British authorities—Rawdon, Balfour, or even Fraser—were toying with Hayne as a cat toys with a wounded mouse or, conversely, that an unfortunate but honest mistake had been made, Fraser returned a half hour later bearing news that Hayne had been granted a temporary stay of execution. Because Lt. Gov. William Bull and a number of others[1] had petitioned Rawdon and Balfour for leniency and because Hayne had been observed treating humanely British officers and soldiers who had fallen into his hands, Rawdon and Balfour granted him a forty-eight-hour reprieve. Hayne returned his thanks for the opportunity to see his children. Fraser departed but returned a short time later— he had actually forgotten part of his message: if General Greene should make any effort to intervene in his favor the reprieve would be terminated and Hayne would be immediately executed.[2]

It is provocative that Greene was mentioned and that his interference was of concern to Balfour and Rawdon, for it was about this time that Greene's deputy commissary general of prisoners, Major Hyrne, departed Charleston to return to the American camp at the High Hills of Santee northwest of Charleston. Whether Hyrne was aware of Hayne's dire predicament is unknown, but it is difficult to imagine that, with Hayne being such a prominent figure, Hyrne would not be cognizant of his imprisonment—unless, of course, Balfour and Rawdon made sure that Hyrne was well clear of Charleston before finally taking action against Hayne. Whether by intention or coincidence, the proceedings against Hayne began about the time Hyrne left town, perhaps the same day.[3]

It is not entirely clear how the majority of Charleston loyalists felt about Hayne's impending execution. Certainly some took a hard line, but there were also expressions of profound regret if not condemnation. Among those who tried to intercede were a few loyalists, Alexander Wright and Robert Powell in particular, whose attempt to circulate a petition on Hayne's behalf was quashed when former attorney general and despised loyalist Sir Egerton Leigh[4] refused to sign, saying he "would rather burn his hand off than do an act so injurious to the King's service." Another loyalist, John Scott, was said to be particularly active in promoting a petition in favor of the condemned man. Hayne's friends were at first filled with false optimism and disbelief over the possibility of an execution from which no present good or future advantage could arise. However, Maj. Harry Barry, the deputy adjutant general and Balfour's secretary, assured one loyalist hopeful "that his cherished expectations would be disappointed, for that the opinions of Lord Rawdon were immutable; and that since his fiat had been death, execution would inevitably follow."[5]

Rawdon later falsely argued that "not one Loyalist of repute could be persuaded to interpose." Rawdon's assertion notwithstanding, the most prominent of all loyalists, Lt. Gov. William Bull, whose promise to sign was at first conditional on the answer of Sir Egerton Leigh, later decided to join his name with those of the patriots. Despite his loyalty to the Crown, Bull was still one of the most beloved men of the province, even during the war, and, though wracked by age and suffering from kidney stones, he had himself conveyed on a litter by his slaves to British headquarters at the Brewton House to make a personal appeal for mitigation. Alexander Garden reported that "on [Bull's] return to his home, the dejection of his countenance at once proclaimed the ill-success of his interference; it was scarcely necessary for him to reply to a friend anxious to know the result of his visit. 'The unfortunate prisoner must die—I have used my best endeavours to save him, but Lord Rawdon is inexorable.'"[6]

Rawdon and Balfour received entreaties from the patriot side, and among them was a letter from certain ladies of Charleston (Appendix D) who professed themselves "deeply interested and affected by the imminent and shocking doom of the most unfortunate Mr. Hayne." The ladies asked the two British officers "in the most earnest manner graciously to avert, prolong or mitigate it," reminding them that humanity was inseparable from courage. A gallant soldier's reluctance to deliberately cause the infliction of death on men in cold blood, they said, should match his zeal in the heat of battle to make his enemies perish by the sword. "He may rejoice to behold his laurels sprinkled with the blood of armed men and resisting adversaries, but will regret to see them wet with the tears of unhappy orphans, mourning the loss of a tender, amiable and worthy parent, executed like a vile and infamous felon."[7]

Alexander Garden claimed that the petition came from the pen of Mrs. Charles Elliott, née Anna Ferguson, daughter of the ardent patriot Thomas Ferguson, who was among those exiled to St. Augustine. A zealot for the cause in her own right, she tempered her feelings and added praise of Rawdon's and Balfour's milder and softer qualities to admiration for their well-known military prowess. As for Hayne, the ladies would not dwell on his most excellent character, the depredations and murders against innocent and unarmed loyalists that he prevented, or "the most grievous shock his numerous and respectable connexions [sic] must sustain by his death." Nor would they do more than remind Rawdon and Balfour "of the complicated distress and sufferings that must befall his young and promising children, to whom perhaps death would be more comfortable than the state of orphanage they will be left in." Instead, the anxious petitioners appealed to Rawdon's and Balfour's spontaneous feelings, humane considerations, and liberal reasoning.[8]

It was all for naught. Balfour answered this petition the same way he answered all petitions for Hayne: he scribbled across the page the name "André," of course referring to his friend Maj. John André. It is said that he answered William Bull verbally to his face the same way but with more venom: "Remember André." Balfour remained bitter for the rest of his life over André's execution as a spy, and whether Balfour and Rawdon were motivated primarily or secondarily by a wish to avenge André is a subject for debate.[9]

During his reprieve Hayne was moved from the cellar of the Exchange to the North East Room[10] off the second floor Great Hall. Here he received visits from friends and family, always maintaining a dignified composure and even on his last night declaring that he was "no more alarmed at the thought of death than of any other occurrence which is necessary and unavoidable." But he did worry that his execution would bring reciprocal retaliation and the shedding of innocent blood.[11]

Hayne's late wife Elizabeth's widowed older sister Mrs. Arthur Peronneau (née Mary Hutson) attempted to save her brother-in-law's life by making a personal appeal to Lieutenant Colonel Rawdon, taking with her three of Hayne's remaining children—Isaac, Sarah, and William Edward, all clad in mourning clothes. Mary Peronneau was no stranger to dealing directly with the British—they had made her home their headquarters in 1779 and reportedly subjected her to every type of insult. Now she forced herself to swallow her pride and conceal her loathing. She and the children presented themselves and, "manifesting the torture of their heart-rending agony," got on their knees in the parlor of the Brewton house and pleaded for the life of her brother-in-law and the children's father. Their display was for naught—Rawdon's resolve was fixed and unchangeable.[12]

Awakened at three A.M. on August 1, Hayne was informed that he had been granted another forty-eight hours to live. This was to be the last bit of good news from the British. On Friday evening, August 3, the British authorities notified Hayne that "the many Cruelt[ies] exercised upon numberless Officers & men of the British Militia, extending even to Death (in many instances) an hour after [their] capture, have induced Lord Rawdon & the Commandant to order his Execution may take place tomorrow morning at 8 o'clock." Resigned to the certainty of his fate, Hayne sent back word that his "earnest desire & his last request was that he might die the death of a soldier taken in Arms," that is, by musketry delivered by a line of marksmen rather than by swinging from the gallows.[13]

During the evening, their Aunt Mary brought the three children to his room—Isaac, the eldest, who was fifteen; Sarah, who was almost eleven; and William Edward, who was just about five. Eight-year-old John Hamden had been spending time with an uncle at Black Swamp in St. Luke's Parish and had been sent for but did not arrive in time. They were all soon to be orphans, and that night they received their affectionate father's tearful farewell hugs and kisses and his last words of advice. It was a heartrending scene. The prisoner remained closely guarded by a Hessian sentinel throughout the night. His coffin, an elongated wooden box covered with black broad cloth and lined with white, had been callously thrust into the room.[14]

Mary Peronneau had diligently and lovingly ministered to Isaac during his confinement, and her unremitting affection and encouragement of religious consolation greatly alleviated his suffering. On the morning of his last day, however, she was so distressed by his circumstances that she sent her twelve-year-old son, William, to ask if he "would spare her the agony of a personal interview which she had not the resolution to support." The condemned man sent back his assurances that her efforts to save him from an ignominious death would be remembered with gratitude to the end and that he was confidant that he would meet her in a better and happier world. It is speculation to suggest that there was a romantic relationship growing between them, but they had known each other for many years and had both lost their spouses, and Mary evidently enjoyed a surrogate relationship with the motherless Hayne children.[15]

On the morning of August 4, before setting off for his final appointment, Hayne delivered to his eldest son, Isaac, a packet containing copies of the accumulated papers relevant to his case, instructing him to deliver them to Mrs. Rebecca Edwards. She was the wife of John Edwards, and Hayne wanted her to forward them to her brother Thomas Bee, who represented South Carolina in the Continental Congress. His last instructions to his son were to recover his body from the place of execution and to see that he was decently buried with his forefathers in the garden cemetery at Hayne Hall.[16]

All too soon a small party of armed redcoats appeared at Hayne's door under orders to deliver him to a place just outside the city. Under Major Fraser's direction,[17] they secured his hands behind his back. Surrounded by guards who escorted him down the stairs, Hayne exited the Exchange into the bright sunshine. Rather than having to bear the indignity of riding in the cart that transported his black-covered coffin, he was allowed to walk to his destination. As he strode west from the Exchange to the cadence of a drumbeat, a melancholy procession consisting of his eldest son, a clergyman, his lawyer, and a few other friends formed behind him, all trailed by the coffin-laden cart. The plodding hoof beats, the grinding of cartwheels into the street, and the rattle and tramp of Hayne's three-hundred-man military escort were the predominant sounds of the solemn parade. Thousands of anxious spectators lined the streets, mostly quiet, some weeping, a few bold enough to call out quiet words of prayerful encouragement. The soldiers' intimidating presence discouraged any form of protest. And certainly there were Tories among the crowd, some but not all believing that Hayne was about to receive his just deserts.[18]

Except for his lawyer, John Colcock, and perhaps two or three others, the identities of the gentlemen who accompanied Hayne on his long last walk are subject to conjecture. The clergyman was probably the loyalist rector of St. Phillip's, Rev. Robert Cooper. A definite third was Isaac Hayne's longtime friend and appointed executor, John Webb. Webb, who was among those who took protection to secure his property after the surrender of Charleston, treated Hayne "with all the tenderness, sympathy and attention of a Brother during his whole confinement," wrote Richard Hutson to the South Carolina senate in 1783. Webb was "indefatigable in his endeavours to ward off Col. Hayne's cruel and immediate Fate," said Hutson, and when he could do nothing else Webb "accompanied him to the last Tragical scene of his Sufferings."[19]

Hayne's intimate friend James Fisher may have been there. He had remained in Charleston acting as an agent for the patriots exiled to St. Augustine by sending them badly needed provisions. Sources dating to the early 1850s suggest that the entourage also included Hayne's close friend Dr. David Ramsay and two brothers-in-law by virtue of their marriage to Hutson sisters, Maj. William Hazzard Wigg and Maj. John Barnwell. Ramsay could not have been present as he was shipboard on the *East Florida* sailing between St. Augustine and Philadelphia. Wigg and Barnwell, along with John Edwards and others, had been confined in Charleston Harbor aboard the prison ship *Pack Horse* since May 1781 but were purportedly sent ashore to attend their friend and comrade in his final moments. This cannot be verified, however Major Wigg's grandson later wrote that Wigg "supported Colonel Hayne upon his arm to the scaffold, received his dying commands and in the presence of the assembled multitude, folded him in his last embrace."[20]

They trudged westward just over a quarter of a mile on Broad and then turned right on King Street. From there it was about three-quarters of a mile to their destination, just beyond the city lines (Boundary Street, now Calhoun, within sight of present-day Marion Square) and very near to where the Orphan House would later be built.[21] As he walked, Hayne maintained his composure and dignity along with a hopeful expectation that his wish for a soldier's death would be honored. But as he passed through the town gates and his place of execution came into view, he saw the gibbet and understood that there would be no firing squad. Crestfallen, he paused for a moment. One of his faithful friends walking alongside whispered softly "'that he hoped he would exhibit an example of the manner in which an American can die.' He answered with the utmost tranquility, 'I will endeavour to do so,'" and pressed onward with firmness, denying his detractors the sight of a quavering coward.[22]

Upon reaching the outskirts, the soldiers formed a hollow square around the scaffold, with the British troops occupying the front and rear and the Hessians on the right and left. "The hangman was unknown to Hayne; he attended at the place of execution, masked and muffled." According to David Ramsay, Hayne climbed up on to the cart without assistance. The hangman placed the noose around his neck but clumsily struggled to pull a cap over Hayne's eyes. He graciously offered to do it himself and did—"I will save you the trouble," he said. Given the opportunity to say his last words, he remarked, almost casually, that he only wished to say goodbye to his friends and then he would be ready. Affectionately shaking hands with three gentlemen, "he recommended his children to their care—and gave the signal for the cart to move."*[23]

Hayne's great-grandson Franklin B. Hayne later observed, "Murderers condemned to death have only about five minutes to keep up their courage from the time they leave their cell until they meet their doom, most of them losing their nerve before the end; but Col. Hayne had to walk with his hands pinioned for [quite a distance] through a weeping populace to the place of his execution, yet not for a moment did he show the slightest fear during this terrible ordeal, and he preserved his dignity and composure to the very end, exciting the admiration and respect of his foes as well as friends."[24]

Of Hayne's final minutes Colcock had plenty to say: "Much has been said of the manner in which many of the old Romans met Death—but I am convinced no Man, on so serious an occasion cou'd have exhibited more Heroick Fortitude & Christian Resignation, than the unfortunate Col. Hayne: His progress to the place of Execution, (on foot, by his request) was like that of any other good Christian, on his Way to the public Service—When arrived at the Gallows, he shook hands, with a few & said Farewell my Friends—The Clergyman then went with him into the Cart and after praying by him, a considerable time took his leave—The provost Master then demanded of him, some signal when he was ready, to which he replied, I am ready at any time—pull'd his own Cap over his Eyes, &——Oh !"[25]

---

*Accounts differ as to whether Hayne's hands were bound in front of or tied behind his back. In one version Hayne had some use of his hand immediately prior to his execution.

Hanging as a method of dispensing capital punishment has existed since biblical times but was not practiced in the eighteenth century as it is generally thought of today. Since the mid–nineteenth century the penalty has been administered in a way that ensures catastrophic fracture of the cervical vertebrae, ensuring a quick and painless death. But prior to that time the weight of the victim simply tightened the noose so that the trachea, carotid arteries, and jugular veins were compressed to the point of occlusion. The condemned died of asphyxiation by strangulation—not always altogether rapid or without attendant suffering. One can only hope that Hayne did not endure a long and agonizing exit and that his friends were not treated to a macabre spectacle.[26]

The grave of Col. Isaac Hayne. The inscription reads: COLONEL ISAAC HAYNE / PATRIOT SOLDIER MARTYR / BORN SEPTEMBER 23, 1745 / MARRIED ELIZABETH HUTSON / JULY 18, 1765 / WAS EXECUTED BY THE BRITISH CONTRARY / TO ALL USAGES OF WAR, / AUG. 4, 1781 / *In life a soldier of his Country, / In death a martyr to her sacred cause, / His memory an undying inspiration to / his fellow countrymen, / His monument the freedom of his Native Land.* Author's collection.

It is said that Hayne's corpse was carted to Hayne Hall by his twenty-year-old body servant Paul and buried in accordance with his wishes that same day. The members of his grieving family, or rather what was left of it, were allowed no respite in their distress. A loyalist foraging party on its way back to Charleston after procuring rice and other foodstuffs for their hospitals camped on the grounds of Hayne Hall on the night after he was buried, and the troops bivouacked close enough to the house to see the fresh grave in the garden. Their choice of a campground was due to happenstance rather than malice, but their presence was no doubt resented.[27]

At first blush it would seem that Isaac Hayne's execution "was a mere accident of his falling into the hands of cruel men, who, disregarding their own laws, put him to an unexpected death." This is not entirely the case, said the historian Edward McCrady. "Though fully understanding the consequences of his action, he determined that, the British having themselves broken the term of his compact of allegiance, as he conceived, he would repudiate its bond and take the field, knowing that in doing so he could neither ask for nor expect any quarter if taken. In doing this . . . he ventured his life not only against the military but the civil power of the enemy; and dared for his country's cause to die even upon the gibbet."[28]

The August 8 issue of the *Royal Gazette* reported that "Mr. Isaac Hayne, who since the capitulation of Charlestown, had taken protection, and acknowledged himself a subject of his Majesty's Government, had notwithstanding been in arms, and at the head of a Rebel Regiment of Militia, was therefore, on Saturday morning last, executed as a Traitor." The *Gazette* was managed by the Scottish-born physician and printer William Charles Wells, who had been persuaded in May 1781 to write a political paper regarding the prominent citizens, "men of rank" Wells called them, who had been sent home on parole after having been taken prisoner and then subsequently appeared in arms against the British. "I therefore was desired to show, by an appeal both to military usage, and the nature of the thing itself," wrote Wells, "that such conduct subjected them to the punishment of death." Balfour repeatedly published this warning in the newspapers, and Wells later thought it probable that it was owing to this warning that Balfour and Rawdon felt justified putting Hayne to death.[29]

Lieutenant Colonel Balfour remained at his post as Charleston's commandant until 1782. Rawdon, in contrast, made an almost immediate departure. Before he left, Lord Rawdon applied in vain to the loyalist Dr. Alexander Garden for a certificate testifying to his inability to continue in the field. The story goes that the good doctor was not impressed by Rawdon's disability—"the anger of Dr. Garden was so highly excited by the scandalous dereliction of duty by Lord Rawdon, that on the manifestation of a design by many tories [*sic*], to pay him the compliment of a farewell address, he boldly protested against it; declaring, that if they would draw up a remonstrance, reprobating his determination to quit the array at a moment that he knew that there was not, in the Southern service, a man qualified to command it, *his* name [Dr. Garden's] should be the first inserted." Dr. Garden was incensed that Rawdon would leave at such a perilous time, when his services were most needed.[30]

Nonetheless, between two hundred and three hundred of the "most respectable characters in Charlestown" signed a testimonial address, published in the *Royal Gazette,* expressing their gratitude for Rawdon's distinguished service and their concern for the impairment of health that was causing his lamented departure. Over Dr. Garden's objections (if the story is credible) and expecting that after a period of convalescence he would return to North American service under Cornwallis, Rawdon boarded a ship that sailed from Charleston bound for England on August 21. His transport, the *Queen Charlotte,* a packet armed with eighteen guns, was only a day out and had not cleared American waters when it was overtaken by a French privateer. Rawdon was taken prisoner.[31]

In dispatches to General Clinton and Lord Germain, Balfour expressed his "infinite regret" over Rawdon's capture, both from public and private considerations. And when Cornwallis learned of Rawdon's capture he wrote Adm. François-Joseph Paul, Comte de Grasse, immediately, inquiring about the state of Rawdon's health and hoping to be allowed to establish communication with his young friend. Rawdon's health notwithstanding, the British were naturally and rightly concerned that he would be subject to retaliation for Hayne's death and other alleged atrocities. De Grasse reassured Cornwallis that Rawdon was in good health "and that he does not fare badly from being with us, notwithstanding his wish to return to his homeland to recover his health since he says he has need of rest, although his misleading appearance belies it." De Grasse's comment about Rawdon's physical condition is telling, given the supposed reason for Rawdon's departure from North America.[32]

British fears over Rawdon's safety were allayed somewhat when New York's *Royal Gazette* reported that "the disaster [Rawdon's capture] was somewhat softened when we reflect that his Lordship is become prisoner to a power ever distinguished by the most elegant manners and the tenderest sensibility." The author of the notice, James Rivington, was referring to the fact that Rawdon had been taken aboard the French flagship *Ville de Paris* in the Chesapeake Bay and had become the guest of the French naval commander Admiral Comte de Grasse.[33]

Subsequent events also contributed to Rawdon's safety. The patriots that Balfour had sent to St. Augustine the year before—including David Ramsay, Richard Hutson, and many of Isaac Hayne's other friends and associates—had recently been released on parole to Philadelphia, but the British soon acquired other high-value hostages. The first was a distant cousin to George Washington, Lt. Col. William Washington, who was captured at the Battle of Eutaw Springs on September 8. Washington had mounted an audacious charge through a thicket, trying to gain the enemy's rear, but when his horse was shot from under him he was pinned underneath, then bayoneted and captured. Four days later, at Hillsborough, North Carolina, a band of loyalists seized North Carolina's governor, Thomas Burke, and a number of Continental and militia officers who accompanied him. Washington and Burke were sent to Charleston, where they provided the British a surety for Rawdon's life and any retaliation for Hayne's death. As will be shown, Washington's life was endangered by a petition to Greene that he himself had signed on August 20 in favor of American retaliation for Hayne, stating that he was cognizant that such retaliation could "involve our own lives in additional dangers."[34]

Rawdon spoke fluent French, and it was through his conversations with Admiral Comte de Grasse that he eventually learned of Cornwallis's entrapment at Yorktown by a combined Franco-American army. He may have observed the finale of the British catastrophe from the deck of a French ship on October 19 when Cornwallis surrendered. Rawdon also had an occasion to practice his French when the Marquis de Lafayette visited the *Ville de Paris* on September 2, though the details of any conversation between him and Lafayette went unrecorded.[35]

Rawdon's uncle Lord Huntingdon was reported in the newspapers as having received letters from Rawdon indicating that his nephew had been received by French officers with not only the highest civility but all the affection of intimate friends. This, according to Huntingdon, Rawdon ascribed to "the circumstance of his having during his captivity in America, produced to Mons. De Grasse the minutes of the proceedings of the court martial with respect to General Haines [*sic*], which were found to be perfectly fair, moderate, and conformant to the laws of nations, and were entirely approved of by the French Admiral and all the officers." Huntingdon was misinformed or misunderstood; Rawdon later asserted that when his capture seemed imminent, he threw his papers overboard, including documents that related to the Hayne case. In any event the letters did not reach England. This fact will be important later.[36]

De Grasse did treat Rawdon with courtesy and kept him safe from American military jurisprudence. That is not to say that retaliation against Rawdon was not suggested—Christopher Gadsden, lieutenant governor of South Carolina, joined by privy council members Richard Hutson, David Ramsay, and Benjamin Cattell, petitioned Congress on that very subject. Rawdon was, they said, "the principal Actor in the Bloody Tragedy," and they ardently urged Congress to secure custody of him from their allies the French.[37]

According to a very colorful, biased, and improbable loyalist account, when the Continental Congress demanded custody, de Grasse peremptorily and summarily refused on the grounds that Congress had no claim to prisoners in French hands. In reality, had this matter actually occurred, it would have been handled strictly through military channels via the French and American commanding officers and would not have involved Congress. In any event, to keep Rawdon out of harm's way after the surrender of Cornwallis at Yorktown, de Grasse shipped him to Brest via the *Survillante*. Rawdon made his way to Paris from Brest and was eventually allowed to return to England on parole to await his exchange.[38]

Rawdon was rather prickly about his recent promotion to brigadier general. In December 1781, when it was decided among General Washington, General Clinton, and the Comte de Rochambeau that he would be exchanged as a colonel, he objected and insisted that he be exchanged at his new, higher rank. It was subsequently decided that Rawdon would be exchanged for Brig. Gen. William Moultrie of South Carolina. When Moultrie was exchanged for Lt. Gen. John Burgoyne, Rawdon was exchanged instead for Brig. Gen. Charles Scott of Virginia, effective July 1782.[39]

Nathanael Greene. Engraving by H. B. Hall & Sons after a painting by
Charles Willson Peale (New York: H. B. Hall & Sons, n.d.).
From the Joshua Danforth Bush Jr. Collection,
Society of the Cincinnati, Washington, D.C.
Reproduced with permission.

Chapter 7

"We seriously lament the necessity of such a severe expedient"

Henry Clinton had initiated the chain of events that culminated in Isaac Hayne's execution, and it fell to Nathanael Greene to try to put the matter to rest in a way that would satisfy Congress, his officers, and the American people. This self-educated Quaker farmer-miller-blacksmith-assemblyman from Rhode Island was born in 1742. His rise was meteoric—from the rank of private in his local militia, he ascended to become George Washington's most trusted lieutenant and second-in-command of the Continental Army. At Washington's urging but contrary to his own desires, Greene served as quartermaster-general of the Continental Army from March 1778 until August 1780. Afterward he presided over the board of fourteen general officers that condemned British Maj. John André to hang as a spy. He was the fifth and most successful commander of the Southern Department, following Generals Charles Lee, Robert Howe, Benjamin Lincoln, and Horatio Gates.[1]

In late 1780 Washington sent Greene south, where he took on Cornwallis in North Carolina. A masterfully calculated retreat by Greene culminated in a tactical loss but a strategic victory over Cornwallis at the Battle of Guilford Courthouse on March 15, 1781. When Cornwallis subsequently marched into Virginia, Greene turned his army south to reclaim South Carolina, engaging the British at Hobkirk's Hill, Eutaw Springs, and Ninety Six. He never decisively defeated the British in battle, but his actions forced the enemy to give up most of South Carolina and to withdraw to the environs of Charleston.[2]

Greene received word of Hayne's untimely demise in a letter from Colonel Harden on or about August 10 and decided that he and he alone would be the one to exact any retribution. This he communicated to General Marion, who had already threatened reprisals for injuries sustained at the hands of the British. Writing on August 10 from his camp at the High Hills of Santee, Greene told Marion not to take punitive measures of his own for he planned to act against British officers instead of loyalist militia. But first he wanted the opportunity to demand an explanation for Hayne's death from the British authorities through official channels.

If their explanations were unsatisfactory—and he was sure they would be—and if they refused to make satisfaction—and he expected they would refuse—then Greene would publish his intention to give no quarter to British officers who fell into his hands.[3]

Marion honored Greene's wishes or, rather, orders, but he still managed to obtain a degree of satisfaction on August 31. Having come to assist Harden at Pon Pon, Marion engaged the British on a causeway leading to Parker's Ferry, a crossing of the Edisto River just shy of six miles northeast of Hayne Hall. A British foraging party consisting of 540 regulars, Hessians, and loyalists under Lt. Col. Ernst Leopold von Borck had camped for two nights on Hayne's property and was returning to the Edisto when 140 of Marion's partisans ambushed and decimated loyalist dragoons led by Maj. Thomas Fraser (whose corps had captured Hayne). The patriot insurgents inflicted more than a hundred total casualties while suffering four, only one of whom was killed. Fraser was badly bruised when his horse was shot from beneath him, and Captain Campbell, who had personally apprehended Hayne, was twice wounded.[4]

Greene was cautious and rather ambivalent about retaliation. He did not want to react against loyalist militia because he believed that the British would use his actions to fan the flames of animosity between Whigs and Tories and incite the two sides to further butchery. Greene also wanted to procrastinate long enough to ensure that sixty-two patriots who had been sent by Balfour to St. Augustine in September 1780 and who were now being exchanged were free and clear of harm before he took any action. "I wish you not to mention the matter to any mortal out of your family," he wrote to Marion, asking for secrecy. In actuality, he need not have worried about the East Florida exiles. They were already safe, having sailed from St. Augustine on July 17, 1781, bound for repatriation in Philadelphia.[5]

Ambivalence notwithstanding, Greene was determined to act decisively if the British pressed him. To Col. William Henderson Greene wrote, "Should you take any British officers keep them close prisoners until you hear farther from me. I shall explain myself fully to you in a few days." He sent much the same message to Henry Lee, adding that if the British persisted in this practice of hanging prisoners he would retaliate on the first person he took captive.[6]

Greene saw retaliation as necessary from a standpoint of policy and justice, but he also wished to know the sentiments of his officers. Lee concurred with Greene except that he recommended that they hang an officer first and then inform the British of what they had done and their reasons why. Lt. Col. William Washington opined that that the execution of Isaac Hayne was unjustified and that retaliation is the "only Argument that will avail with Men whose Minds are calloused to every Sentiment of Humanity." Still Greene remained doubtful and privately struggled with his uncertainty. On one hand, he feared that without retaliation the militia would be discouraged and quit the service. On the other hand, he did not want to precipitate an escalation in the brutality of giving no quarter for officers of either side.[7]

Responding to Greene's request for their views concerning the British treatment of Hayne, his subordinate officers wrote and signed a petition agreeing that retaliation was warranted to prevent further atrocities on the part of the British. The petition touched on British violations of the articles of capitulation signed at the surrender of Charleston and the prisoner exchange cartel that was in force, but the officers were at their perceptive best when they summed up their view of British policy from the time of surrender to the present: "We conceive forms of protection which are granted one day, and retracted, violated, disclaimed or deserted the next, can enjoin no such condition or obligation upon persons who accept them."[8]

They were also willing to put themselves at risk: "Permit us to add, that while we seriously lament the necessity of such a severe expedient, and commiserate the sufferings to which individuals will necessarily be exposed, we are not unmindful that such a measure may in its consequences, involve our own lives in additional dangers; but we had rather forego temporary distinctions, and commit ourselves to the most desperate situations than prosecute this just and necessary war upon terms so unequal and so dishonorable." Greene informed Georgia's governor, Nathan Brownson, that his officers were "very willing to become common sufferers with the Militia," adding that "it is a free will offering, dictated as well from affection as policy."[9]

Writing to the president of the Continental Congress, Thomas McKean, on August 25 to seek approval for the measures he was taking, Greene informed McKean that he had stopped prisoner exchanges. He avowed his intention to retaliate and reported that he would therefore issue a proclamation setting forth the reasons for his actions. Referring to this "disagreeable business," Greene told McKean that "Col. Haynes [*sic*] was a most amiable character, highly respected and had a most extensive influence," adding that "nothing could strike deeper at the root of Independence than this measure [Hayne's hanging]." Retaliation was necessary, and Greene did not doubt that Congress would sanction the steps he was taking—"let them lead to what consequences they may."[10]

If there was one person in particular upon whom Greene would have liked to first exact retribution, it was Rawdon. Greene sincerely believed that Rawdon had been the driving force behind Hayne's execution. "It appears it was done by order of Lord Rawdon just before he set sail for England where he expected to leave an ocean of 3000 miles between him and us to prevent a just retaliation," he said to Lafayette on August 26, adding that "there is no man I would wish it [retaliation] fall on sooner than him." To Thomas McKean he wrote, "Lord Rawdon was the principal instigator of Hayne's execution, and there is hardly a mile from Camden to Charles Town in which he has not left monuments of his barbarity, by arbitrary & savage executions, most of which happened even without the form of [a] trial."[11]

Greene knew not where the affair would lead, but if he did not react he feared the militia would all desert. Writing on August 26, Greene informed George Washington of the matter. "I am determined to retaliate," he told his commanding officer, "and as the enemy are indifferent about their militia officers I mean to retaliate on the [B]ritish officers, as the surest way of putting a stop to the practice that can only serve to gratifying private revenge."[12]

When Greene wrote still another letter on August 26, this one to Nisbet Balfour, it was the second letter in a month to Charleston's commandant on the subject of British violations of the prisoner exchange cartel. Since the first letter, Greene said, he had been "informed of a more flagrant violation . . . in the cruel and unjust execution of Col Hanes [sic] for which I mean an immediate retalliation [sic] unless you can offer some thing more to justify the measure than I am informed of or is mentioned in the Charles Town paper." Greene's wish was "to have all considered as prisoners of war who should be found in Arms and made captives on either side; and . . . that they should be exchanged as such." On this point he was firmly convinced that he and Cornwallis were in one accord.[13]

It was solicitude for the honor of humanity, an abhorrence of cruelty, and "a desire to give every man an opportunity to act agreeable to his principles and inclination" that had thus far moved Greene to charity. But no more, he told Balfour: "I shall take the earliest opportunity of informing his Lordship [Cornwallis] of the violence done to the business of exchange and the disagreeable necessity I am laid under to retalliate [sic]; and of its being my determination not only in this instance but to repeat it as often as any violence is done to the good people who adhere to our cause."[14]

Keeping a promise he made to Balfour (and to Congress) that he would publish his intentions— those being "the principles upon which I proceed and the objects I mean to retaliate upon who are British Officers and not tory Militia"— he composed and released a proclamation summarizing Hayne's capture and imprisonment in Charleston, stating that Hayne was "most cruelly and unjustifiably condemned and executed, in open violation of the cartel agreed upon between the commanders of the two armies, for the relief and exchange of all prisoners of war." Greene maintained that the sentiments and measures "were supported by the opinion and wish of the whole Army." Furthermore, he was suspending prisoner exchanges until this matter was resolved to his satisfaction.[15]

Greene was not only decrying Hayne's execution, he was also using Hayne's death as a platform from which he could vent his outrage over British tactics in general. In Greene's view the British were employing terrorism to prevent the people "from acting in conformity with their political interests and private inclinations," and he believed that these methods were "no less opposite to the spirit of the British constitution, than they are an unwarrantable attack upon the laws of humanity, and the rights of the free citizens of the United States."[16]

Through his proclamation Greene expressly declared his "intention to retaliate for all such inhuman insults, as often as they may occur . . . [on] Regular British Officers, and not the deluded inhabitants [loyalists] who have joined their army." Concluding his proclamation, he lamented "the necessity of appealing to measures so hurtful to the feelings of humanity, and so contrary to those liberal principles on which I would choose to carry on the war." Balfour and the British were thus given fair warning of the consequences of a repeated offense.[17]

In his letter to Lafayette, Greene had pointed out that if Cornwallis attempted to justify Rawdon's and Balfour's actions and allowed such measures to continue, "it will open the door for great cruelties and much distress, as I am determined to persevere at the risque of my life and everything that is dear and valuable." The same day he wrote to Lafayette (and to Washington and Balfour), Greene sent Cornwallis a letter containing much the same wording found in his proclamation, along with copies of his correspondence regarding Hayne. It had been eight months since he had complained about Cornwallis's orders to hang captured militiamen who had borne arms for Britain and subsequently defected back to American service. Greene had warned that "punishing capitally for breach of military parole is a severity that the principles of modern war will not authorize." Greene now hoped to persuade Cornwallis to halt such harsh measures because of the adverse effects they would have on the prisoner exchange cartel.[18]

On August 29 South Carolina delegate John Mathews laid before Congress information that he had received from fourteen-year-old Isaac Neufville, who had been an eyewitness to Hayne's hanging. Young Neufville was the son of John Neufville, a wealthy Charleston merchant and patriot who was one of those exiled to St. Augustine in 1780. The elder Neufville was aboard the schooner *East Florida* en route to Philadelphia at the time of Hayne's execution. By edict announced in the *Royal Gazette* on June 27, 1781, the families of the St. Augustine exiles had been banished from Charleston and South Carolina; Isaac Neufville and his mother were therefore reunited with John in Philadelphia.[19]

Congress was highly interested in Isaac Neufville's account of Isaac Hayne's death, delivered in the form of a deposition taken by Thomas McKean on August 30 and delivered to Congress the next day. Neufville's rendition is completely consistent with other American accounts: that Hayne "being surprized by a detached party of the British cavalry was taken and carried down to Charlestown. That he was there thrown into the Provost, and as it was publicly reported, was without even the formality of a trial sentenced to death by the British Commandant there." According to the boy, "something like a court had been appointed for the purpose of proving the identity of his person," and, "at the intercession of several persons among whom were many British officers he was respited for 48 hours." Furthermore, "a Petition for his pardon was signed and presented by those gentlemen to the Commandant but without effect."[20]

The young deponent reported that "early on the morning of Thursday the second of this instant a Messenger was sent to Col. Haines [sic] to acquaint him that his execution was to take place within an hour, and that it was left to his choice either to walk or ride to the place of execution." Again Hayne was "respited without any interposition in his behalf and without any assigned cause till the fourth instant." When that day arrived, "in the morning he was escorted by a party of soldiers to a gallows erected without the lines of the town with his hands tied behind, and there hung up till he was dead."[21]

Infuriated by the story told by Neufville, on August 29 Mathews made a motion, seconded by George Walton of Georgia, that, Congress having "obtained the most indubitable proof of . . . the horrid murder of Col. Haynes [sic] an officer in the militia of the State of So. Carolina, . . . the Commander in Chief be directed to cause a British officer, now a prisoner within these United States in the line of the British army not under the rank of a Major immediately to suffer the same death that was inflicted on Col. Haynes [sic]." The question of whether Congress would actually order General Washington to hang a British officer to atone for Hayne was sent to committee for further consideration.[22]

The amended resolution that came out of committee on August 31 resolved instead to send a copy of Isaac Neufville's deposition to General Greene with a request that "he make full enquiry into all the circumstances, attending the execution of Colo. Isaac Haynes [sic], by order of the British Commandant in Charles Town, and that if thereupon it shall appear that such execution was contrary to the laws of war, he cause a British officer, not under the rank of major to be executed in a like manner, retaliation to be made in such manner, as is warranted by those laws, and will in his opinion have the most probable tendency to restrain the enemy from such acts of cruelty in the future."[23]

In his return letter to Greene on September 3, Balfour admitted that he and Rawdon had ordered the execution of Isaac Hayne, but he emphatically stated that they had acted on the most explicit directions from Lord Cornwallis "in regard to all those who shou'd be found in Arms after being at their own requests received as Subjects," especially those who accepted commissions and participated in the revolt of the country. Therefore, Balfour said, it was Cornwallis to whom Greene should properly address his objections (which Greene had done). Since in Balfour's opinion Cornwallis was "answerable for this measure, the appeal will more properly be made, & in such appeal, I must not doubt every fit satisfaction will be render'd."[24]

Balfour thus admitted his (and Rawdon's) culpability. Intentional or not, his pronouncement to Clinton in May 1781 to "to make the most striking examples of such, as having taken protection, snatch every occasion to rise in arms against us" was a perversion of Cornwallis's order in August 1780 that "every militia man who has borne arms with us and afterwards joined the enemy, shall be immediately hanged." Hayne never served with the British before fighting against them. To the contrary, a refusal to bear arms against his former comrades was the stipulated condition of his declaration of allegiance given under duress. The accounts of Ramsay and Moultrie support the assertion that though he took British protection, Hayne never took up arms in their service. "[A]s far as negative proof can go," wrote William Dobein James, who served with Francis Marion, "this should be conclusive."[25]

Facts notwithstanding, Balfour was willing to match threat with threat, telling Greene that retaliation risked serious and disagreeable consequences. He insisted that "on the subjection [subjugation] of any Territory the Inhabitants of it owe Allegiance to the conquering Power" and that to withdraw that allegiance on any account "is justly punishable with Death, by whatever Law, either Civil or Military." In Balfour's mind the validity of retaliation required parity in all circumstances, "without such every shadow of justice is removed, & Vengeance only points to indiscriminate Horrors." Balfour argued that executing a captured British officer was not the same as executing Hayne for treason and that reprisal would only beget more reprisal. Balfour also reminded Greene that many American officers in different parts of the Continent were under British authority. He had exercised restraint when loyalist officers taken prisoner were killed by their American captors, whom he denounced as licensed and protected murderers. "Britain will loudly claim retribution for the Blood of her Officers, when causelessly shed," he warned.[26]

Having the last word with Balfour on September 19, Greene disputed Balfour's contention that there should be a parity of circumstances: "Retaliation presupposes an act of violence having been committed, and that it is adopted to punish the past and restrain the future; and therefore whatever will produce these consequences, is warranted by the Laws of retaliation." He also took issue with Balfour's proposition that the inhabitants of a country owed their allegiance to a conqueror, and he put forth that "there are no instances, where the inhabitants are punished capitally for breach of parole given under these circumstances." Balfour's and Rawdon's actions were therefore all the more egregious because they had lost Hayne's part of the country. Upon their own principles, the inhabitants and therefore Hayne owed allegiance to the new conqueror.[27]

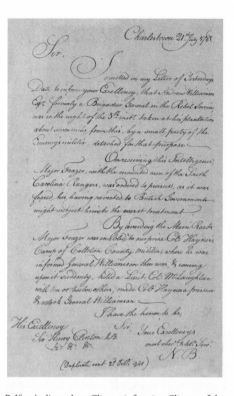

Balfour's dispatch to Clinton informing Clinton of the
rescue of Williamson and the capture of Hayne. Letter book of Lt. Col.
Nisbet Balfour, Robert Charles Lawrence Fergusson Collection, Society of the
Cincinnati, Washington, D.C., fol. 44r. Reproduced with permission.

By his own word Greene had never authorized or countenanced an execution
except for the crime of desertion. "On the contrary," he said, "I have taken all the
pains in my power to soften the resentments of the inhabitants, towards each other
and to prevent as much as possible, the dreadfull [sic] calamity of private murders.
It has been my object to reclaim, not to destroy even such of the inhabitants as
have been opposed to the interest of their Country." Greene later admittedthat his
answer to Balfour was "in softer terms, than I should have written, had our affairs
in Virginia [against Cornwallis] not have worn the most flattering prospects; for I
have always thought it cowardly to insult people in adversity."[28]

Unaware that within a fortnight he would find himself under siege at Yorktown by General Washington's Franco-American army, Cornwallis replied to
Greene that he had heard nothing of the matter from Balfour. Neither would
his good opinion of his subordinate allow him to believe that Balfour could be
guilty of an act of cruelty or injustice. He admonished Greene "to take time to

investigate this business with coolness & temper before you proceed to retaliation, as the consequences of it may be very fatal to many innocent individuals on both sides." That Balfour had not communicated anything to Cornwallis of the Hayne affair is plausible. He told Clinton of Hayne's capture in a July 21 letter, but in his subsequent official correspondence he did not mention Hayne or the execution.[29]

The American public had learned of Hayne's death during the first week in September with the republication of the report in the August 8 issue of Charleston's *Royal Gazette*. By midmonth, the papers that Isaac Hayne had entrusted to his son—copies of the correspondence between Hayne and his captors in the days leading to his execution, the legal opinions rendered by John Colcock, and the ladies' petition to Balfour—had reached Philadelphia (Appendices B–D).[30] Exactly when Rebecca Edwards reached Philadelphia is unknown—it was through her that Isaac Hayne intended to forward the packet to her brother Thomas Bee in the Continental Congress. Whether she conveyed them in person or sent them to Philadelphia via Harden, Rutledge, and Greene cannot be determined. But their subsequent release to the press in tandem with General Greene's August 26 proclamation was a propaganda coup that transformed Hayne's execution from an incident of local or provincial concern in South Carolina to a matter of national outrage. Balfour and Rawdon were universally execrated for their actions.[31]

On October 24 the congressional delegates in Philadelphia received word from George Washington's headquarters in Virginia confirming the surrender of Cornwallis at Yorktown on October 19. Washington's messenger, Col. Tench Tilghman, reported back to his commander that Congress was perfectly satisfied with the articles of capitulation agreed upon, "except the So. Carolinians, whose animosities carry them to the length, that they think no treatment could have been too severe for the Garrison—the Officers and Ld Cornwallis in particular." The following day South Carolina's Arthur Middleton made a motion, seconded by Isaac Motte, "that General Washington be directed to detain Earl Cornwallis, and the officers captured in the garrisons of York and Gloucester, till the further order of Congress." South Carolina's four delegates unanimously approved the motion, the two Georgia delegates split their votes, but the eight other delegations (New York was not represented) all voted no, and the motion was defeated. Tilghman explained the motion's rejection by observing that had it passed it would have been an affront to Washington, a violation of the articles of capitulation, and a violation of the national honor of the Americans and of the French.[32]

The journal of New Jersey delegate Elias Boudinot gives the episode color that is otherwise lacking in the congressional record and from Tilghman's account. As a consequence of Cornwallis's "great Cruelty to the Citizens" while commanding in South Carolina, the delegates from that state wanted him specially charged with the murder of Isaac Hayne as an atrocity committed under pretext of martial law. "This enraged the Gentlemen from the Southward, & particularly a Mr. Middleton and soon after Lord Cornwallis' Capture, a Motion was made in Congress, that General Washington should cause his Lordship to be executed in retaliation of Col Haines [*sic*] and other cruelties committed by him." Boudinot recorded that "this motion was strongly advocated by a very large party in the House and the prospect of its success greatly alarmed many moderate Members of Congress." The moderates maintained that Washington, having entered into a capitulation with Cornwallis in good faith "after the facts committed, & having knowledge of them," would be exposed "to the necessity of resigning his Command or forfeiting his Honor & Reputation &c &c &c." According to Boudinot (but not the record), the debate continued back and forth for several days, and it was only with great difficulty that the moderates "succeeded in putting a negative on it, by a small Majority."[33]

Except for trying to shift responsibility to Cornwallis, Balfour had not backed down to Greene. But if he believed that his and Rawdon's treatment of Colonel Hayne was justified by law, circumstances, and the intent of Cornwallis's orders, the affair had made his presence in Charleston increasingly uncomfortable. Lt. Gen. Alexander Leslie, who succeeded to command of the southern district in late 1781, closed a March 1782 letter to General Clinton thus: "Col. Balfour presses me to remind your Excellency on the subject of his leave, the circumstance of Haine's [*sic*] execution renders his situation here very unpleasant." In another letter that included copies of the Balfour-Greene correspondence, Leslie communicated a sense of urgency created by the threat of reprisal if Balfour were to be captured: "The very disagreeable predicament which Lt. Colonel Balfour and other officers of rank in this army stand in, from this business, renders it necessary for me to receive your Excellency's commands upon that point as soon as possible."[34]

General Greene's proclamation had excited a well-founded state of alarm and apprehension among the British officers who were already held captive and those who were still at large in and around Charleston. A group of officers reportedly presented a memorial to Balfour expressing their dissatisfaction with the changed condition of the war and were given an assurance that the ruthless precedent would never be repeated. Rawdon later gave a different version of events, claiming that "the story of remonstrance from the British officers to Lieutenant-Colonel Balfour shows how lamentably [the Americans] were deceived in every respect by the fabrications in the province. That recurrence [protestation] of the British officers to the commandant, was for the purpose of urging him to secure objects for retaliation, in case of Greene's carrying into effect his outrageous threat." Rawdon could not have been a witness to the occasion, however, because by that time he was a guest of the French.[35]

Clinton may not have fully appreciated the gravity of the "disagreeable predic-ament" in which Balfour and other officers of rank in the southern British army found themselves by virtue of Greene's threats of reprisals. It is, however, conceiv-able, given his strained relationship with Balfour, that he took some small amount of satisfaction in Balfour's discomfiture. In either case he promised on April 15 to inform Leslie of his sentiments at the earliest opportunity, but he never followed through. Instead he turned command of British forces in North America over to Lt. Gen. Sir Guy Carleton on May 8 and returned home to England.[36]

On June 27, 1782, Leslie notified Carleton that he was sending Balfour to New York, "there to inform your Excellency of the state of the miserable loyalists here of these two provinces." Balfour was replaced as commandant of Charleston by Lt. Col. Isaac Allen and sailed from Charleston in July. Prior to his departure, the *Royal Gazette* published two addresses, one from the officers of the militia and one from a committee of loyalists, both thanking him for the services he had rendered, particularly to the refugees who had fled to Charleston for protection. Balfour thanked them all for their kindness and declared that he reciprocated their warm feelings of respect and esteem.[37]

Part III

Francis Lord Rawdon, Marquis of Hastings. George Parker's engraving after the painting by
Martin Archer Shee (London: Peter Jackson, n.d.). From the Joshua Danforth Bush Jr. Collection,
Society of the Cincinnati, Washington, D.C. Reproduced with permission.

Chapter 8

Rawdon's Fantastic Shipboard Recollections

Public outrage aside, and even though the Continental Congress had approved of reprisal in principle, Greene never actually executed a British officer in retaliation for Isaac Hayne's death. As time passed he grew more resolute in his ambivalence and equivocation, telling George Washington in November 1781 that he wished to act decisively but did not think himself "at liberty on a matter of such magnitude but from the most pressing necessity[,] and as the Enemy did not repeat the offense I have been at a loss how to act." While waiting for more definite instructions from Congress on whether to retaliate in the absence of a second offense, the hesitant Greene sought Washington's guidance.[1]

"I really know not what to say on the subject of retaliation," Washington told Greene, and he offered little else except for one important admonition: "Of this I am convinced," he said, "that of all Laws it is the most difficult to execute, where you have not the transgressor himself in your possession[.] Humanity will ever interfere and plead strongly against the sacrifice of an innocent person for the guilt of another." This was probably the best advice Greene received, and he took it to heart, telling General Leslie in February 1782 that while the matter was still before Congress, he was persuaded that retaliation would not be ordered "because of the author's not being in our Power."[2]

The execution of Isaac Hayne initially had its desired effect of intimidation on many of those individuals who had accepted British protection. "Indeed, a much greater Effect than you can conceive," wrote John Rutledge, "for, a great many Protection Men, who had joined [Col. William] Harden, thereupon deserted him & again submitted themselves, to the British Government & Mercy." But American successes in the South Carolina lowcountry, said Rutledge, combined with "Gen¹. Greene's well timed Proclamation, & spirited Determination, in Consequence of Hayne's Death, has removed the Apprehensions of our Militia, (most of whom had taken Protection, especially those in the lower parts of the Country,) of suffering in like Manner, if taken Prisoners."[3]

By threatening retaliation, Greene not only was able to counteract the impression that the execution was calculated to produce; he also deterred the British from carrying out any further executions. And perhaps of equal importance is that American militiamen sitting on the sidelines returned to the fight with even greater zeal. In the end, American outrage was never satisfied by the type of justice demanded in payment for Hayne's sacrifice. The war between the mother country and its former colonies wound to a close, making Isaac Hayne's tragic fate and the thought of retribution easier to put aside.[4]

In another context, the Hayne affair was the flashpoint among complicated and contentious issues that resulted in a temporary suspension of prisoner exchange, so, in effect, captives on both sides experienced hardship on account of his execution. Prisoner exchanges resumed by the fall of 1782, and, with the end of the war approaching, the issue of Hayne's hanging became moot. Francis Rawdon and Nisbet Balfour never suffered any direct consequences for their actions. Nevertheless, noted Kinloch Bull, the resultant storm of protest on the North American continent and in the British Parliament left a permanent stain on the reputations of both men. "Hayne's case was not overly different from that of many others during the confused period following the fall of Charleston," explained Bull, "but it became a *cause célèbre* because Hayne was a member of the gentry and because high-level civil and military officials were involved."[5]

Rawdon made landfall in England in December 1782. His good treatment at the hands of the French had had a salutary effect on his health. The American war had left intact if not enhanced his military reputation, and he did not sully it by becoming involved in the bitter squabbles between his former commanding officers Clinton and Cornwallis. For him the war against the despised rebels was over, but he continued to support his beloved Volunteers of Ireland even to his own financial detriment. At Rawdon's urging, the provincial regiment was placed on the British establishment as the 105th Regiment of Foot and brought home to Ireland in 1782. It was disbanded in 1783. About the time Rawdon was making his way from France back to England, he was elected in absentia to the Irish House of Commons. Nonetheless, he chose to live in England rather than Ireland, and he would eventually take a seat in the English House of Lords.[6]

If Rawdon thought he had put the Hayne affair behind him when he departed North America, he was mistaken. Copies of American newspapers and a corresponding narrative supplied by a gentleman from Charleston named John Bowman had come into the hands of Charles Lennox, Duke of Richmond, who had long been a supporter of the American colonists during the war. The facts of Hayne's execution, Richmond stated, "so far as he could judge it, appeared to be extremely objectionable, when sanctioned by a British officer." Not having received any official information from the ministry, Richmond suspected a coverup and demanded that the cabinet ministers produce the proceedings of Hayne's court of enquiry.[7]

Henry Laurens confirmed for Richmond the veracity of Bowman's account of the Hayne affair. Laurens had a particular interest in the incident. He was a South Carolinian and former president of the Continental Congress who had been captured at sea in 1780 while en route to Holland to negotiate a treaty. He was subsequently charged with treason and imprisoned in the Tower of London. Recently exchanged for Lord Cornwallis, Laurens had been acquainted with Isaac Hayne back home in South Carolina.[8]

Armed with Bowman's letter and the public prints of the correspondence between Hayne and his captors, the legal opinion of John Colcock, and a copy of General Greene's proclamation threatening retaliation against British officers, Richmond proposed an inquiry into the execution of Isaac Hayne. "If colonel Haynes [sic] died by the force or virtue of any existing law, he of course fell a just victim to his own crimes," said Richmond. If, however, "he was put to death contrary to law, or indeed without the mere outward forms of a legal trial," perhaps this was a greater crime than any act Hayne committed. Richmond pointed out that not only Greene but even the loyalists[9] in Charleston and South Carolina "did not hesitate to denominate it murder, and that of the foulest complexion."[10]

The debates in the House of Lords occupied most of January 31 and February 4, 1782, and included a heated exchange with references to Hugo Grotius's 1625 treatise *De jure belli ac pacis* (*On the Law of War and Peace*). Willoughby Bertie, Earl of Abingdon, another proponent of American liberty, minced no words when he raised the salient question and provided his own answer: "for what is the case, my Lords? It is the case of a cruel barbarous murder of an individual." In contrast, Wills Hill, Earl of Hillsborough, was concerned about impugning the honor of a gallant officer and observed that the brave and promising young nobleman "who had distinguished himself so brilliantly in the course of the war, on such a variety of occasions, and who was in a responsible position at Charles-town, when the circumstance happened, was now absent. . . . Why not wait his return? Lord Rawdon as a *viva voce* witness, could give the noble Duke [Richmond] and the House the fullest information on the subject."[11]

Rawdon's uncle the Earl of Huntingdon quickly rose to his nephew's defense. Having forgotten to ask Rawdon for details while he was still in England, Huntingdon reported that he had applied to the office of the colonial secretary for information but found that the ministry had received no official papers whatever respecting the execution of Hayne. No, the papers had been thrown overboard prior to Rawdon's capture by the French—there was no coverup. Then

Huntingdon strenuously contended that Rawdon was junior to Balfour in rank and could not be held responsible for the conduct of or decisions made by his superior officers. Adding strength to his arguments was that he had been visited by Lord Cornwallis, who gave him "authority to declare, that lord Rawdon had acted in respect to Colonel Haynes [*sic*] exactly as he should have done himself, had he been in Charles-town at the time, and that he had executed several persons taken in arms, after having broken their parole, upon whom the same sort of court of inquiry had sat." At the conclusion of debate a ballot was taken, and the proposed inquiry into the execution of Isaac Hayne was soundly defeated by a nearly three-to-one margin. There would be no official inquiry into Hayne's execution despite the numerous expressions of opinion unfavorable to Rawdon and Balfour.[12]

At the time of the debates Rawdon was in Ireland tending to family matters. From what he read in the newspapers and in letters from Huntingdon, he was mortified to learn of Richmond's remarks in the House of Lords. At his uncle's urging, Rawdon immediately returned to England, arriving on February 21. He took great umbrage and rejected with disdain such "vague surmises, and unsupported insinuations" against the character of a British officer brought about by the duke's inquiry into the execution of Isaac Hayne. Rawdon was aggrieved by the injury to his reputation and humanity and could not bear becoming the subject of their Lordships' criticism or censure. To counter what he termed an illiberal advantage of his absence, Rawdon demanded that Richmond make a public apology in terms that he would dictate. "If your Grace had rather abet your malignity with your sword," Rawdon warned, "I shall rejoice in bringing the matter to that issue."[13]

The Duke of Richmond stood his ground at first, refusing to receive Rawdon's letter because of its tone. Instead, he responded through an intermediary that it was never his intention to say anything in the House of Lords that could be misconstrued to be a personal attack on Rawdon. Richmond countered that if the chancellor of the House of Lords could recollect any expression during the course of the debate that could be considered injurious to the character of Lord Rawdon, he would publically disavow such intention—but only if Rawdon made known his desires in more admissible language. Otherwise, as Rawdon had not specified any singular word or expression of Richmond's that was offensive, Richmond had nothing more to say on the matter.[14]

Rawdon conceded that it was not one specific expression of Richmond's but rather "the general cast of the proceedings which has publicly exposed him to the suspicion of wanton severity and abuse of power." For this Richmond must openly disavow in the House of Lords any idea of casting aspersions upon his conduct. And not only that—Rawdon demanded the right to dictate Richmond's recantation. Richmond categorically denied Rawdon's charges. He again offered to refer the matter to the chancellor or any other unprejudiced peer and stated that he would apologize if he were found to be in the wrong but then countered that "a moment's reflection must satisfy Lord Rawdon that the Duke of Richmond cannot suffer himself to be dictated to by any man."[15]

The pugnacious Rawdon refused to be denied satisfaction and issued an ultimatum to Richmond: make an apology in person before the full House of Lords or accept the alternative option—an interview on the field of honor. For whatever reason, Richmond acceded to Rawdon's demand for a public apology: "I find that my motion, for the enquiry into the execution of Isaac Haynes [sic], has been considered as provoking a suspicion against Lord Rawdon's justice and humanity. I solemnly protest, that I did not conceive that it could throw the most distinct insinuation upon his Lordship's conduct; nor did I ever mean to say any thing that could have that tendency. Since I learn that the matter is thought liable to bear a false construction, I declare that I am very sorry to have introduced it upon authority, to which (at the time of making my motion) I said I could affix no degree of credit."[16]

Richmond was well connected and an old soldier in his own right, having served honorably during the Seven Years' War. He had been promoted to the rank of lieutenant general in 1770 and would be promoted to full general a few months after this exchange with Rawdon. But perhaps the prospect of facing a man on the dueling ground who was nearly twenty-years his junior and in the prime of life was too daunting. Adding to Richmond's humiliation was that the day he caved in to Rawdon was his forty-seventh birthday.[17]

What has been presented in the narrative of Hayne's condemnation and the events leading to the execution of his sentence is mainly derived from sources that originated on the American side. But what of the British viewpoint? The backcountry loyalist Alexander Chesney believed that Hayne was executed "for having communicated with the rebels whilst a British commissary." Lt. Roderick MacKenzie of the Seventy-first Regiment thought Hayne was guilty of all manner of treachery. Other than correspondence between Lieutenant Colonel Balfour and General Greene, the only extant document that gives any view from the actual perspective of Hayne's captors is a letter written by Francis Rawdon to Henry Lee in 1813. By this time Rawdon had ascended to the barony of Hastings and succeeded his father as the second Earl of Moira in the peerage of Ireland. In June 1813, as the newly appointed governor-general and commander in chief of the forces in India, Rawdon (or Moira, as he was now known) was shipboard en route to Calcutta.[18]

Lee had sent him a copy of his *Memoirs of the War in the Southern Department of the United States,* published the previous year. Rawdon received the book while busily arranging his embarkation from Portsmouth. Once under way, he retrieved it from the hold, where it had been accidently placed underneath a quantity of other packages. He then took advantage of his long sea voyage to peruse its pages and collect his thoughts. In a polite but voluminous letter to Lee—a missive as long as a chapter of this book—the remorseless and unrepentant Rawdon attempted to correct what he alleged were factual errors contained within Lee's narrative. An initial point he made was that in a war the loser rarely had an opportunity to controvert charges fabricated against him by the victors. Rawdon maintained that, though easily proved incorrect, "misrepresentations thus become an article of political creed" seemingly exempt from scrutiny. After waxing philosophic about the nature of truth in the history of war, particularly his part in the American war, he provided Lee with an alternative version of the Hayne affair—as noteworthy for the provocative and self-serving nature of his assertions as for the clarity of his thirty-two-year-old recollections rendered without the aid of documents or personal papers while he was shipboard.[19]

Rawdon makes many points in his letter, but a few are especially worthy of consideration. First, he argued from the British perspective that the recovery of British-held territory by the Americans did not release Hayne from his sworn obligations to the British.[20] Second, to the assertion made by Lee that it was Clinton's proclamation that created the conditions for Hayne's untenable situation, Rawdon said, "Could, however, that proclamation have had the effect of annulling any of the conditions on the faith of which Charleston was surrendered [which it did], it would have stamped indelible disgrace on him who issued it, and would have been deeply disreputable to the country which in that act he represented. The part which [Hayne] had to take, as a prisoner on parole under the capitulation, was clear. He had only to repair to Charleston, and surrender himself, till the remonstrance of Congress could be exerted with Sir Henry Clinton, upon so gross an infraction of public faith. The non-existence of any such reclamation on the part of Congress, whose view would not be restricted to the single case of Hayne, sufficiently rebuts the construction you put upon the proclamation."[21]

It was simple to Rawdon. Taking up arms after taking protection was treason: "[Hayne] made his choice with all the obligations inseparable from it, and spontaneously rendered himself liable to all penalties attached to a breach of those obligations." As for Hayne's conditional fidelity, Rawdon asked rhetorically, "Where was the British officer to be found, who could have inducement, or disposition, or competence, to allow of a limited oath of allegiance to his sovereign! The tale carried falsity on the very face of it. . . . Were the possibility admitted of his having established the stipulation to which you allude, it would not alter his criminality. When summoned to bear arms (if he ever were so), he would have to say that he had made a condition, that he abided by the reservation, and that he was prepared to meet any consequence of adhering to it. If, instead of that course, he chose to enter into secret negotiation with the enemy, he did it knowingly under all the peril connected with the act."[22]

Third, Rawdon also considered Hayne guilty of espionage. The documents produced by Hayne at the court of enquiry meant to establish his claim of being treated as an American officer were to Rawdon but evidence of his crime: "He was, from his correspondence with the enemy, while within our posts [at Hayne Hall], a spy in the strictest sense of the word; and to that guilt was added the further crime of his having debauched a portion of our enrolled militia, at the head of which he menaced with death all persons of the vicinage [vicinity], who would not join him in arms against us, and actually devastated the property of those who fled from participation in the revolt."[23]

Midway through the letter, Rawdon's narrative took a tangential turn that portrayed him as a benevolent advocate for Hayne. "The way I came to have any part in the affair was this," began Rawdon's opening to a fantastic story. He explained that when Lord Cornwallis marched into North Carolina, he gave Rawdon command of operations in South Carolina. At the same time his lordship entreated him, as a proof of their friendship, to act cordially and cooperatively with Balfour, from whom Cornwallis knew Rawdon had suffered some estrangement. Rawdon promised to give Balfour his most zealous support. Not long afterward Balfour informed Rawdon that he wanted to make an example of the captured leader of an insurrection that had taken place in the rear of the British army. He sought Rawdon's concurrence, "that it might vouch to Sir Henry Clinton, with whom he was on ill terms." Rawdon replied that there could be no doubt of the justice of the necessity of the measure, to which he would readily give the sanction of his name.[24]

"Collateral circumstances were then unknown to me," he said. According to Rawdon, immediately after arriving in Charleston he was approached by a number of ladies who asked him to save Hayne from his impending execution. "Ignorant of the complicated nature and extent of the crime," wrote Rawdon, "I incautiously promised to use my endeavors toward inducing Lieutenant-Colonel Balfour to lenity." As a favor to Rawdon, an officer of Balfour's staff, perhaps deputy adjutant-general Maj. Harry Barry, drew up a petition for the ladies to sign that Rawdon would use as basis for his address to the commandant (ostensibly the same petition that Alexander Garden said was penned by Anna Ferguson Elliot). But when he broached the issue with Balfour, the astonished commandant furnished Rawdon with particulars of which Rawdon had no knowledge. It must have been a terribly awkward moment. Instead of acquiescing, Balfour suggested that Rawdon not only better inform himself of the details of Hayne's case but also seriously consider that failure to exact a severe penalty for Hayne's offense was sure to be ascribed to timidity.[25]

Rawdon admitted to Lee that he had made a grievous error by not immediately yielding to Balfour's reasoning, "instead of still attempting to realize the hope, which I had suffered the ladies so loosely to entertain. I unluckily persevered in the effort to reconcile a pardon with some appearance of propriety." It was at this time that he met with Mary Peronneau: "I frankly told her what had passed between me and Lieutenant-Colonel Balfour, stating the embarrassment in which I found myself, from the enormity of [Hayne's] transgression." Nonetheless, he promised her he would continue to act on her brother-in-law's behalf.[26]

"As a mode of gaining time, I solicited Lieutenant-Colonel Balfour to have the particulars of the case ascertained by a court of inquiry for my satisfaction, alleging the chance (though I could not really believe the existence of any such), that circumstances might have been distorted by the animosity of Hayne's neighbors." Rawdon's rationale was that the same form of investigation been used in the case of Maj. John André. But it was an injudicious move, he said, "because it afforded a color for perversion, by seeming to imply that there might be a doubt as to the amount of guilt; whereas by all the recognized laws of war, nothing was requisite in the case of Hayne, but to identify his person previous to hanging him on the next tree."[27]

In Rawdon's mind there remained no possible excuse for a reduction of Hayne's punishment—"it would have been baseness in me toward Lieutenant-Colonel Balfour, and a forfeiture of my plighted assurance to Lord Cornwallis, had I withheld my name from the measure." At this point intervention for Hayne on Rawdon's part was out of the question. That Hayne received a death sentence "was deeply necessary for the public service . . . no shadow of palliation could be found."[28]

Surprisingly, Rawdon attempted to deflect responsibility by submitting to Lee that Balfour was the senior officer. Balfour came first on the army's list of officers, and Rawdon's provincial rank of colonel "did not alter that relation, as the colonels on the provincial establishment were subordinate to the youngest lieutenant-colonels of the line." He had been, he said, completely dependent on Lieutenant Colonel Balfour "for subsistence, for military stores, for horses, for arms, and for those reinforcements which were indispensable from the expenditure of men, in the unceasing activity of our service." Moreover, he had had no interest or management whatsoever in the case of Hayne while he was in the field; "in fact, I never heard of the insurrection which he instigated, till its suppression was communicated to me by Lieutenant-Colonel Balfour."[29]

On the matter of retaliation, Rawdon again tried to circumvent culpability by maintaining that he and Balfour had several direct orders from Lord Cornwallis "to check by retaliation the merciless severity with which your civil governments treated the loyalists who fell into their power." Then he claimed that he and Balfour had not followed orders wholeheartedly. Each of them, he claimed, with numbers of prisoners in their hands, "had taken it upon himself to dispense with that injunction; not from any doubt of its equity, but from a fear that our obedience would only extend the calamity, and from a hope, that the difference of our procedure would be the best corrective of the inhumanity." His fellow British officers, he said, were of a different mind and were extraordinarily dissatisfied at the seeming hesitation to punish Hayne: "They viewed it as a feebleness, and a dishonest desertion of the interests which our army was bound to uphold."[30]

"This sentiment was so strong," he told Lee, "that at a dinner which Lieutenant-Colonel Balfour gave to the staff and principal officers on the eve of my embarkation, I thought myself bound in justice toward the commandant, to address the company, to confess that the apparent demur was imputable to me alone, to own that I had sought to find grounds to excuse a remission of the punishment, and to admit that I had been wrong in the endeavour." Rawdon was emphatic that his public acknowledgment was sincere and that years of reflection had made him feel no less than culpable for not having immediately given due consideration to the factors that so patently demanded the example made by Hayne's execution.[31]

In a single letter full of contradictions, Rawdon asserted that Hayne was guilty of being both a traitorous British subject *and* an American officer acting as a spy. He maintained that subsequent to asserting in writing to Balfour that there could be no doubt as to the necessity of making an example of a captured rebel officer (he would readily give the sanction of his name), he had tried to intercede on Hayne's behalf to the point of embarrassment, that he was a reluctant participant, and that the credit (not blame) for Hayne's execution belonged more to Balfour and Cornwallis than to him. And according to Rawdon's timeline he was assisting the ladies with their petition for leniency at the same time that Major Fraser was delivering communications to Hayne in his and Balfour's name informing him that he was to be executed by their authority.[32]

Robert Y. Hayne, senator from South Carolina and Isaac Hayne's distant cousin, pointed out in a 1828 critique of Rawdon's specious arguments that the spy André, captured behind American lines in a civilian disguise, had received an "open and deliberate investigation . . . before a Court composed of the most respectable officers in the army, and proceeding with all the forms recognised by the usages of war." Contrast this with the case of Isaac Hayne, who was taken at the head of his men while in uniform, received a hurried inquiry without counsel or witnesses, and was summarily hanged. How could he thus be construed to be a spy or compared to André at all?[33]

Rawdon's memory was faulty. Hayne was informed—and this is supported by the correspondence between Balfour and Greene—that the pretext for his execution was that he had been found in arms after taking protection—treason and treason only—not that he was a spy. Either way he was sentenced to death by a joint order, not "in consequence of any sentence of the Court of enquiry but by their Authority which is invested in them as Commander in Chief of the Army in South Carolina, & Commandant of Charlestown." Whether considered an American officer or a British subject (depending on one's point of view, American or British), he was executed without a trial and without appeal, all contrary to the laws and constitution of England.[34]

Rawdon's attempt to convince Lee that he was Balfour's subordinate goes against all evidence to the contrary. Referring back to the ladies' petition, it is important to note that their supplication is addressed primarily to him: "To the right honorable Lord Rawdon, Commander-in-chief of his Majesty's forces in South Carolina, and to Col. Balfour, Commandant at Charles Town." Furthermore, in a communiqué to the condemned Hayne, Rawdon and Balfour are referred to respectively as "Commander in Chief of the Army in South Carolina, & Commandant of Charlestown." Cornwallis considered Rawdon to be Balfour's superior officer—it was to Rawdon that Cornwallis left command in the field while Balfour languished in Charleston. Lt. Gov. William Bull made his strongest application on Hayne's behalf to Lord Rawdon, not to Balfour. In the correspondence between Hayne and his captors, Hayne always names Rawdon first as a matter of protocol, and it was Rawdon whom Nathanael Greene considered most responsible for Hayne's execution.[35]

It is unfortunate for history that Balfour never had an opportunity to respond to Rawdon's assertions. Rawdon's letter to Henry Lee was first published in 1824, the year after Balfour's death, in a book written by Henry "Black Horse Harry" Lee IV, the namesake son of Henry "Light Horse Harry" Lee. It was purported that shortly after the war Balfour dined in London with the loyalist James Penman. When the execution of Colonel Hayne was mentioned, Balfour supposedly said, "It has been whispered abroad, that Lord Rawdon, since his return to Europe, has endeavoured to throw the odium of that harsh measure on me. But let the blame rest where it ought—*on himself.* He was immoveably [*sic*] fixed in his purpose to destroy, and I conscientiously believe, delayed the sailing of the Packet, in which he was to embark for Europe, *till the execution took place,* from the apprehension—that I would be induced, after his departure, to grant a pardon."[36]

Robert Y. Hayne's provocative 1828 analysis and criticism of Rawdon's letter to Lee concluded that there was no *necessity* for Isaac Hayne's execution and that it was, quoting Rawdon's own words, "an atrocious act." The condemned patriot's distant cousin, a senator from South Carolina at the time (and a future governor of his state), called the deed "a sacrifice from which, in fact, it was morally impossible that any advantage could be derived to the British cause." Rawdon and Balfour, he said, were motivated by "vindictive feelings produced by the unexpected reverses of the British arms" and by the desire to offer a victim to the memory of Maj. John André—all fueled by indignation over the bold capture of General Williamson, who had retired to the supposed safety of Charleston. "It was *an act of vengeance,* executed by men, who had been, of late, too much accustomed 'to feel power and forget right,' and had waded so deep in blood, that the execution of one rebel more, could hardly disturb the serenity of their feelings, even though that rebel was Colonel Isaac Hayne."[37]

The Hayne family cemetery, near Jacksonboro, S.C., where Hayne Hall once stood. Author's collection.

Chapter 9

"In South Carolina no one even knows where he is buried"

In 1902 the preeminent South Carolina historian Edward McCrady summarized the essence of the Isaac Hayne story in a manner that bears repeating:

> The tragic circumstances of Colonel Hayne's case from its inception to his death, the cruel conditions under which he had given his allegiance to the King, his honorable conduct in adhering to his word under the strongest inducements to have renounced its obligation, his decision at last that he was released from its obligation, and the gallant and brilliant action with which he at once accompanied that decision, the romantic incidents of his capture, his quiet, gentle, and dignified bearing throughout his imprisonment and trial and while waiting only the pleasure of his judges as to his doom, his firm and heroic conduct in meeting the ignominious death to which he was devoted, all tended to excite the deepest interest and to call for the most heartfelt sympathy for the noble gentleman who thus died for his country. Colonel Hayne was indeed a martyr to its cause.[1]

"But after all," noted McCrady, "notwithstanding the intense feeling which this unfortunate affair excited at home, and the indignation with which it was regarded by all the friends of America in Europe, notwithstanding the bitter denunciations with which it has been treated by the historians of America, if a state of war warrants the infliction of death whenever necessary to secure its ultimate object, it can scarcely be questioned that it was a military necessity in this instance." Rawdon, Balfour, Cornwallis, and probably Clinton would have agreed, but it is unfair to use the example given by McCrady to say that the Americans would have established this barbaric precedent first had not a loyalist named Captain William

Green escaped after his capture at the Battle of Kings Mountain on October 7, 1780. By slipping away during the night, Green avoided the execution of a death sentence pronounced by a drumhead court-martial for having "violated his oath as an officer to support the governments of the state of North Carolina and the United States by accepting a British commission and fighting at King's Mountain." The comparison is not valid—Hayne never served in a loyalist regiment.[2]

The case of Isaac Hayne did, however, bring to a head a vital question, one to which the two sides never reconciled an answer, and that was the question of the status of those who had given their paroles or taken British protection. "Were these persons released from the binding efficacy of the pledges given by them because the Americans had recovered possession, though temporary it might be, of the territory in which they lived?" asked McCrady, who followed with an answer: "If so, every raiding force was a recruiting party to the rebels. It was the practical reversal of Sir Henry Clinton's policy of conquering America by the Americans. It was conquering the British by the means of these reclaimed subjects." To the Americans the answer to the question was a resounding "yes," but the British thought otherwise,[3] and, as they gave up territory in South Carolina and the ranks of the Americans began to swell, Balfour and Rawdon decided that an example was necessary for the sake of deterrence. The legality and justification under military law or the constitutionality under civil law can be debated endlessly, but the simple fact for the unfortunate Isaac Hayne is that he fell into British hands at a most inopportune time.[4]

Francis Lord Rawdon (1754–1826) received a promotion to the regular army rank of colonel and an appointment to the post of aide-de-camp to the king on November 20, 1782. He was an early and very active advocate on behalf of the many loyalists who came to England after the war seeking compensation for their service and losses. On March 5, 1783, in the House of Lords, he was ceremonially created an English peer by George III, becoming Baron Rawdon of Rawdon in the county of York. In 1790 Rawdon fulfilled a stipulation of his uncle's will when he took the surname of Hastings in addition to his own surname of Rawdon. Francis Rawdon-Hastings succeeded his father as the second Earl of Moira in the peerage of Ireland in 1793. The same year he was promoted to major general, and on the recommendation of Cornwallis he was named to command an expeditionary force that campaigned effectively for a short time in Flanders during 1793 and 1794. He was promoted to lieutenant general in 1798. Because of the renewed war with France, in 1803 he was elevated to full general and appointed commander in chief of the forces in Scotland, where he prepared for an expected attack that never materialized. He enjoyed serving in Scotland and was exceedingly popular there.[5]

Early in his career in the House of Lords he was aligned politically with Prime Minister William Pitt, but his later estrangement from Pitt and his close personal friendship with George, the Prince of Wales (later King George IV), led to a change in his political allegiance. He was considered for prime minister in the formation of a new government in 1797, but this came to naught. While serving in the House of Lords he pressed for a more humane and liberal administration of his native Ireland. In 1806 he was admitted to the privy council and appointed to the lucrative and honorific offices of master of the ordnance and constable of the Tower of London. He backed the regency of the Prince of Wales when George III was incapacitated by mental illness and was unable to fulfill the duties of the monarch. In 1812 the prince invested Moira, as he was now known, with the Order of the Garter, Britain's oldest, highest, and most prestigious order of chivalry.[6]

In 1812 Moira was appointed governor-general and commander in chief of the British forces in India. His administration in Calcutta was marked by fairness and a devotion to civil and financial duties, to which he tended with great industry and ability despite allegations of impropriety involving a certain mercantile house. During his tenure he successfully waged the Anglo-Nepalese War (1814–1816). For his service in India, particularly the military operations against Nepal, he received the thanks of both houses of Parliament in 1817 and was created Viscount Loudoun, Earl of Rawdon, and Marquess of Hastings in the peerage of the United Kingdom. The honors continued; in 1818 he was made a Knight Grand Cross, Hanoverian Order, and a Knight Grand Cross of the Order of the Bath.[7]

In 1804 the forty-nine-year-old bachelor married a twenty-four-year-old Scottish noblewoman, Flora Muir Campbell, Countess of Loudoun in her own right. The couple had six children, to whom he was a devoted father. He tended toward pecuniary extravagance, and it was owing to the poor condition of his finances that the aging Moira accepted the post of governor and commander in chief of Malta, to which he was appointed in 1824. While in Malta he fell from his horse and sustained injuries of a magnitude that led to his death aboard the HMS *Revenge* off the coast of Naples, Italy, in 1826 at the age of seventy-two. A letter found among his papers contained the instruction that upon his death his right hand should be severed and preserved until the death of his wife, after which it was to be placed with her in her coffin. His wishes were honored.[8]

Lt. Col. Nisbet Balfour (1743–1823) sailed for England aboard the frigate *Southampton* bearing dispatches from General Clinton and arrived in London in October 1782. Like Francis Rawdon, he found that his notoriety in North America had little bearing on his future career. For his service in America he received a promotion to the rank of colonel and an appointment to the post of aide-de-camp to the king on November 20, 1782. He also served on a commission to distribute funds granted by Parliament to loyalist claimants who had suffered during the war. His reputation seems not to have been diminished because of the Hayne affair; he was held in high esteem by his contemporaries and moved in the best military circles. Through the influence of his only sister, who had married well, he obtained a seat in Parliament, where he served from 1790 to 1802. When war broke out between England and France in 1793, he was promoted to major general in command of a brigade in a force led by his old comrade Lord Rawdon, now Lord Moira. Though he never again saw active service, Balfour was promoted to lieutenant general in 1798 and to full general in 1803. He retired to his family seat at Dunbog, in the shire of Fife, in Scotland, where he died at the age of eighty, in October 1823.[9]

Henry Clinton (c.1730–1795) returned to England in 1782 to find himself the scapegoat for the surrender of Cornwallis at Yorktown, which he insisted was his subordinate's fault. In 1783 the ever-argumentative Clinton ignited a war of pamphlets with Cornwallis when he published his *Narrative of the Campaign of 1781 in North America,* in which he blamed Cornwallis for the failures of British forces in the southern theater of North America in 1781. When Cornwallis responded in kind, Clinton attempted to have the last word with *Observations on Some Parts of the Answer of Earl Cornwallis to Sir Henry Clinton's Narrative.* Clinton had been elected to Parliament in 1772, and he resumed his seat, serving intermittently until 1794. He generally had good relations with his children by his wife as well as with his out-of-wedlock son, whom he sired with Mary Baddeley, his married Irish housekeeper, with whom he began a lifelong liaison in Boston in 1775. Sir Henry was promoted to full general in 1793, and in 1794 he was appointed governor of Gibraltar. Poor health prevented him assuming his post. He died in England in 1795.[10]

Charles Cornwallis (1738–1805) was trapped behind defensive works at Yorktown, Virginia, and besieged by a Franco-American force led by Gen. George Washington, Major General Comte de Rochambeau, and Admiral Comte de Grasse. He surrendered more than eight thousand British soldiers and sailors on October 19, 1781, feigning illness to avoid the humiliation of personally attending the surrender ceremony. Much as General Clinton had denied Gen. Benjamin Lincoln's request that Charleston's surrendering garrison be allowed to march out with the honors of war—muskets held at shoulder-arms, drums beating and fifers fifing, colors flying—the same courtesy was denied to Cornwallis and his army by General Washington. Adding insult to injury, the transport *Greyhound* on which he was sailing to England was captured by French privateers. On December 31, 1781, Cornwallis was exchanged for Henry Laurens and returned to England, where he received a hero's welcome. Once home, he countered Clinton's charges with *An Answer to That Part of the Narrative of Lieutenant-General Sir Henry Clinton, K.B.: Which Relates to the Conduct of Lieutenant-General Earl Cornwallis during the Campaign in North-America in the Year 1781,* published in 1782.[11]

The end of the war in America did not end Cornwallis's public service and military career. Between 1783 and his death in 1805, he served as governor-general of India (1786–1793) and lord-lieutenant of Ireland (1798–1801). In both cases he put down rebellions while establishing a reputation as a fair and wise reformer. He was appointed to the office of master of the ordnance in 1795, invested with the Order of the Garter in 1786, created first Marquess Cornwallis in 1792, and promoted to the rank of full general in 1793. As envoy plenipotentiary he negotiated and signed the Treaty of Amiens between England and France in 1802, temporarily ending the French Revolutionary Wars. He left retirement at age sixty-six to accept a second posting to India but became ill and died there shortly after his arrival in 1805.[12]

Nathanael Greene (1742–1786) briefly returned to Rhode Island in 1783 and was elected the first president of the state's chapter of the Society of the Cincinnati. He had received grants of money and land from South Carolina, North Carolina, and Georgia but was by no means wealthy. In fact, the opposite was true—he was heavily in debt from guaranteeing financial obligations incurred while supplying clothing and provisions for his ragged troops in the Southern Department late in the war. He finally settled with his wife and five children at Mulberry Grove, a plantation of more than twenty-one hundred acres located twelve miles upriver from Savannah, deeded to him for his war service by a grateful Georgia legislature. He died on June 19, 1786, just shy of forty-four years of age, presumably of sunstroke suffered while touring a neighbor's rice plantation. He was buried with full military honors in Savannah. His wife, Catherine Littlefield Greene (1755–1814), or "Caty," who was a favorite of George Washington, worked hard to make Mulberry Grove a success and to settle her late husband's debts. She accomplished both. Hard times eventually forced her to sell the plantation, but not before her boarder, an inventor named Eli Whitney, constructed his prototype of the cotton gin while residing there. It has been proposed that Mrs. Greene conceived the idea of such a machine herself but did not pursue the patent because in that day and time it would have been unseemly for a lady of her social station to make any attempt at outside industry.[13]

Isaac Hayne (1766–1802), eldest son of Col. Isaac Hayne and heir to Hayne Hall, buried the remains of his father in the family cemetery. In February 1782 his uncle Richard Hutson wrote to Founding Father and preeminent American physician

Dr. Benjamin Rush asking Rush to direct young Hayne in the study of "physic" (medicine). Hutson made the request "confident that your feelings will be interested in behalf of one of the Orphans of that Martyr to Liberty & his Country." To Nathanael Greene, Hutson appealed for financial patronage on behalf of the aspiring doctor, writing that he was "straining every nerve to fulfill the ardent wish [of his deceased friend] to have his Children qualified to figure on the Stage of Life, as useful Members of Society."[14]

After completing his medical studies, Dr. Hayne returned home. The Privy Council in August 1787 named him among a number of gentlemen recommended as commissioners of the roads in sundry parts of the state, his being the Parker's Ferry Road near his home. In 1790 he attended the state's constitutional convention, in Columbia. He married Mary Hopkins in 1793, and the couple had four children, but sadly none survived to adulthood. He practiced medicine and engaged in agricultural pursuits in Colleton County until his death in 1802, at the age of thirty-six. He was interred with his father, mother, grandfather, and great-grandfather in the burial ground at Hayne Hall. A story attributed to a Rev. M. Beckwith circulated in the 1820s and after claimed that the shock and horror of witnessing his father "struggling in the halter," coupled with the recent loss of his mother, had driven the younger Isaac Hayne to insanity and that when he died, "in his last moments often called on his father in terms that brought tears from the hardest hearts." This report has not been substantiated.[15]

William Edward Hayne (1776–1843), youngest son of Col. Isaac Hayne, also attended the state's constitutional convention in Columbia in 1790. Like so many lowcountry families, the Hayne family had seen Isaac Hayne's once splendid fortune ruined by the war. The Aera Furnace added to the family debt that burdened the Hayne siblings. In 1798 William Edward Hayne entered into a new partnership with William Hill and was actively involved in the business until about 1806.[16]

William Edward Hayne was elected comptroller general of South Carolina in 1839. He had six children with his first wife, Eloisa Davidson Brevard, and eight with his second wife, his cousin Elizabeth Peronneau Hayne (daughter of his aunt Mary Hutson Peronneau). His eldest son by his first wife, Isaac William Hayne (1809–1880), was the secretary of South Carolina's Nullification Convention in 1832–1833 and an outspoken advocate of secession. In January 1861 Governor Francis W. Pickens sent Isaac William Hayne to President James Buchanan as a special envoy to negotiate an amicable and peaceful transfer of Fort Sumter to the state of South Carolina. The mission failed. During the Civil War, Hayne was appointed commandant of the Conscriptions Department headquartered in Columbia. He served as attorney general of South Carolina from 1848 to 1868.[17]

Sarah Hayne (1770–1800) married Thomas Simmons of Johns Island. She died in 1800, leaving behind a daughter and a son.[18] John Hamden Hayne (1773–1824 or 1825) died unmarried and without issue.[19] John Colcock (1744–1782), Col. Isaac Hayne's attorney, remained in British-controlled Charleston until his death in 1782, a little more than a year after the execution of his friend and client. He left behind a wife, Milicent Jones Colcock, a daughter, Milicent, and a son, Charles Jones Colcock (1771–1839), who would have a distinguished career as a lawyer, legislator, jurist, banker, and president of the board of trustees of the Medical College of South Carolina.[20]

Brig. Gen. Andrew Williamson (c.1730–1786) suffered a certain amount of notoriety after the war, in part as a consequence of the execution of Isaac Hayne, an event he no doubt greatly lamented and for which he tried to atone. In 1782 Gen. Nathanael Greene notified Gov. John Mathews of South Carolina that while behind British lines Williamson had been employed in the business of providing intelligence: "He has faithfully served the Army; and has given generally the best information we have had, being very much in the confidence with the enemy and a man of sense and observation. . . . Mr. Williamson has run every risque to render his information useful. . . . I hope the political offenses of an individual may be cancelled where he employs all his powers for the safety of that people whom he may have offended; and where he was exposed to greater dangers and of much longer duration than he could be in discharge of his duty in common with other Citizens[.]" As a result of Greene's testimony, Williamson was removed from the confiscation list but was assessed a financial penalty (amercement). He died on March 21, 1786, at his Horse Savannah plantation.[21]

Captain Archibald "Mad Archy" Campbell (?–1782), Isaac Hayne's battlefield captor, possessed a violent temper but was otherwise known as a brave and honorable man. It is said that he was "indignant at the execution of his gallant prisoner, and declared that if he could have suspected such might be his fate, he would rather have killed him, in the pursuit, with his own hand, that he at least might have died the death of a soldier." Campbell was unhorsed and taken captive during the Battle of Videau's Bridge, on January 3, 1782. Disregarding a sentry's order to halt, Campbell was shot to death while trying to escape.[22]

No monument in honor of Col. Isaac Hayne was erected in the eighteenth or nineteenth century. Other important matters took precedence: forging a new nation, wars in 1812, 1861, 1898, and 1917. Hayne Hall burned down prior to the death of Dr. Isaac Hayne in 1802, the rest of the property fell into the disarray of disuse, and the family cemetery was eventually overgrown with weeds. That Hayne's burial site was forgotten is not unprecedented. Much the same happened to the grave of Gen.

William Moultrie, who died in 1805 and was interred at Windsor Hill plantation some fifteen miles northwest of Charleston. The burial site was lost and forgotten until the twentieth century.[23]

In 1904 Charleston attorney, judge, and historian Theodore D. Jervey published a genealogy of the Hayne Family in *The South Carolina Historical and Genealogical Magazine*. Isaac Hayne's great-grandson Franklin B. Hayne of New Orleans provided details that Jervey used to complete the lineage. In 1905 Frank Hayne lamented to Jervey that "if Col. Isaac Hayne had been executed in Boston instead of Charleston, a monument would have been erected to him quite as high as the Bunker Hill monument, while in South Carolina no one even knows where he is buried."[24]

Moreover, Frank had a bone to pick with the late historian Edward McCrady. He thought McCrady had presented a faithful rendering of the circumstances leading up to the capture and concluding with the hanging of Isaac Hayne in the second volume of his two-volume history of the Revolutionary War in South Carolina. But he considered his ancestor a martyr and took exception to the way McCrady seemed to excuse the British for hanging his forbear as a military necessity. He vehemently protested "against the idea that [Isaac Hayne] was in the same class with Nathanael Hale or Major [John] Andre, and that his execution was justifiable." He greatly admired McCrady but believed that the historian had done his family a great injustice. Only the historian's death in 1903, a year before Frank Hayne read McCrady's history, prevented the great-grandson from protesting directly to the author.[25]

To honor his ancestor, Frank Hayne enlisted the help of Edward T. H. Shaffer, a Walterboro, South Carolina, businessman and farmer who had distinguished himself as a historical researcher and author. Shaffer had rediscovered the unmarked and terribly neglected Hayne burial site. The Daughters of the American Revolution were willing to place a government marker at the grave but suggested that the family erect something more substantial in Isaac Hayne's memory. Frank Hayne disagreed, declaring that his ancestor deserved more than a monument from one of his descendants: "The nation furnished a monument to Nathan Hale, and his native state erected more than one in addition. I think my ancestor has much more right to be considered a 'Martyr of the Revolution' even than Nathan Hale, as great a patriot as he was. Therefore if this generation of South Carolinians do not see fit to honor his memory by erecting a monument, I do not care to do so but would rather have his tomb unnoticed, hoping that some future generations may consider it their duty to do what the last two generations have neglected."[26]

Working with Shaffer, Frank Hayne secured the deed to the burial ground, cleaned up the property, and placed over the grave a simple marble slab that told the story of his ancestor's martyrdom. An appropriations bill passed by the South Carolina legislature in 1929 funded the erection of a monument to Isaac Hayne. A granite stone was ceremoniously unveiled on November 19, 1929, and dedicated in the presence of a crowd of five hundred spectators and dignitaries, including representatives of numerous patriotic organizations, the military branches, and the civil government. Of course Franklin B. Hayne was the chief speaker for the occasion of the unveiling, and he made full use of the opportunity to once again rail against his perception of inaccuracies in the accounts of the historians Edward McCrady and Mary Simms Oliphant. In addition to the South Carolina state seal and a fitting inscription, the monument bore the Hayne family crest and the motto "*TE-NAX PROPOSITI*," meaning "firm of purpose." Also inscribed was the Latin phrase "*DULCE ET DECORUM EST PRO PATRI MORI*," which roughly translates to "it is sweet and right to die for your country."[27]

The Isaac Hayne monument, dedicated on November 19, 1929. In addition
to the Hayne family crest and the motto *"TENAX PROPOSITI,"* meaning "firm of purpose,"
on the obverse, the reverse bears the South Carolina state seal, a fitting inscription, and
the Latin phrase *"DULCE ET DECORUM EST PRO PATRI MORI,"* which roughly translates to "it is
sweet and right to die for your country." Author's collection.

Chapter 10

A Survey of the Story of
Isaac Hayne in Art and Literature

As he walked to the gallows and into eternity, Isaac Hayne also took his rightful place in the pantheon of his country's heroes. Indeed, American historians of the late eighteenth, nineteenth, and early twentieth centuries were sure to include Isaac Hayne in their narratives. Not unexpectedly, his case received scant attention across the Atlantic beyond parliamentary histories that recounted the debates in the House of Lords over the criminality of Francis Rawdon's actions toward Hayne. In parallel with the historians, other branches of the humanities found fertile ground in the tragic end of South Carolina's patriot-martyr.[1]

First were the artists. A print made from a woodcut titled *Capture of Hayne and Death of M'Laughlin* appeared in Horatio Newton Moore's *The Life and Times of Gen. Francis Marion,* published in Philadelphia in 1845. The illustration is surprisingly accurate; Hayne is trapped by his horse, King Herod, while McLaughlin fends off British dragoons with his sword. The Ford house, rice field, and fence appear in the background.[2]

The Charleston artist John Blake White (1781–1859) painted the most important and well-conceived work on the subject of the Hayne execution. Though born in 1781, too late to participate in the Revolutionary War, White felt an intimate connection to his nascent country's struggle. The artist's father, Blake Leay White, owned White Hall plantation, adjacent to the plantation of Gen. Francis Marion, and according to family lore, as a child John bounced on Marion's knee during the general's frequent visits.[3]

Early in his career White painted under the tutelage of Benjamin West in London. Despite being discouraged by the acclaimed American artist John Trumbull, who on multiple occasions advised him to quit painting and return to the legal profession, White doggedly pursued his passion. During a career that spanned five decades he produced among his body of work a number of oil paintings depicting memorable scenes of the Revolutionary War in South Carolina: *The Betrayal of Nathan Hale* (c.1810), *The Battle of Eutaw Springs* (1825), *The Battle of Fort Moultrie*

(1826), *General Marion Inviting a British Officer to Share His Meal* (1836), *Sergeants Jasper and Newton Rescuing American Prisoners from the British* (1837), *Mrs. Motte Directing Generals Marion and Lee to Burn Her Mansion to Dislodge the British* (1839), and *General Marion and His Men Fording the [Pee Dee]* (1840).[4]

In 1850 White prepared two canvases for exhibition at the South Carolina Institute Fair: *The Capture of André* and a companion piece, *The Martyrdom of Hayne*. Neither piece survived the Civil War, so all that remains of *The Martyrdom of Hayne* are two contemporaneous descriptions. According to a notice published in the *Charleston Courier*, "the scene . . . is laid in the second story of the Provost (now the Exchange or Customs House), where the martyred Hayne was imprisoned, and the moment chosen is when a British officer, attended by the executioner, with all the dread paraphernalia of his office, announces to the illustrious captive that he is to be led to immediate execution. The doomed patriot, attended by his faithful friend and executor, John Webb, and his equally faithful servant Paul, receives the intelligence with patriotic firmness and Christian resignation; and imagination is left to supply the terrible catastrophe." The fair's judges awarded White a silver medal for the best historical paintings in oil.[5]

The vivid details given to describe the painting in the fair's catalog of exhibited articles may have come from the pen of the artist and are worth repeating in their entirety since the painting itself is lost:

> The picture represents Hayne a prisoner in the Provost, now the Custom House, in the City of Charleston. He is standing at a window of the Surveyor's Apartment, in an easy, composed posture, his right arm resting on the Bible. A British Colonel, one of his own rank, respectfully approaches, holding in his left hand the Warrant for his immediate execution. He announces to the prisoner that he comes to execute this painful duty, to which Hayne is said to have replied with consummate firmness, "Well, Sir, I am ready." The other personages of the group are two devoted friends, John Webb, and James Fisher, Esq; also his faithful body servant Paul, who await the issue, with calm, but intense interest. They accompanied him to the scaffold, and Paul, it is said, bore the sacred remains of his master to the family cemetery in the country. A little to the right of the Prisoner stands the Executioner, with grim and sullen composure; having in his right hand a halter, and in his left, the sable hood or cap of Jack Ketch,[6] a Sentinel stands at his back—a full blown rose lies on the window sill, expressive of the quietness of the scene, and the calm composure with which the patriot can meet death when about to die in the service of his country's cause.[7]

It was more than 123 years before another painter applied brush to canvas in memory of Isaac Hayne. James Lewis Kirby, a descendant of Maj. William Hazzard Wigg and a longtime supporter of the South Carolina Historical Society in Charleston, commissioned a work by the noted artist Carroll N. Jones Jr. (1917–2009). The result was *Isaac Hayne Being Led from the Exchange to the Scaffold*, a colorful and panoramic image that has hung in the reading room of the Society's Fireproof Building on Meeting Street since 1974. In the painting Hayne walks west from the Exchange, crossing East Bay onto Broad Street, taking a route that will ultimately lead to his final destination on the outskirts of town. His hands are bound behind his back. He is accompanied by two of his brothers-in-law, Major Wigg and Maj. John Barnwell, and by another man, who is perhaps his attorney, John Colcock. Onlookers are held back by British soldiers. It is said that Kirby had Jones paint likenesses of himself and his family into the far right of the scene as characters who solemnly watch the sad procession.[8]

Aside from a sketch by Mary A. Anderson that illustrates Miller and Andrus's *Charleston's Old Exchange Building: A Witness to American History*, it appears that no artist has attempted the subject of Hayne's death since Carroll Jones. Anderson portrayed Hayne on the eve of his execution bidding farewell to his children in the North East Room, off the second-floor Great Hall of the Exchange. His coffin is in the foreground.[9]

When the South Carolina Department of Parks, Recreation and Tourism developed the family cemetery at Hayne Hall as a historical site in 2005, designers of an informational brochure were unable to find a pictorial rendering of Hayne's execution. Instead, they modified an engraving after the painting by the English artist William Hamilton (1751–1801) titled *The Unfortunate Death of Major André*, which appeared as an illustration in Edward Barnard's *The New, Comprehensive and Complete History of England*, published in London in 1783. This adaptation was used to illustrate an interpretive marker installed at the site in 2007; the military uniforms in the image were colorized so that the victim of the hanging (originally André, now Hayne) is wearing a blue coat and the executioner and watching soldiers (originally American, now British) wear redcoats.[10]

The first appearance of the Isaac Hayne story in literature occurred in 1838 with the three-installment serial publication in *The Lady's Book*[11] of a closet drama, the five-act Shakespearean-like tragedy *Ormond Grosvenor*, by the magazine's editor Sarah Josepha Buell Hale (1788–1879). According to Hale, "this drama was written to illustrate the spirit of the American Revolution; or struggle between the principles of civil Liberty—then first developing their power in this country—and the proscriptive privileges of aristocratic domination in the old world." The plot centers around the capture and execution of Hayne and the dilemma of his fictional protégé, Grosvenor, who renounces his claim to British nobility to support the American cause. The author's use of blank verse allowed her characters to articulate the lofty Enlightenment ideals of American republicanism and the unity of the North and the South in establishing these ideals at a time when sectional tension had not yet risen to a fever pitch.[12]

Hale's career of more than fifty years as writer and editor, philanthropist, proponent of education for women, and antisuffragist put her in the role of America's prototypical Victorian woman and matriarch of maternal feminism. As such, she was arguably the most influential woman of the nineteenth century. Her editorials prompted Abraham Lincoln to proclaim Thanksgiving Day a national holiday in 1863, and she included among her numerous published works the nursery rhyme "Mary Had a Little Lamb."[13]

True to the form of a Shakespearean tragedy, *Ormond Grosvenor* is a wartime love story gone awry in which the protagonist makes a fatal decision and suffers the consequences. Lord Rawdon is portrayed as cruel and severe. Nisbet Balfour is depicted as a most devious and blackhearted scoundrel who plots murder to satisfy his lust for Ormond Grosvenor's sister Julia. So severely traumatized is Isaac Hayne's eldest son that he is driven mad by the sight of his father's execution; he is dead before the conclusion of the final act, presumably by his own hand.[14]

George Lippard (1822–1854) took Hale's notion of an immediately insane oldest son to the next level in his melodramatic "The Martyr of the South," published in 1847 in *Legends of the American Revolution: Or, Washington and His Generals.* Lippard described his romantic historical fiction "as an earnest attempt to embody the scenes of the Past, in a series of Historical pictures." He narrates the scene of Isaac Hayne's execution as a bystander and does an admirable job of re-creating the morose mood of the day. Rawdon is portrayed as an unfeeling bureaucrat who at the end receives mercy from General Washington at Yorktown. Of Hayne's son, Lippard wrote, "he beheld that manly form suspended to the gibbet, with the cap over his brow, while the distorted face glowed horribly in the sun. That was his FA-THER! That boy did not shriek, nor groan, but instantly—like a light extinguished suddenly—the fire left his eye, the color his cheek. His lips opened in a silly smile. The first word he uttered told the story—'My father!' he cried, and then pointed to the body, and broke into a laugh. Oh, it was horrible, that laugh, so hollow, shrill, and wild. The child of the Martyr was an idiot."[15]

Quite the dashing and colorful character, Lippard was a dramatist, journalist, and social justice advocate who hailed from Philadelphia, to which he gave the sobriquet the "Quaker City" in his controversial book of the same name. In his writing Lippard played loosely with the facts, and, though now largely forgotten, his sensationalistic stories were widely read and immensely popular in his day. He died of tuberculosis at the young age of thirty-two.[16]

Lippard used George Washington returned from the dead as a literary device in "The Entranced, or the Wanderer of Eighteen Centuries," a story serialized in 1849. The Arisen Washington accompanies Lucius, a condemned Christian nobleman from the court of Nero who emerges from a trance at intervals across the centuries to view the progress of Christianity. Washington's purpose, as he guides Lucius, is to look upon the fruits of his labors, and he is not well pleased with what that he sees. When Washington hears an unnamed senator from South Carolina (undoubtedly John C. Calhoun) speaking in favor of perpetuating the evils of slavery, "his cheek grew warm with a sudden glow, and his heart beat violently within his mean attire. 'From what part of this land, does that great man come?' he asked of a spectator by his side. 'From Carolina'—was the answer—'a great man indeed, and an honest one! Would to God we had more of such.' 'Carolina,' murmured the Arisen Washington, with the voice of one who thinks aloud: 'The land of the Martyr Hayne! And Hayne was hung some seventy years ago, by the creatures of a Tyrant, in order that words like those uttered by the Senator, might be spoken to-day, in the Senate of a redeemed People!'" [17]

In 1849 another noteworthy and popular female author and editor of the era published a historical dramatic sketch in her collection *Verses of a Life Time*. Caroline Howard Gilman (1794–1888) was born in Boston but relocated to Charleston in 1819 with her husband, the Unitarian minister Rev. Samuel Gilman. There she embraced the South and became the southern counterpart of Sarah Josepha Hale. For "Isaac Hayne, or, The Patriot Martyr of South Carolina," she gathered material from Ramsay's *History,* Garden's *Anecdotes,* Lee's *Memoirs,* and Robert Young Hayne's 1928 account published in the *Southern Review.* Consequently, her sketch demonstrates close fidelity to the facts. Like her contemporary Hale, with whom she differed on the issue of slavery, Gilman promoted domestic tranquility and North-South reconciliation in her writing. As a reflection of their times and their writing in general, Gilman's "Isaac Hayne" and Hale's *Ormond Grosvenor* richly reflect women's limited supporting roles in marriage, society, and warfare.[18]

During the mid-1800s readers were offered a pair of poems on the subject of the death of Isaac Hayne. First, in 1850 the Bowdoin College professor and poet Rev. Thomas C. Upham (1799–1872) published "a series of poems illustrative of American scenery, and of the associations, feelings, and employments of the American cottager and farmer" under the title *American Cottage Life.* Included was "Death of Colonel Hayne," in which Upham portrayed Hayne as undaunted, even defiant unto death. Upham mirrors Sarah Hale's *Ormond Grosvenor* by depicting Hayne's oldest son as becoming woefully insane immediately after his father's

hanging. "These are thy fearful scenes, oh War!" penned Upham, who wrote philo-
sophically of the influence of war on domestic life: "the distracted sister, mourning
in her distant home over her fallen brother; or to the mother weeping in solitude
over her beloved son; or to the wife, lamenting, with inexpressible grief, the untimely death of her husband!"[19]

Next was the Charleston attorney William Gilmore Simms (1806–1870).
Simms was South Carolina's, if not the entire South's, preeminent poet, novelist,
and historian of the nineteenth century. He published "Hayne: A Dirge" (later
renamed "Hayne—Let the Death-Bell Toll") in his critically acclaimed 1860 collection, *Areytos, or Songs and Ballads of the South.* Simms delivered a melancholy
and doleful tribute to Hayne that is at the same time patriotic and uplifting—"
A mortal agony first, and then / A glad release to the realms of peace."[20]

The most important and enduring works of literature to adapt the Hayne
story to fiction were brought to the reading public by Simms who published
an eight-volume prose epic of the Revolutionary War in South Carolina. First
composed was *The Partisan: A Tale of the Revolution* (1835), which focused on the
crushing American defeat at Camden in 1780 and the guerrilla warfare tactics employed by partisan commanders as they continued the struggle against their British oppressors. Alongside historical characters such as Francis Marion, Horatio
Gates, Francis Rawdon, Banastre Tarleton, and Charles Cornwallis, Simms introduced the recurring fictional characters Colonel Richard Walton; Walton's lovely
daughter, Katharine, an avowed rebel; and Colonel Walton's nephew, Maj. Robert
Singleton, the brave and gallant title character who is also his cousin Katharine's
love interest.[21]

Colonel Walton is closely modeled after Isaac Hayne, and like Hayne he is
placed in a precarious position by Clinton's proclamations that revoked parole and
demanded British allegiance. "You must buckle on the sword," Singleton tells Walton, "—you must take up arms for or against your people, and in either case at the
expense of all that comfortable quiet for which you have already made quite too
many sacrifices." Some of *The Partisan* is purely the product of Simms's imagination, particularly where Colonel Walton is concerned, but much is factually based.
The knowledgeable and respected historian Simms constructed plots and dialogues
as they well may have actually happened. The author, who was quite sensitive to
the critical and commercial reception of *The Partisan,* later commented that "the
work was treated with indulgence by the critics [such as Edgar Allan Poe], and was
welcomed with kindness by its readers."[22]

In 1850 Sarah Hale and *Godey's Lady's Book* published another Simms novel in
eleven serial installments. *Katharine Walton,* a Revolutionary romance set in British-
occupied Charleston, was the prequel to *The Partisan.* Opinions vary regarding the

book's literary merits, but in its day *Katharine Walton* received favorable reviews and sold well in the North and the South. Intentional or not, Simms's inclusion in his narrative of an undercurrent of social and political commentary relevant to the sectional politics of the 1850s and to Charleston social life has intrigued scholars for a century. *Katharine Walton* was published in book form in 1854.[23]

A portrait of Lt. Col. Nisbet Balfour has not been found. The only known artistic depiction of Balfour is a fictional scene illustrated by artist F.O.C. Darley and engraved by Whitney, Jocelyn, and Annin for William Gilmore Simms's 1854 edition of *Katharine Walton; or, the Rebel of Dorchester.* Author's collection.

One can only wonder if, when editing *Katharine Walton* for publication in *Godey's,* Sarah Hale noticed a peculiar similarity between her *Ormond Grosvenor,* published a decade earlier, and Simms's novel. In both works Lieutenant Colonel Balfour is portrayed as an immoral, depraved, and loathsome character who is willing to sacrifice or trade someone else's life to coerce an unwilling lady into marriage. In *Ormond Grosvenor* Balfour plots murder to possess Julia Grosvenor. In *Katherine Walton* he offers to spare the title character's father, Colonel Walton, from perishing on the gallows in exchange for her promise to wed. Kate Walton is a heroine on the horns of a dilemma. Offered the choice of union with a villain to save the colonel, she finally relents: "I consent, Colonel Balfour—only save him—hasten, before it is too late!"[24]

The plot twists and turns to foil Balfour's plan, and at the climax of *Katharine Walton* Colonel Walton suffers Isaac Hayne's fate—execution by hanging. Simms the historian had covered the Hayne affair a decade earlier in *The History of South Carolina*. Ever the stickler for accuracy, he stated in his notes that he had interviewed actual witnesses to Hayne's hanging, and so the scene leading up to Colonel Walton's demise can be considered historically correct. He included some of this factual information in the notes that accompanied his aforementioned poetic dirge about Hayne's death.[25]

There is no question that William Shakespeare was an important literary influence on William Gilmore Simms. His characters sometimes mimic Shakespeare's characters, his works contain many Shakespearian quotations and allusions, and in 1848 he edited and published a volume of apocryphal Shakespearean plays. The thirteen Shakespearean references and quotations that are strewn through *Katharine Walton* begin with an epigraph on the title page—a quotation from *Henry IV, Part 2*. Others are drawn from *The Merchant of Venice, Macbeth, As You Like It, Hamlet, A Midsummer Night's Dream, Romeo and Juliet,* and *Much Ado about Nothing.*[26]

When Simms infused the fictionalized story of Isaac Hayne into *Katharine Walton,* he wove it into a subplot that closely follows the 1604 Shakespearean tragicomedy *Measure for Measure,* in which the villain, Angelo, becomes Nisbet Balfour, Katharine Walton becomes a version of and the heroine, Isabella, and Isaac Hayne represents Isabella's brother, Claudio. Angelo, who lusts after Isabella, promises to halt the execution of Claudio if she will surrender her virginity to him in exchange. Whether he realized it or not, Simms's rendition of this theme was of the sixth generation. Shakespeare's inspiration for the play seems to have come from both George Whetstone and his Italian predecessor G. B. Giraldi Cinthïo, each of whom produced both dramatic and narrative versions during the mid-to late 1500s.[27]

Perhaps the most bizarre use of the Isaac Hayne story as a literary device was published in 1861 in *Faulkner's History of the Revolution in the Southern States* as "The Dream of John C. Calhoun," a tale attributed to Joseph A. Scoville, a *New York Herald* reporter and Senator Calhoun's private secretary. As the story goes, the senator from South Carolina relates to his friends a disturbing dream from the preceding night; further, since awakening, whenever he looks at his right hand he sees a dark spot on the back of it. Calhoun explains that in his dream he was working long into the night writing a plan for the dissolution of the American union. An intruder—an apparition of George Washington dressed in his general's uniform—suddenly appears before him. Grasping Calhoun's right hand, Washington asks, "[W]ith this right hand you would sign your name to a paper declaring the Union dissolved?" Calhoun applies affirmatively. At that same moment a black spot appears upon the back of his hand—an inky blotch.[28]

"What is that?" demands an alarmed Calhoun upon noticing the mark. Washington, dropping Calhoun's hand, tells him that the stain "is the mark by which Benedict Arnold is known in the next world." Washington then dumps a pile of bones on Calhoun's table, saying, "There are the bones of Isaac Hayne, who was hung at Charleston by the British. He gave his life to establish this Union. When you put your name to the declaration of a dissolution, why, you may as well have the bones of Isaac Hayne before you. He was a South Carolinian; so are you. But there was no blotch on his hand!" And so in the story Washington shames Calhoun for his disunionism.[29]

Sometime prior to his death the Swedish-American poet Oliver Allstorm (1878–1963) composed eight verses that he titled "Death of Isaac Hayne." This poem was appended to David K. Bowden's 1977 monograph *The Execution of Isaac Hayne*. Devoid of flowery verbiage—characteristic of many of the aforementioned works—that tends to obscure meaning for the modern reader, Allstorm's stanzas convey the story of the martyr Hayne with simplicity and patriotic verve. The copy in the South Caroliniana Library at the University of South Carolina is undated.[30]

In the course of the twentieth and the twenty-first centuries there have been few important uses of the Isaac Hayne story as a literary device. Summer stock productions of *The Liberty Tree* by the acclaimed Southern Appalachian playwright Kermit Hunter (1910–2001) ran from 1968 to 1970. The portrayals of Isaac Hayne and other South Carolina Revolutionary War characters were purely historical.[31]

In 2009 Gerald G. Stokes Jr. published *Letters for Catherine*, a work of historical fiction of the modern "young adult" genre. Like William Gilmore Simms, Stokes penned a Revolutionary War trilogy, of which *Letters to Catherine* was the final installment. In his coming-of-age novel of romance and adventure Stokes managed to stay close to the facts, basing his story in part on the memoir of Maj. William Hazzard Wigg, a friend of Isaac Hayne who may have been present at Hayne's hanging. Stokes used the Hayne affair at the climax of a plot that unfolds aboard the notorious prison ships *Pack Horse* and *Torbay* in Charleston harbor, where American prisoners were confined under miserable conditions by the British during the occupation summer of 1781.[32]

Early in the twentieth century a fictional element was added to the Hayne story in popular literature that has persisted to the present time. Accounts that began with Harriott Horry Ravenel's 1922 *Charleston, the Place and the People* are generally accurate until Hayne makes his dreary trek to the gallows. Walking up Meeting Street, he passes the junction with Atlantic Street. On one corner is the home of his sister-in-law Mary Peronneau, "and she, standing at the north window, cried to him in agony, 'Return, return to us.' He replied, 'I will if I can,' and walked on." Ravenel reported that, according to the legend, "ever after, any one standing at the north window after nightfall would hear a ghostly voice in the street below, and steps sounding on the stair and in the hall, as of a man returning,—never going down, always up!"[33]

Other versions of the story vary in minute details: balcony versus window, presence or absence of the Hayne children, but all have provided material for Charleston's numerous "ghost tours" enjoyed by the city's visitors. And while it is entirely possible that Hayne and his entourage walked up Meeting Street to reach his final destination (this author prefers a King Street route for previously offered reasons), it seems to bother no one that the intersection of Meeting and Atlantic is well south of the Exchange and would not have been passed by the north-bound procession.[34]

Appendix A

The Proclamations of Lt. Gen. Sir Henry Clinton

Handbill issued after the Surrender of Charles town.

When the roal [*sic*] army arrived in South Carolina, the commander in chief avoided, as much as possible, every measure which might excite the loyal inhabitants to rise in favour of government, and thus bring danger and trouble upon themselves, at a time when the King's army, being employed in the reduction of Charles town, could not assist or second their struggles.

The blood of the loyalists that had been unhappily shed, and the severities which had been inflicted on them by the rebels, in consequence of the former spirited but ill-timed insurrections of the King's numerous friends on the back of both Carolinas, had already occasioned too much grief and regret to His Majesty, and the fellow subjects in Europe, for him wantonly to bring again into hazard the lives and happiness of men who deserve so well of their country.

But Charles town, with its harbour, and fort Moultrie, being now reduced, and their garrisons, to the amount of six thousand men, with all their arms, stores, artillery, and ships of war, being in possession of His Majesty's forces, the time is come when it is equally the interest and duty of every good man to be in readiness to join the King's troops, and assist them in establishing justice and liberty, and in restoring and securing their own property, whenever they shall march to support them against the small rebel parties that still linger at a distance in the province.

After so much disorder, violence, and oppression, the helping hand of every man is wanted to re-establish peace and good government; and as the commander in chief wished not to draw the King's friends into danger, when any doubt could remain of their success; so now that that is certain, he trusts that one and all will heartily join, and, by a general concurrence, give effect to such necessary measures for that purpose, as, from time to time, may be pointed out to them. And they

Tarleton, *History of the Campaigns of 1780 and 1781,* 70–78.

may rest assured that every means will be used to avoid giving them any trouble but what is necessary to secure to them peace, liberty, and prosperity.

In order to attain these happy ends, it is the duty of all men, who wish well to themselves and their country, to be ready at a moment, with their arms, to regain their just rights, and support the free constitution of their forefathers, under which we all increased and prospered.

Those who have families will form a militia to remain at home, and occasionally to assemble in their own districts, when required, under officers of their own chusing, for the maintenance of peace and good order. Those who have no families, and can conveniently be spared for a time, it is hoped will chearfully assist His Majesty's troops in driving their rebel oppressors, and all the miseries of war, far from the province.

For this purpose it is necessary that the young men be ready to assemble when required, and serve with the King's troops for any six months of the ensuing twelve that may be found requisite, under proper regulations. They may chuse officers to each company to command them, and will be allowed, when on service, pay, ammunition, and provisions, in the same manner as the King's troops. When they join the army, each man will be furnished with a certificate, declaring that he is only engaged to serve as a militia man for the time specified; that he is not to be marched beyond North Carolina and Georgia; and that when the time is out, he is freed from all claims whatever of military service, except the common and usual militia duty where he lives.

He will then have paid his debt to his country, and be entitled to enjoy, undisturbed, that peace, liberty, and property, at home, which he had contributed to secure.

South Carolina.

By his excellency Sir Henry Clinton, Knight of the most honourable order of the Bath, general commander in chief of all His Majesty's forces within the colonies lying on the Atlantic ocean, from Nova Scotia to West Florida inclusive.

Proclamation.

Whereas, notwithstanding the gracious offers, which have been made to receive to His Majesty's peace and protection, with pardon and oblivion for their past offences, all those his deluded and infatuated subjects, who should return to their duty, and a due obedience to the laws, yet there are some wicked and desperate men, who, regardless of the ruin and misery in which the country will be involved, are still endeavouring to support the flame of rebellion, and, under pretence of authority derived from the late usurped legislatures, are attempting, by enormous fines, grievous imprisonments, and sanguinary punishments, to compel His Majesty's faithful and unwilling subjects to take up arms against his authority and government; and it is therefore become necessary, as well for the protection of the loyal subjects, as to procure the establishment of peace and good government in the country, to prevent, by the terror of example, such enormous offences being committed in future: I have therefore thought fit to issue this my proclamation, to declare, that if any person shall hereafter appear in arms, in order to prevent the establishment of His Majesty's government in this country, or shall, under any pretence or authority whatsoever, attempt to compel any other person or persons to do so, or who shall hinder or intimidate, or attempt to hinder or intimidate, the King's faithful and loyal subjects from joining his forces, or otherwise performing those duties their allegiance requires, such person or persons so offending shall be treated with that severity so criminal and hardened an obstinacy will deserve, and his or their estates will be immediately seized, in order to be confiscated. And for the encouragement of the King's faithful and peaceable subjects, I do again assure them, that they shall meet with effectual countenance, protection, and support; and whenever the situation of the country will permit of the restoration of civil government and peace, they will, by the commissioners appointed by His Majesty for that purpose, be restored to the full possession of that liberty in their persons and property which they had before experienced under the British government. And that so desirable an event may be the more speedily accomplished, I do hereby, in His Majesty's name, require and command all persons whatsoever to be aiding and assisting to his forces, whenever they shall be required, in order to extirpate the rebellion, and thereby restore peace and prosperity to this, at present, desolated and distracted country.

Given under my hand, at head quarters, in Charles town, the 22d day of May, 1780.

(Signed) H. Clinton.
By his excellency's command,
(Signed) Nathaniel Philips,
Assisting Secretary.

South Carolina.

By Sir Henry Clinton, Knight of the Bath, general of His Majesty's forces, and Mariot Arbuthnot, Esquire, vice-admiral of the Blue, His Majesty's commissioners to restore peace and good government in the several colonies in rebellion in North-America.

Proclamation.

His Majesty having been pleased by his letters patent, under the Great Seal of Great Britain, to appoint us to be his commissioners, to restore the blessings of peace and liberty to the several colonies in rebellion in America, we do hereby make publick his most gracious intentions, and in obedience to his commands, do declare to such of his deluded subjects as have been perverted from their duty by the factious arts of self-interested and ambitious men, that they will still be received with mercy and forgiveness, if they immediately return to their allegiance, and a due obedience to those laws and that government which they formerly boasted was their best birthright and noblest inheritance; and upon a due experience of the sincerity of their professions, a full and free pardon will be granted for the treasonable offences which they have heretofore committed, in such manner and form as His Majesty's commission doth direct.

Nevertheless, it is only to those, who, convinced of their errors, are firmly re-solved to return and to support that government under which they were formerly so happy and free, that these gracious offers are once more renewed; and therefore those persons are excepted, who, notwithstanding their present hopeless situation, and regardless of the accumulating pressure of the miseries of the people, which their infatuated conduct must contribute to increase, are nevertheless still so hardened in their guilt, as to endeavour to keep alive the flame of rebellion in this province, which will otherwise soon be reinstated in its former prosperity, security and peace.

Nor can we at present resolve to extend the royal clemency to those who are polluted with the blood of their fellow citizens, most wantonly and inhumanly shed under the mock forms of justice, because they refused submission to an usur-pation which they abhorred, and would not oppose that government with which they deemed themselves inseparably connected: And in order to give quiet and content to the minds of His Majesty's faithful and well-affected subjects, we do again assure them, that they shall have effectual countenance, protection, and sup-port, and, as soon as the situation of the province will admit, the inhabitants will be re-instated in the possession of all those rights and immunities which they heretofore enjoyed under a free British government, exempt from taxation, except by their own legislature: And we do hereby call upon all His Majesty's faithful subjects, to be aiding with their endeavours, in order that a measure so conducive to their own happiness, and the welfare and prosperity of the province, may be the more speedily and easily attained.

Given under our hands and seals, at Charles town, the 1st day of June, in the twentieth year of His Majesty's reign, and in the year of our Lord 1780.

H. Clinton,
M. Arbuthnot.
By their excellencies command,
James Simpson, Sec.

SOUTH CAROLINA.

By his excellency Sir Henry Clinton, Knight of the most honourable order of the Bath, general and commander in chief of all His Majesty's forces within the colonies lying on the Atlantic ocean, from Nova Scotia to West Florida inclusive, &c. &c. &c.

PROCLAMATION.

WHEREAS after the arrival of His Majesty's forces under my command in this province, in February last, numbers of persons were made prisoners by the army, or voluntarily surrendered themselves as such, and such persons were afterwards dismissed on their respective paroles; and whereas since the surrender of Charles town, and the defeats and dispersion of the rebel forces, it is become unnecessary that such paroles should be any longer observed; and proper that all persons should take an active part in settling and securing His Majesty's government, and delivering the country from that anarchy which for some time past hath prevailed; I do hereby issue this my proclamation, to declare, that all the inhabitants of this province, who are now prisoners upon parole, and were not in the military line, (those who were in fort Moultrie and Charles town at the times of their capitulation and surrender, or were then in actual confinement excepted) that from and after the twentieth day of June instant, they are freed and exempted from all such paroles, and may hold themselves as restored to all the rights and duties belonging to citizens and inhabitants.

And all persons under the description before mentioned, who shall afterwards neglect to return to their allegiance, and to His Majesty's government, will be considered as enemies and rebels to the fame, and treated accordingly.

Given under my hand, at head quarters in Charles town, the 3d day of June, 1780, and in the twentieth year of His Majesty's reign.

(Signed) H. Clinton.

By his excellency's command,

(Signed) Peter Russel,

Assisting secretary.

Appendix B

The Correspondence between
Col. Isaac Hayne and His British Captors

No. 1

[Thursday morning, July 26, 1781][1]

Sir

I am directed by the Commandant to acquaint you, that a Board of Field officers will assemble tomorrow, at ten o'clock, at the State House, for your trial.

I am Sir

Your Most Obed^t Servt

Chas Fraser   Town Major

Mr Isaac Hayne[2]

No. 2

Thursday Evening 26 July 1781

Sir

I am directed by the Commandant to acquaint you, that, instead of a Board of Field Officers, as is mentioned in my letter of this morning, a Court of Enquiry, consisting of four field officers, and five captains, will assemble tomorrow at 10 o'clock, at the State House, for the purpose of ascertaining in what point of view you are to be looked upon—Paper Pen and Ink will be allowed you, immediately, and any person you may name will be permitted to attend you as your Counsel, at the above place and hour.

I am Sir

Your Most Obed^t Hble Servt

Chas Fraser Town Major

Mr Isaac Hayne

in the Provost[3]

No. 3

Memorandum Sunday 29th July 1781

The Town Adjutant will be so good as to wait on Col⁰ Hayne, in the Provost, and acquaint him, that, in consequence of the Court of Enquiry held on him, yesterday, and the Preceeding [*sic*] day, Lord Rawdon and the commandant have come to a resolution, that he shall be executed on [T]uesday the 31st inst, at six o'clock, for having been found in arms, and levying a Regiment to oppose the British Government, notwithstanding he had become a subject, and taken protection, under that Government, after the reduction of Charles Town.

Chas Fraser

Town Major⁴

No. 4

Provost 29th July 1781

My Lord & Honble Sir,

I was on [T]hursday morning last, favored with a billet from Major Fraser, informing me, that a Board of Field Officers would assemble the next day for my trial, and, in the evening of the same day, I received another from same gentleman, acquainting me, that instead thereof a Court of Enquiry would sit for the purpose of ascertaining in what point of view I was to be looked upon. I was also told that any person I should name should attend me as my Counsel—Having never had any idea or heard of one entertained, of a Court of Enquiry but that it was to precede a Court-Martial or some other Court for the more extensive examination of facts, except in the case of a spy, and, Mr Jarvis,⁵ the Deputy Provost Marshal being unsuccessful in attempting to meet with the Gentleman I had named for my Counsel, I was not anxious to have witnesses summoned, of whom, tho indeed I had but little time, I could have produced many, and attended this Board without assistance —

When before the Board, I was further convinced that I was right in my conjecture, as I found that the Members were not sworn, and Witnesses were not examined upon oath, and, it must have been obvious to every Member, and other Persons present, from my request and general conduct that I had not the least conception, of being upon a trial or examination for my life or death, nor do I believe the Members themselves, or any Person there present, had any such.

In the case of spies, a court of Enquiry is all that may be necessary, because the single fact, whether a spy or not, is all that is inquired into, and his entering the lines of the Enemy's Encampment or Garrison subjects him to Military execution—as this neither is, or ever was a charge against me, I humbly apprehended, from the information I received, that the Court was to inquire, what point of view I was to be considered in, and from my having no warning of being intended for trial, that it was only meant to inquire, whether I was to be considered as a British or American Subject, if the former, to be intitled to a fair and legal trial, if the latter, to be admitted to Parole —

Judge then, my Lord and Sir, of my astonishment, when I found that I had been surprised into a trial, without knowing it to be such, and deprived of making a defence, which I can, both in law and fact; and of the assistance of Counsel, and witnesses, being Just informed, that I was, on the proceedings of the Court, adjudged to die, and that on a very short day —

Immediately on the receipt of this notice, I sent for the Gentleman of the law, who I had originally intended should be my counsel—his opinion, in point of Law, of the proceedings had against me, I've inclosed, and beg leave to refer to it—I can, and do, sincerely assure you, that I had, and have much to alledge in my defence, if I shall be favour'd with a trial. If I should not, (which, from your Justice and equity, I cannot suppose), I have to request, as I earnestly do, that the time of my execution may be extended, that I may take a last farewell of my Children, and prepare for the awful change. —

I shall hope for a speedy answer; and am with respect

Your Lordships & Honors Obed^t H^{ble} Servt

Isaac Haynes.

Lord Rawdon &

The Honble

Nisbett Balfour Esqr^6

No. 5

Lord Rawdon's and the Commandants Answer to my Letter of the 29th, delivered by the Town Major on Monday the 30th at 1 o'clock. —

I am to inform you that you was not ordered for Execution in consequence of any sentence of the Court of enquiry but by their Authority which is invested in them as Commander in Chief of the Army in South Carolina, & Commandant of Charlestown—therefore their resolutions remain unaltered —

(I then requested)

That Major Fraser would earnestly entreat Lord Rawdon and the Commandant for a respite until I could send for my Children, and take a final leave of them —

At 3 o'clock the Town Adjutant, M^r [Edward] Cooper returned for answer that my request was denied —^{7}

No. 6

Tuesday July 31—One o'clock AM —

The Deputy Provost Marshal entered & informed me to Prepare for Death as he had just received Orders to that effect & that I must quit the room at 5 o'clock —

In less than half an Hour Major Fraser entered & delivered the following message —Colonel Hayne I am to inform you from the Commandant that in consequence of a Petition signed by Governor Bull & a number of others; Your request yesterday & the humane treatment you observed to such British Officers & Soldiers which fell into your hands, that you have a respite for 48 hours —

I then returned thanks to the Commandant, for the respite as it gave me an opportunity of seeing my Children —

He had not gone out long before he returned & said he had forgot part of his Message —Viz[t]. That the moment any representation was made to the Commandant by General Green[e] in your behalf the respite ceased & you would be immediately ordered for execution —[8]

No. 7

Aug[t]. 1, 1781—3 o'clock A.M. —

M[r] Cooper, Town Adjutant came in and read the following message— viz[t].— Lord Rawdon & the Commandant have agreed to grant a respite to M[r] Hayne for 48 hours longer—

I returned for Answer—I was obliged to them —[9]

No. 8

Memorandum—Friday Evening 3d August 1781 —

The Town Adjutant will be so good as to wait upon M[r] Hayne in the Provost, & acquaint him, that the many Crueltys [sic] exercised upon numberless Officers & Men of the British Militia, extending to death (in many instances) an hour after that capture, have induced Lord Rawdon & The Commandant to order his Execution may take place tomorrow morning at 8 o'clock.

C Fraser   Town Major

Recd Friday Evening 11 o'clock —[10]

No. 9

I (M[r] Hayne) desired the Town Adjutant to wait upon the Lord Rawdon & the Commandant & inform them that his earnest desire & his last request was that he might die the death of a Soldier taken in Arms.[11]

Appendix C

Case of Colonel Hayne

The Colonel being in the Provost, taken as is said in Arms against His Majesty; received on Thursday Evening intimation from Major Fraser in these words "A Court of Enquiry consisting of 4 Field Officers & 5 Captains will assemble tomorrow at 10 o'clock at the State House for the purpose of ascertaining in what point of view you are to be looked upon." The Court met the next morning & the Prisoner attended— Neither the Members or Witnesses were sworn—The Prisoner not conceiving it more than A Court of Enquiry previous to a Trial neither availed himself of the leave given him for having Counsel or produced Witnesses to a great many Facts necessary for his defence, for which indeed he had but little time.—He has this Morning received Notice that Lord Rawdon & the Commandant have come to a resolution in consequence of the Court of Enquiry that he shall be Executed on Tuesday the 31st Inst.—The Prisoner enquires, Whether the proceedings had are warranted by any Law & the sentence thereupon Legal?

1st^{ly}   That in the notification of your intended examination before the Court of Enquiry, there is not even by Military rule a sufficient certainty or charge expressed to be considered by the Court, or defended by you. —

2d^{ly}   That no Enemy is liable to suffer Death by the Articles of War or any other Military rule or Law of which I have ever had cognizance without Trial, except Spies, who are by the Articles of War expressively deprived of that right. —

3d^{ly} That no Subject is liable or can be deprived of his Life, Liberty or property but by the Judgment of his Peers or the Law of the Land, & that there is no Law that I know of which warrants such a Trial & Condemnation as has been had in this case. —

That it is a fixed rule in Law that a Man is to be presumed innocent 'till found Guilty. That even being found or taken in Arms is not such a proof of Guilt as prevents a defence upon proof of compulsion or otherways & that many so taken have been on such proof acquitted. —

John Colcock, Legal brief, "Case of Colonel Hayne, 1781," South Carolina Historical Society.

4th^ly   That I am therefore clearly of opinion that considering you as an Enemy
          (not a Spy) the proceedings had against you are not warranted by Law & that
          as a Subject they are directly repugnant and contrary thereto. —
Jno Colcock
          Charlestown July 29, 1781.

Appendix D

Ladies' Petition for Colonel Isaac Hayne

To the right honorable Lord Rawdon, Commander-in-chief of his Majesty's forces in South Carolina, and to Col. Balfour, Commandant at Charles Town.

My Lord and Sir:

We should have reason to reproach ourselves of having omitted a proper occasion of manifesting the tenderness peculiarly characteristic of our sex, if we did not profess ourselves deeply interested and affected by the imminent and shocking doom of the most unfortunate Mr. Hayne, and if we do not entreat you in the most earnest manner graciously to avert, prolong or mitigate it. We do not even think, much less do we intend to imply, in the remotest degree, that your sentence is unjust; but we are induced to hope, that every end it proposes may be equally answered, as it carried into execution; for to us it does not appear probable that any whom it is intended to influence and deter from similar delinquency, will be encouraged with the hope of impunity, by reason of any favor shewn him, as they must surely reflect that it was owing to certain causes and circumstances that will not apply to them. We presume to make this intercession for him, and to hope that it will not prove fruitless, from the knowledge of your dispositions in particular, as well as from the reflection in general, that humanity is rarely separable from courage, and that the gallant soldier feels as much reluctance to cause, by deliberate decrees, the infliction of death on men in cold blood, as he does ardour in the day of battle and heat of action to make the enemies of his country perish by the sword. He may rejoice to behold his laurels sprinkled with the blood of armed men and resisting adversaries, but will regret to see them wet with the tears of unhappy orphans, mourning the loss of a tender, amiable and worthy parent, executed like a vile and infamous felon[.]

To the praises, that men who have been witnesses and sharers of your dangers and services in the field, may sound of your military virtues and prowess, we trust you will give the ladies occasion to add the praises of your milder and softer virtues

"Ladies Petition for Colonel Hayne [n.d.]," in Gibbes, *Documentary History of the American Revolution* (1853), 112–13.

by furnishing them with a striking proof of your clemency and politeness in the present instance. May the unhappy object of our petition owe to that clemency and politeness, to our prayers and to his own merits in other respects, what you may think him not entitled to if policy and justice were not outweighed in his behalf. To any other men in power than such as we conceive you both to be, we should employ on the occasion more ingenuity and art to dress up and enforce the many pathetic and favorable circumstances attending his case, in order to move your passions and engage your favor, but we think this will be needless, and is obviated by your own spontaneous feelings, humane considerations and liberal reasonings. Nor shall we dwell on his most excellent character, the outrages and excesses, and perhaps murders prevented by him, to which innocent and unarmed individuals were exposed in an extensive manner; nor shall we here lay any stress on the most grievous shock his numerous and respectable connexions must sustain by his death, aggravated by the mode of it; nor shall we do more than remind you of the complicated distress and sufferings that must befall his young and promising children, to whom perhaps death would be more comfortable than the state of orphanage they will be left in[.] All these things we understand have been already represented, and we are sure will have their due weight with men of your humane and benevolent minds. Many of us have already subscribed to a former petition for him, and hope you will regard our doing it again not as importunity, but earnestness; and we pray most fervently that you will forever greatly oblige us by not letting us do it in vain.

   We are, my lord and sir, with all respect,

   Your very anxious petitioners and humble servants.

Notes

Preface

1. Billias, Review of *The Execution of Isaac Hayne*, by David K. Bowden, 139–40; Higgin-botham, Review of *The Execution of Isaac Hayne*, by David K. Bowden, 151.

2. Lee, *Memoirs of the War in the Southern Department*, 450.

3. Wilson, *Southern Strategy*, xiii.

4. Franklin, "The North, the South, and the American Revolution," 5–23.

5. Buchanan, *Road to Guilford Courthouse*, ix.

6. "I only regret that I have but one life to give for my country."

7. Bowden, *Execution of Isaac Hayne*, 11.

8. Ibid., 47.

9. Ibid., 13 (first quote), 72, 76n16; Franklin B. Hayne to Theodore D. Jervey, June 3, 1905, Isaac Hayne (1745–1781), Mss P, 3000, South Caroliniana Library (second quote); "Col. Isaac Hayne Cruelly and Unjustly Hanged by British, Descendent [*sic*] Says," *Charleston Evening Post*, November 23, 1929.

10. The term "redcoat" is used in this narrative to refer to British soldiers in a general sense with the understanding that certain British forces engaged in the southern campaigns wore green coats and that some Hessian soldiers wore blue or green coats.

11. Bowden, *Execution of Isaac Hayne*, 12; Urban, *Fusiliers*, xiii (quoted).

12. Piecuch, *Three Peoples, One King*, 275.

Prologue

1. Simms, "Hayne: A Dirge," 247n*; Simms, *Katharine Walton*, 469. The prologue is largely the paraphrased words of William Gilmore Simms (1806–1870), who interviewed actual witnesses to Hayne's hanging. The friend carrying the umbrella over Hayne's head is not substan-tiated, nor are the number and composition of the accompanying British detachment. Bowden, *Execution of Isaac Hayne*, 71.

2. Ramsay, *History of the Revolution of South Carolina*, 2:283; Simms, "Hayne: A Dirge," 248n† and 248n‡; Simms, *Katharine Walton*, 469. The dialogue quoted is an invention of the author's imagination.

3. Simms, "Hayne: A Dirge," 248n‡ and 248n†.

4. Simms, *Katharine Walton*, 470.

Chapter 1: The British Violate Their Terms and Rule by Edict

1. Stephen and Lee, *Dictionary of National Biography*, 4:550–51; Wyatt and Willcox, "Sir Henry Clinton: A Psychological Exploration in History," 4–26.

2. Billias, *George Washington's Generals and Opponents*, 2:73–76; Stephen and Lee, *Dictionary of National Biography*, 4:550–51.

3. Entry for May 25, 1780, "Sir Henry Clinton's 'Journal of the Siege of Charleston, 1780,'" 174.

4. Ibid.; Kolb and Weir, *Captured at Kings Mountain,* xxv–xxvi, xxx; Wilson, *Southern Strategy,* 1–2; Josiah Martin to William Legge, Earl of Dartmouth, June 30, 1775, in Davies, *Documents of the American Revolution,* 9:209–16.

5. Bragg, *Crescent Moon over Carolina,* 51–52, 58, 64–65, 71–72, 80–81.

6. Wilson, *Southern Strategy,* 238–39.

7. Articles of capitulation, May 12, 1780, in Moultrie, *Memoirs,* 2:99–103 (first quote); Johnson, *Traditions and Reminiscences,* 267 (second quote).

8. Lee, *Memoirs of the War in the Southern Department,* 449–50.

9. Clinton, *American Rebellion,* 174, 440–41; "Handbill issued after the surrender of Charlestown," in Tarleton, *History of the Campaigns of 1780 and 1781,* 70–72; Ramsay, *American Revolution,* 2:157–58; McCrady, *Revolution 1775,* 549–50; Stedman, *American War,* 2:190–91; *Annual Register,* 223–24 (quoted).

10. The June 1 proclamation was issued by Clinton acting jointly with Vice Adm. Mariot Arbuthnot in their appointed roles of commissioners for restoring peace in the North American colonies.

11. Clinton, *American Rebellion,* 174–75; Stedman, *American War,* 2:191; Proclamations, May 22 and June 1, 1780, in Tarleton, *History of the Campaigns of 1780 and 1781,* 73–74 (first quote), 76–78 (second and third quotes).

12. Proclamations, May 22 and June 1, 1780, in Tarleton, *History of the Campaigns of 1780 and 1781,* 73–74 (second and third quotes), 76–78 (first quote).

13. Clinton, *American Rebellion,* 181; Proclamation, June 3, 1780, Tarleton, *History of the Campaigns of 1780 and 1781,* 75–76 (quoted); Nadelhaft, *Disorders of War,* 56.

14. Proclamation, June 3, 1780, in Tarleton, *History of the Campaigns of 1780 and 1781,* 75–76; Hayne, "The Execution of Colonel Isaac Hayne," 81; Nadelhaft, *Disorders of War,* 56, 59–60.

15. Stephen and Lee, *Dictionary of National Biography,* 4:1159–61; Billias, *George Washington's Generals and Opponents,* 2:193–204.

16. Stephen and Lee, *Dictionary of National Biography,* 4:1159–61; Billias, *George Washington's Generals and Opponents,* 2:193–204.

17. Charles Cornwallis to Nisbet Balfour, June 11, 1780, *Cornwallis Papers,* 1:83.

18. Ramsay, *History of the Revolution of South Carolina,* 2:115 (first quote); Moultrie, *Memoirs,* 2:210 (second quote). Moultrie includes a quote from Ramsay, *History of the Revolution of South Carolina,* 2:116.

19. McCrady, *Revolution 1775,* 556–57 (quoted); Clinton, *American Rebellion,* 177.

20. Ramsay, *History of the Revolution of South Carolina,* 2:116 (second quote), 121, 158 (first quote).

21. Ibid., 2:117.

22. Clinton, *American Rebellion,* 181.

23. Proclamation, May 22, 1780, in Tarleton, *History of the Campaigns of 1780 and 1781,* 73–74; Nadelhaft, *Disorders of War,* 56, 58, 59–60.

24. Josiah Martin to George Germain, August 18, 1780, in Davies, *Documents of the American Revolution,* 18:139–40 (first quote); Clinton, *American Rebellion,* 181–82 (second quote).

25. Moultrie, *Memoirs,* 2:210–11 (first quote), 325–26 (second quote).

26. Charles Cornwallis to John Harris Cruger, August 18, 1780, in Ross, *Correspondence of Charles, First Marquis Cornwallis,* 1:56–57.

27. Ramsay, *History of the Revolution of South Carolina,* 2:157–58; "Letters [between George Washington and Henry Clinton during October 1780, with enclosures from Rawdon and Cornwallis] concerning the transactions of Lord Cornwallis and Lord Rawdon in the Carolinas," *Writings of George Washington* (Sparks, ed.), 7:552–58; James, *Sketch of the Life of Brig. Gen. Francis,* 130; Wickwire and Wickwire, *Cornwallis and the War of Independence,* 178–81.

28. Simms, *Life of Francis Marion,* 60–62, 113, 162 (quoted), 189; Moultrie, *Memoirs,* 2:354–55; Busick, *A Sober Desire for History,* 47–48, 56–57.

29. Busick, *A Sober Desire for History,* 48, 75–76; Simms, *Life of Francis Marion,* 186, 189.

30. Nisbet Balfour to Henry Clinton, May 6, 1781, in Cornwallis, *An Answer,* 97–98 of appendix part 6.

31. Ibid.

Chapter 2: A Proud and Haughty Scot Takes Command of Charleston

1. Stephen and Lee, *Dictionary of National Biography,* 1:976–77.

2. Ibid.; "Fourth (or the King's Own) Regiment of Foot," *United Service Journal and Naval and Military Magazine,* 1830, part 2, 559; Adams, *Famous Regiments of the British Army,* 130; Cowper, *King's Own,* 1:229, 245.

3. Stephen and Lee, *Dictionary of National Biography,* 1:976–77; Cowper, *King's Own,* 1:247, 256; Entry for October 10, 1775, *General Sir William Howe's Orderly Book,* 108; *A List of the General and Field Officers* [1778], xv; Urban, *Fusiliers,* 81; William Howe to George German, September 21, 1776, in Davies, *Documents of the American Revolution,* 12:229.

4. Simcoe, *Simcoe's Military Journal,* 56; Entry for October 5, 1777, "Diary of Robert Morton," *Pennsylvania Magazine of History and Biography* 1, no. 1 (1877): 15; Urban, *Fusiliers,* 136, 138.

5. Urban, *Fusiliers,* 111–12, 126, 136, 177 (quoted); Stephen and Lee, *Dictionary of National Biography,* 1:976–77; Lamb, *Memoir of His Own Life,* 90–91.

6. Undated journal entry, Nisbet Balfour correspondence, 1780–1781, Library of Congress, Washington, D.C. (quoted); Urban, *Fusiliers,* 137–38, 166–80; Balfour, Nesbit. Will, proved December 3, 1823, PROB 11/1678/109, National Archives [United Kingdom], Richmond, Surrey, UK.

7. Trevelyan, *Purchase System in the British Army,* passim.

8. Ibid., 3–5; Urban, *Fusiliers,* 137, 177, 193, 195.

9. *A List of All the Officers of the Army* [1781], 11; Urban, *Fusiliers,* 137, 150; Cary and McCance, *Regimental Records of the Royal Welch Fusiliers,* 1:118.

10. Urban, *Fusiliers,* 154, 160, 189, 255–57; Charles Cornwallis to Henry Clinton, May 26, 1781, Charles Cornwallis to George Germain, April 18, 1781, in Cornwallis, *An Answer,* 46, 83–84; Clinton, *American Rebellion,* 227n23, 272, 284–86, 289n15; Stevens, *Campaign in Virginia,* 1:12n25, 34n4, 62n7, 68n6, 69n8, 109n5, 240, 242, 266, 300, 331nn1–2, 341nn1–5, 343nn25–26, 353, 422nn18–19, 490–91; Cary and McCance, *Regimental Records of the Royal Welch Fusiliers,* 1:171.

11. Urban, *Fusiliers,* 166–67; James Rivington to Richard Cumberland, November 23, 1778, in Davies, *Documents of the American Revolution,* 15:266; Crary, "The Tory and the Spy," 61–72.

12. Urban, *Fusiliers,* 166–67; Rivington to Cumberland, November 23, 1778, in Davies, *Documents of the American Revolution,* 15:266.

13. Urban, *Fusiliers,* 168–71, 175–80.

14. Clinton, *American Rebellion,* 151, 153–54, 159; Moultrie, *Memoirs,* 2:44; Wilson, *Southern Strategy,* 205, 239–41.

15. Clinton, *American Rebellion,* 160–64 (quoted); William Moultrie to a friend, March 26 and April 3, 1780, in Moultrie, *Memoirs,* 2:61–62, 62n; Wilson, *Southern Strategy,* 206–7, 238–39.

16. Urban, *Fusiliers,* 181, 188–89; Entry for April 18, 1780, "Sir Henry Clinton's 'Journal of the Siege of Charleston, 1780,'" 162; Nisbet Balfour to "Lewis," May 15, 1780, Nisbet Balfour correspondence, 1780–1781, Library of Congress, Washington, D.C. (quoted).

17. Urban, *Fusiliers,* 190–93; Entry for May 2, 1780, "Sir Henry Clinton's 'Journal of the Siege of Charleston, 1780,'" 172 (quoted); Nisbet Balfour to Charles Cornwallis, November 5 and 17, 1780, Charles Cornwallis to Nisbet Balfour, November 12 and 17, 1780, *Cornwallis Papers,* 3:63, 71, 75–76, 86.

18. Urban, *Fusiliers*, 193; Chesney, *Journal of Alexander Chesney*, 83.

19. Urban, *Fusiliers*, 191–93, 195; Entry for May 2, 1780, "Sir Henry Clinton's 'Journal of the Siege of Charleston, 1780,'" 172; Nisbet Balfour to Charles Cornwallis, May 20 and 30 and June 24, 1780, *Cornwallis Papers*, 1:72, 73–74, 237, 239.

20. Urban, *Fusiliers*, 196–97, 198–99; Nisbet Balfour to Charles Cornwallis, June 24, 1780, *Cornwallis Papers*, 1:239; Charles Cornwallis to George Germain, August 20, 1780, in Ross, *Correspondence of Charles, First Marquis Cornwallis*, 1:502–5.

21. "General Andrew Williamson," in Chesney, *Journal of Alexander Chesney*, 76–78; Simms, *Katharine Walton*, 485n19.34; Nisbet Balfour to Charles Cornwallis, June 24, 1780, *Cornwallis Papers*, 1:239–40 (quoted).

22. Ramsay, *History of the Revolution of South Carolina*, 2:194.

23. Ibid., 194–95.

24. Urban, *Fusiliers*, 198–99, 213; Charles Cornwallis to Nisbet Balfour, July 17, 1780, *Cornwallis Papers*, 1:250 (quoted).

25. Nelson, *Francis Rawdon-Hastings*, 87–88, 202n1; Charles Cornwallis to Nisbet Balfour, November 12, 1780, Charles Cornwallis to George Germain, August 20, 1780, in Ross, *Correspondence of Charles, First Marquis Cornwallis*, 1:68–69 (quoted), 502–5; Lord Moira (Francis Rawdon) to Henry Lee, June 24, 1813, in Lee, *Memoirs of the War in the Southern Department*, 616.

26. Ramsay, *History of the Revolution of South Carolina*, 2:263–64.

27. Ibid., 161–66, 299–301, 458–59n22–23; Tarleton, *History of the Campaigns of 1780 and 1781*, 159–60; List of persons transported to St. Augustine, enclosed with Nisbet Balfour to Charles Cornwallis, September 4, 1780, *Cornwallis Papers*, 2:77–78; "Charlestown, 25th June, 1781," *Royal Gazette* (Charleston), June 27–30; "Charlestown, July 11th, 1781," *Royal Gazette* (Charleston), August 18–22, 1781.

28. Urban, *Fusiliers*, 216, 253, 254–55; Borick, *Relieve Us of This Burthen*, 18, 116, 137n45; Nisbet Balfour to Francis Rawdon, October 26, 1780, quoted in Ranlet, "In the Hands of the British," 744 (quoted), 744n51; William Moultrie to Nisbet Balfour, September 1, 1780, and March 21, 1781, in Moultrie, *Memoirs*, 2:138–39, 193–94; Nisbet Balfour to Charles Cornwallis, October 22 and 29, 1780, *Cornwallis Papers*, 2:130, 139; Nisbet Balfour to Charles Cornwallis, May 21, 1781, *Cornwallis Papers*, 5:277; Charles Cornwallis to Henry Clinton, December 3, 1780, in Davies, *Documents of the American Revolution*, 18:247.

29. Charles Cornwallis to Nisbet Balfour, February 21, 1781, *Cornwallis Papers*, 4:41–42; William Moultrie to Nisbet Balfour, April 3 and May 3, 1781, in Moultrie, *Memoirs*, 2:194–95, 197.

30. Charles Cornwallis to Nisbet Balfour, September 3 and 6 and October 7, 1780, Nisbet Balfour to Charles Cornwallis, September 4 and October 1, 1780, Nisbet Balfour to Francis Rawdon, October 29, 1780, *Cornwallis Papers*, 2:73, 74, 114, 116, 138; Charles Cornwallis to Nisbet Balfour, November 4, 18, and 22, 1780, Nisbet Balfour to Charles Cornwallis, November 17 and 30, 1780, *Cornwallis Papers*, 3:60–68, 79, 84, 87, 101–4; Charles Cornwallis to Nisbet Balfour, April 5, 21, 22 and May 3, 1781, *Cornwallis Papers*, 4:42–44, 121–22, 176; Nisbet Balfour to Charles Cornwallis, May 21, 1781, *Cornwallis Papers*, 5:277; *Cornwallis Papers*, 5:275; Urban, *Fusiliers*, 221, 222, 250, 251, 253, 255; Borick, *Relieve Us of This Burthen*, 19–20, 32.

31. Moultrie, *Memoirs*, 2:252.

32. George Benson to William Moultrie, September 4, 1780, William Moultrie to Nisbet Balfour, November 22, 1780, Nisbet Balfour to William Moultrie, November 28, 1780, in Moultrie, *Memoirs*, 139 (first quote), 142 (third quote), 143–45 (second quote), 300; Nisbet Balfour to Charles Cornwallis, September 27, 1780, *Cornwallis Papers*, 2:111; Nisbet Balfour to Charles Cornwallis, November 15, 1780, *Cornwallis Papers*, 3:76; Borick, *Relieve Us of This Burthen*, 55–56.

33. Nisbet Balfour to William Moultrie Jr., January 14, 1781, James Fraser to William Moultrie, January 28, 1781, William Moultrie to James Fraser, February 2, 1781, in Moultrie, *Memoirs,* 2:149–50, 152, 154–55.

34. Urban, *Fusiliers,* 214–16.

35. Nisbet Balfour to Francis Rawdon, November 1, 1780, Nisbet Balfour to Charles Cornwallis, November 5, 1780, *Cornwallis Papers,* 3:62, 64–65; Urban, *Fusiliers,* 221–22, 223; Borick, *Relieve Us of This Burthen,* 99, 150n37; Charles Cornwallis to Nisbet Balfour, April 24, 1781, Nisbet Balfour to Charles Cornwallis, April 20, 1781, *Cornwallis Papers,* 4:122, 172; Nisbet Balfour to Charles Cornwallis, May 21, 1781, *Cornwallis Papers,* 5:274–75, 277.

36. Urban, *Fusiliers,* 265–66; Nisbet Balfour to Charles Cornwallis, April 26, 1781, *Cornwallis Papers,* 4:177–78; Nisbet Balfour to Charles Cornwallis, May 21, 1781, *Cornwallis Papers,* 5:274–78; William L. Pierce Jr. to St. George Tucker, August 26, 1781, in Coleman, "Southern Campaign of General Greene 1781–2," 434 (quoted).

37. Nisbet Balfour to "the militia prisoners late on parole in Charleston, now on board a prison-ship," May 17, 1781, Stephen Moore and John Barnwell to Nathanael Greene, May 18, 1781, in Ramsay, *History of the Revolution of South Carolina,* 2:535–37, 541; Urban, *Fusiliers,* 265–66; Nisbet Balfour to Henry Clinton, May 6, 1781, in Cornwallis, *An Answer,* 97–98 of appendix part 6.

Chapter 3: A Fierce and Unrelenting Soldier Comes in from the Field

1. Nelson, *Francis Rawdon-Hastings,* 17, 18–19 (quoted), 194nn7–8.

2. Ibid., 20–22, 24, 194–95nn9–13; Stephen and Lee, *Dictionary of National Biography,* 9:117–22; Garden, *Anecdotes,* 1:253, McCrady, *Revolution 1780,* 403n1.

3. Stephen and Lee, *Dictionary of National Biography,* 9:117–22; Nelson, *Francis Rawdon-Hastings,* 20, 22–24, 195nn13–15; Ross-of-Bladensburg, *Marquess of Hastings,* 7–8, 13 (quoted).

4. Stephen and Lee, *Dictionary of National Biography,* 9:117–22; Nelson, *Francis Rawdon-Hastings,* 22–25, 195nn14–15.

5. Nelson, *Francis Rawdon-Hastings,* 24–27, 195n16, n19; Cannon, *Historical Record of the Fifth Regiment of Foot,* 42.

6. Frothingham, *Centennial: Battle of Bunker Hill,* 113 (first quote); Cannon, *Historical Record of the Fifth Regiment of Foot,* 42–43 (second quote); Stephen and Lee, *Dictionary of National Biography,* 9:117–22; Nelson, *Francis Rawdon-Hastings,* 27–28, 195–96nn19–21; John Burgoyne to Thomas Stanley, June 25, 1775, in Force, ed., *American Archives,* ser. 4, 2:1094–95 (third quote).

7. Nelson, *Francis Rawdon-Hastings,* 29 (quoted), 30–32, 196n21, n24.

8. Ibid., 34–41 (quoted), 42, 196n1, 197n8; "General Orders by Major General the Honourable William Howe," entry for January 15, 1776, in Kemble, *Journals of Lieut. Col. Stephen Kemble,* 297.

9. Richard Hutson to Isaac Hayne, June 24, 1776 [typescript], Richard Hutson letter book, 1765–1777 (34/559), SCHS.

10. Alexander Garden was the estranged patriot son of Charleston's famous Scottish-born physician, botanist, and ardent loyalist, Dr. Alexander Garden. Dr. Garden will appear later in the narrative.

11. Ibid. (first and second quotes); Garden, *Anecdotes,* 2:114 (third quote).

12. Nelson, *Francis Rawdon-Hastings,* 44, 46, 197n13.

13. Ibid., 25–26, 32–33, 36 (first quote), 38, 42–43, 49, 54, 195n18, 196n24, n4, 197n7, n9; Conway, "To Subdue America," 394; Francis Rawdon to Francis Hastings, Earl of Huntingdon, August 5, 1776, in Commager and Morris, eds., *Spirit of Seventy-Six,* 424 (second and third quotes).

14. Nelson, *Francis Rawdon-Hastings,* 46, 49 (quoted), 197nn11–13; Conway, "To Subdue America," 381, 393–94.

15. Conway, "To Subdue America," 381, 383–85; Dull, *Diplomatic History of the American Revolution,* 47, 53. For more on the Howe brothers as peace commissioners see Ira D. Gruber, *The Howe Brothers and the American Revolution* (Chapel Hill, N.C., 1972), passim.

16. Nelson, *Francis Rawdon-Hastings,* 55, 60–61, 198nn5–6; Clinton, *American Rebellion,* 58, 61; Gottschalk, *Lafayette Comes to America,* 89.

17. Nelson, *Francis Rawdon-Hastings,* 60–62 (quoted), 65, 199n15, n17, 200n25; "All Gentlemen Natives of Ireland," *Royal Gazette* (New York), April 3, 1779; Clinton, *American Rebellion,* 110–11; Ross-of-Bladensburg, *Marquess of Hastings,* 15–16; Henry Clinton to George Germain, October 23, 1778, in Davies, *Documents of the American Revolution,* 15:227–28; Alexander Innes to Henry Clinton, September 22, 1779, in Davies, *Documents of the American Revolution,* 17:47, 219; Journal entries for May 1 and 2, 1778, and "Gen. Sir Henry Clinton's Orders," entries for May 25 and 30, 1778, in Kemble, *Journals of Lieut. Col. Stephen Kemble,* 150, 586, 587.

18. Nelson, *Francis Rawdon-Hastings,* 62–63, 199n15, nn18–20; Journal entry for June 27, 1778, and "Gen. Sir Henry Clinton's Orders," entry for June 19, 1778, in Kemble, *Journals of Lieut. Col. Stephen Kemble,* 153, 595–96.

19. Nelson, *Francis Rawdon-Hastings,* 38, 63, 65–69, 71–72, 200nn26–30, n32, 201nn3–5; Stephen Kemble to Henry Clinton, September 6, 1779, in Kemble, *Journals of Lieut. Col. Stephen Kemble,* 183–84; Henry Clinton to George Germain, June 3, 1780, George Germain to Henry Clinton, July 5, 1780, in Davies, *Documents of the American Revolution,* 16:342–43, 359.

20. Nelson, *Francis Rawdon-Hastings,* 70–71, 200–1nn1–2; "New-York, March 18," *Royal Gazette* (New York), March 18, 1780; Clinton, *American Rebellion,* 166–67.

21. Nelson, *Francis Rawdon-Hastings,* 73–75, 201nn5–7; Charles Cornwallis to George Germain, August 20, 1780, in Ross, *Correspondence of Charles, First Marquis Cornwallis,* 1:502–3; Stedman, *American War,* 2:195–96; Clinton, *American Rebellion,* 175–76.

22. Nelson, *Francis Rawdon-Hastings,* 74–76, 201n9; Francis Rawdon to Charles Cornwallis, June 22, 1781, *Cornwallis Papers,* 1:183 (quoted).

23. Francis Rawdon to Charles Cornwallis, July 7, 1781, *Cornwallis Papers,* 1:193–94 (quoted); Nelson, *Francis Rawdon-Hastings,* 76–77.

24. Francis Rawdon to Henry Rugeley, July 1, 1780, in Ramsay, *History of the Revolution of South Carolina,* 2:132–34 (quotes); George Washington to Henry Clinton, October 16, 1780, *Writings of George Washington* (Sparks, ed.), 7:553, 554–55n†. *See also* Wickwire and Wickwire, *Cornwallis and the War of Independence,* 178–81.

25. Lord Moira (Francis Rawdon) to John McMahon, January 19, 1801, in George IV, *Correspondence of George, Prince of Wales,* 4:192–97; Nelson, *Francis Rawdon-Hastings,* 77–80, 80–89, 201n12; Gordon, *South Carolina and the American Revolution,* 90–94; Charles Cornwallis to Henry Clinton, August 10 and 18, 1780, Charles Cornwallis to George Germain, August 20 and 21, 1780, in Ross, *Correspondence of Charles, First Marquis Cornwallis,* 1:54–57, 503–9; Piecuch, *Battle of Camden,* 146–47.

26. Lord Moira (Francis Rawdon) to John McMahon, January 19, 1801, in George IV, *Correspondence of George, Prince of Wales,* 4:192–97; Nelson, *Francis Rawdon-Hastings,* 81–82; Gordon, *South Carolina and the American Revolution,* 92–94.

27. Nelson, *Francis Rawdon-Hastings,* 82–83, 202n18; Josiah Martin to George Germain, August 18, 1780, in Davies, *Documents of the American Revolution,* 18:142; Charles Cornwallis to George Germain, August 20 and 21, 1780, in Stevens, *Campaign in Virginia,* 1:241–48 (first quote), 249–56; Lord Moira (Francis Rawdon) to John McMahon, January 19, 1801, in George IV, *Correspondence of George, Prince of Wales,* 4:193 (second quote); Piecuch, *Battle of Camden,* 55–61.

28. Nelson, *Francis Rawdon-Hastings*, 82–85, 202nn21–22; Francis Rawdon to Alexander Leslie, October 24, 1780, Francis Rawdon to Henry Clinton, October 29, 1780, in Stevens, *Campaign in Virginia*, 1:271–75, 277–80.

29. Nelson, *Francis Rawdon-Hastings*, 86–91; Francis Rawdon to Charles Cornwallis, March 7 and 24, 1781, *Cornwallis Papers*, 4:47–49 (quoted), 51–52.

30. Nelson, *Francis Rawdon-Hastings*, 90–95; Francis Rawdon to Charles Cornwallis, April 26, 1781, in Davies, *Documents of the American Revolution*, 20:122–24.

31. Nelson, *Francis Rawdon-Hastings*, 96–97; Charles Cornwallis to Francis Rawdon, May 20, 1781, *Cornwallis Papers*, 5:286–87 (quoted); Lord Moira (Francis Rawdon) to Henry Lee, June 24, 1813, in Lee, *Memoirs of the War in the Southern Department*, 615–16.

32. Charles Cornwallis to Francis Rawdon, May 20, 1781, *Cornwallis Papers*, 5:286–87 (first and second quotes); "By the Right Honourable Francis Lord Rawdon . . . and Nesbit Balfour," *Royal American Gazette* (New York), June 28, 1781 (third quote).

33. Nelson, *Francis Rawdon-Hastings*, 98–102; Nisbet Balfour to George Germain, June 27, 1781, in Davies, *Documents of the American Revolution*, 20:163–64.

34. Nelson, *Francis Rawdon-Hastings*, 101–3; Lord Moira (Francis Rawdon) to Henry Lee, June 24, 1813, in Lee, *Memoirs of the War in the Southern Department*, 616 (quoted).

35. Nelson, *Francis Rawdon-Hastings*, 97–102; Lord Moira (Francis Rawdon) to Henry Lee, June 24, 1813, in Lee, *Memoirs of the War in the Southern Department*, 615.

Chapter 4: "I do not mean to desert the cause of America"

1. Edgar and Bailey, *Biographical Dictionary*, 310; Jervey, "The Hayne Family," 167, 169, 180–81.

2. Jervey, "The Hayne Family," 181; Edgar and Bailey, *Biographical Dictionary*, 310; Will of Isaac Hayne (n.d.) [typescript], Biographical and genealogical research on Isaac Hayne (30-4 Hayne), SCHS.

3. Will of Isaac Hayne (n.d.) [typescript], Biographical and genealogical research on Isaac Hayne (30-4 Hayne), SCHS; Hayne, Isaac Hayne Ledger, 1765–1781 (34/561), SCHS.

4. Hayne, "The Execution of Colonel Isaac Hayne," 77–78 (quoted); Harrison, *Charleston Album*, 44; "Colonel Isaac Hayne," *Army and Navy Chronicle*, 161–62.

5. Hayne, "The Execution of Colonel Isaac Hayne," 77–78.

6. South Carolina Historical Society, "Records Kept by Colonel Isaac Hayne," 14–23; Richard Hutson to Isaac Hayne, January 28, 1767 [typescript], Richard Hutson letter book, 1765–1777 (34/559), SCHS. The number of slaves owned by Isaac Hayne is unknown and is not specified in his last will and testament. Will of Isaac Hayne (n.d.) [typescript], Biographical and genealogical research on Isaac Hayne (30-4 Hayne), SCHS.

7. Richard Hutson to Isaac Hayne, August 29, 1767 [typescript], Richard Hutson letter book, 1765–1777 (34/559), SCHS; Hutson, "The Hutson Family of South Carolina," 128; Shaffer, *To Be an American*, 27, 59–60.

8. The Circular Church. The Hutson family patriarch Rev. William Hutson served as the church's pastor from 1757 to 1761. Hutson, "The Hutson Family of South Carolina," 127–28.

9. Hutson, "The Hutson Family of South Carolina," 127–28; Salley, *Marriage Notices*, 29; Jervey, "The Hayne Family," 181; William Edward Hayne to Jeremiah A. Yates, December 23, 1835, William Edward Hayne (1776–1843), Mss P, 2340, South Caroliniana Library. The children of Isaac and Elizabeth Hayne were Isaac Hayne (1766–1802), Mary Hayne (1768–1768), Sarah Hayne (1770–1800), John Hamden Hayne (1773–1825), Elizabeth Hayne (1774–1776), Mary Hayne (1776–1780), William Edward Hayne (1776–1843), and Eliza Hayne (c.1779–1780).

10. Richard Hutson to Isaac Hayne, May 27, 1776, Richard Hutson to Isaac Hayne, June 24, 1776, Richard Hutson to Isaac Hayne, March 22, 1777 [typescripts], Richard Hutson letter book, 1765–1777 (34/559), SCHS; Glover, *All Our Relations,* 80–81.

11. Edgar and Bailey, *Biographical Dictionary,* 310; "Charles-town, January 2," *South-Carolina Gazette and Country Journal* (Charleston, S.C.), January 2, 1770; Cooper, *Statutes at Large,* 4:323–26.

12. Edgar and Bailey, *Biographical Dictionary,* 310; Richard Hutson to Isaac Hayne, January 18, 1777 [typescript], Richard Hutson letter book, 1765–1777 (34/559), SCHS (quoted).

13. Richard Hutson to Isaac Hayne, January 18, 1777 [typescript], Richard Hutson letter book, 1765–1777 (34/559), SCHS (quoted); Edgar and Bailey, *Biographical Dictionary,* 310; Howe, *History of the Presbyterian Church in South Carolina,* 1:475.

14. Hemphill and Wates, *Extracts from the Journals of the Provincial Congresses of South Carolina,* 15–19, 35–42.

15. Edgar and Bailey, *Biographical Dictionary,* 310; South Carolina Historical Society, "Journal of the Second Council of Safety," 185; Salley, "Papers of the First Council of Safety," 6; Moultrie, *Memoirs,* 1:120; Lee, *Memoirs of the War in the Southern Department,* 449n (quoted); Hayne, "The Execution of Colonel Isaac Hayne," 76.

16. Articles of agreement between William Hill and Isaac Hayne, October 22, 1778, Thomas Addis Emmet Collection, 1483-1876, MssCol 927, New York Public Library; Hemphill and Wates, *Extracts from the Journals of the Provincial Congresses of South Carolina,* 226; Stevens and Allen, *Journals of the House of Representatives, 1791,* 133–35; Stevens, *Journals of the House of Representatives, 1792–1794,* 390–92; Drayton, *View of South-Carolina,* 152; Lander, "The Iron Industry in Ante-Bellum South Carolina," 339, 339n5, 355; Cowan, "William Hill and the Aera Ironworks," 8, 28n35.

17. Articles of agreement between William Hill and Isaac Hayne, October 22, 1778, Thomas Addis Emmet Collection, 1483-1876, MssCol 927, New York Public Library; South Carolina Historical Society, "Records Kept by Colonel Isaac Hayne," 15–19; Cowan, "William Hill and the Aera Ironworks," 8, 28n35.

18. Drayton, *View of South-Carolina,* 150–52; Stevens and Allen, *Journals of the House of Representatives, 1791,* 134; Cowan, "William Hill and the Aera Ironworks," 21; "The Aera Furnace," *Gazette of the State of South Carolina* (Charleston, S.C.), November 24, 1779 (quoted).

19. Stevens, *Journals of the House of Representatives, 1792–1794,* 391–92 (first quote); Hill, *Col. William Hill's Memoirs of the Revolution,* 8 (second quote); Edgar, *Partisans and Redcoats,* 59; Charles Cornwallis to Henry Clinton, June 30, 1780, in Tarleton, *History of the Campaigns of 1780 and 1781,* 120; Ramsay, *History of the Revolution of South Carolina,* 2:159.

20. "The Round O section [of Colleton County] has been known as such since 1709. According to the late Mr. Alex S. Salley, it was named for the Round-O Creek which preserved the 'moniker of a famous Indian Chief who had a purple medallion tattooed on his shoulder. The English traders found it easier to call him by his ornament than by his lengthy name.'" Neuffer, *Names in South Carolina, Vols. I–XII, 1954–1965,* 111, 191 (quoted).

21. James Hamilton to Captain Isaac Hayne, July 6, 1777 [typescript], Biographical and genealogical research on Isaac Hayne (30-4 Hayne), SCHS; Howe, *History of the Presbyterian Church in South Carolina,* 1:476; Ramsay, *History of the Revolution of South Carolina,* 2:278; Hayne, "The Execution of Colonel Isaac Hayne," 76; "Colonel Isaac Hayne," in Chesney, *Journal of Alexander Chesney,* 94–95; Lee, *Memoirs of the War in the Southern Department,* 449–50.

22. Bowden, *Execution of Isaac Hayne,* 19–20, 23nn18–20; Note re Isaac Hayne, September 4, 1781, Letters from Maj. Gen. Nathaniel [*sic*] Greene, 1776–85, Papers of the Continental Congress (hereinafter cited as PCC), NA microfilm series M247, roll 175 (vol. 2), 348–50 (quoted).

23. Ramsay, *History of the Revolution of South Carolina*, 2:278.

24. Lee, *Memoirs of the War in the Southern Department*, 449–50 (quoted); "Colonel Robert Ballingall," in Chesney, *Journal of Alexander Chesney*, 94.

25. Lee, *Memoirs of the War in the Southern Department*, 450; William Edward Hayne to Jeremiah A. Yates, December 23, 1835, William Edward Hayne (1776–1843), Mss P, 2340, South Caroliniana Library; Jervey, "The Hayne Family," 181.

26. Lee, *Memoirs of the War in the Southern Department*, 450.

27. Enclosure, John Rutledge to John Dickinson (n.d.), Letters relating to Colonel Hayne, box 5, folder 7, John Dickinson Papers, Library Company of Philadelphia. (See also Smith, *Letters of Delegates to Congress, 18:697–701);* Lee, *Memoirs of the War in the Southern Department*, 449; McCrady, *Revolution 1780*, 131.

28. Ramsay, *History of the Revolution of South Carolina*, 2:278. The given time frame is predicated on the date of Clinton's last proclamation (June 3, 1780) and the facts that Patterson was still commandant of Charleston (a post he held until about mid-July) and that David Ramsay had not yet been arrested by the British (this arrest occurred on August 27, 1780).

29. Ibid., 2:278–79.

30. Ibid.

31. Ibid., 2:280 (quoted); Enclosure, John Rutledge to John Dickinson (n.d.), Letters relating to Colonel Hayne, box 5, folder 7, John Dickinson Papers, Library Company of Philadelphia (first quote); Lee, *Memoirs of the War in the Southern Department*, 450–51; Hayne, "The Execution of Colonel Isaac Hayne," 81. According to South Carolina's revolutionary governor John Rutledge, Hayne did not sign an *oath* of allegiance to King George III, "the Practice having been for those who applied for protection or requested to be admitted as British Subjects." Rather he signed a *declaration* of allegiance, albeit under extreme duress. The British did not make such a distinction.

Chapter 5: The Captor Becomes the Captive

1. Mackenzie, *Strictures on Lt. Col. Tarleton's History of the Campaigns of 1780 and 1781*, 140n* (quoted); Murray, *English Review*, 407–14. An incident similar to what MacKenzie reports is found in Tarleton, *A History of the Campaigns of 1780 and 1781*, 95–96.

2. Barnwell, *Story of an American Family*, 36; Salley, *Journal of the House of Representatives of South Carolina. January 8, 1782–February 26, 1782*, 91–92; Daso, "Colonel William Harden," 96–98, 97n9; William Harden to Francis Marion, April 7, 1781, in Gibbes, *Documentary History of the American Revolution* (1853), 49–51; McCrady, *Revolution 1780*, 133, 318; Ripley, *Battleground*, 184.

3. Harden to Marion, April 7 and 18, 1781, in Gibbes, *Documentary History of the American Revolution* (1853), 49–51 (quoted), 55; McCrady, *Revolution 1780*, 133–34; Lee, *Memoirs of the War in the Southern Department*, 451–52.

4. Ramsay, *History of the Revolution of South Carolina*, 2:280–81; Enclosure, John Rutledge to John Dickinson (n.d.), Letters relating to Colonel Hayne, box 5, folder 7, John Dickinson Papers.

5. Enclosure, John Rutledge to John Dickinson (n.d.), Letters relating to Colonel Hayne, box 5, folder 7, John Dickinson Papers.

6. Ramsay, *History of the Revolution of South Carolina*, 2:280–81; William Harden to Francis Marion, April 18, 1781, in Gibbes, *Documentary History of the American Revolution* (1853), 53–55; Hayne, "The Execution of Colonel Isaac Hayne," 87–88; McCrady, *Revolution 1780*, 132–33, 319 (first quote), 330 (second quote), 383; Lee, *Memoirs of the War in the Southern Department*, 452; Chesney, *Journal of Alexander Chesney*, 24.

7. Garden, *Anecdotes,* 1:250–51; Lambert, *South Carolina Loyalists,* 150–51, 153n29.

8. "Particulars respecting Col. Haynes [*sic*], lately published in the London papers," *Scots Magazine* 43:704; William Bull to George Germain, July 2, 1781, in Davies, *Documents of the American Revolution,* 20:168–69.

9. Moss, *Roster of South Carolina Patriots,* 998; "General Andrew Williamson," in Chesney, *Journal of Alexander Chesney,* 76–78; Nisbet Balfour to Charles Cornwallis, June 6 and 24, 1780, *Cornwallis Papers,* 1:77, 77n12, 239–40; Johnson, *Traditions and Reminiscences,* 144–53, 361; Davis, "The Feather Bed Aristocracy," 141; Lee, *Memoirs of the War in the Southern Department,* 452; LeRoy Hammond to Nathanael Greene, May 15, 1782, Andrew Williamson to Nathanael Greene, June 24, 1782, *Papers of General Nathanael Greene,* 11:195, 368n1.

10. "Charlestown, July 11," *Royal Gazette* (Charleston), July 7–11, 1781; Lord Moira (Francis Rawdon) to Henry Lee, June 24, 1813, in Lee, *Memoirs of the War in the Southern Department,* 618; Ramsay, *History of the Revolution of South Carolina,* 2:280–81; Johnson, *Traditions and Reminiscences,* 361 (quoted); McCrady, *Revolution 1780,* 319.

11. "Charlestown, July 11," *Royal Gazette* (Charleston), July 7–11, 1781; Lord Moira (Francis Rawdon) to Henry Lee, June 24, 1813, in Lee, *Memoirs of the War in the Southern Department,* 618; Nisbet Balfour to Henry Clinton, July 21, 1781, Letter book of Lt. Col. Nisbet Balfour, MSS L2001F617, Society of the Cincinnati; McCrady, *Revolution 1780,* 319.

12. Johnson, *Traditions and Reminiscences,* 361–62; McCrady, *Revolution 1780,* 319–20; Simms, *Katharine Walton,* 515n341.23; Glover, *Colonel Joseph Glover,* 28–29; Pattillo, *Carolina Planters on the Alabama Frontier,* 433–34; Glover, *Narratives of Colleton County,* 29–30; Lee, *Memoirs of the War in the Southern Department,* 452–53. Johnson gives the distance from Parker's Ferry to Woodford as four miles. An examination of contemporary and modern maps reveals that the distance was perhaps a little more than twice that far.

13. "Charlestown, July 11," *Royal Gazette* (Charleston), July 7–14, 1781 (first quote); Enclosure, John Rutledge to John Dickinson (n.d.), Letters relating to Colonel Hayne, box 5, folder 7, John Dickinson Papers, Library Company of Philadelphia (second quote). See also Smith, *Letters of Delegates to Congress, 18:700.*

14. Johnson, *Traditions and Reminiscences,* 362; McCrady, *Revolution 1780,* 320, 592, 592n1; Glover, *Colonel Joseph Glover,* 28–29, 698n46; Pattillo, *Carolina Planters on the Alabama Frontier,* 433–34; Glover, *Narratives of Colleton County,* 30–31; Lee, *Memoirs of the War in the Southern Department,* 452–53; Muster rolls for Captain Archibald Campbell's Company, South Carolina Light Dragoons, April 24 and October 24, 1781, in Clark, *Loyalists in the Southern Campaign of the Revolutionary War,* 1:89–91; Harrison, *Charleston Album,* 47–48. It appears from the various accounts that Harden lost about fourteen killed and several others wounded.

15. Thompson and Lumpkin, *Journals of the House of Representatives, 1783–1784,* 341; Moultrie, *Memoirs,* 2:85, 85n[*]; "The President," *City Gazette,* May 14, 1791.

16. McCrady, *Revolution 1780,* 382 (quoted); "Charlestown, 25th June, 1781," *Royal Gazette* (Charleston, S.C.), June 27–30, 1781; "Charlestown, July 11th, 1781," and "Charlestown, August 12th, 1781," *Royal Gazette* (Charleston, S.C.), August 11–15, 1781.

17. McCrady, *Revolution 1780,* 382–83; Urban, *Fusiliers,* 266.

18. "Articles of a Cartel," in Moultrie, *Memoirs,* 2:198–200; Knight, "Prisoner Exchange and Parole," 209–10; McCrady, *Revolution 1780,* 409–10; "General Exchange," June 22, 1781, in Gibbes, *Documentary History of the American Revolution* (1853), 122–23.

19. "General Exchange," June 22, 1781, in Gibbes, *Documentary History of the American Revolution* (1853), 122–23; Edmund M. Hyrne to Nathanael Greene, August 1, 1781, Nathanael Greene to Nisbet Balfour, August 2, 1781, Nisbet Balfour to Nathanael Greene, August 18, 1781, *Papers*

of General Nathanael Greene, 9:123, 123n1, 124–25, 125–26n1, 202, 202nn3–4; Johnson, *Sketches of the Life and Correspondence of Nathanael Greene,* 2:201.

20. Charles Fraser, a second lieutenant in the Royal Welch Fusiliers, occupied the post of "town major." As the commandant's executive officer, as head of the military police, and in command of the jail and guards, he was charged with keeping good order. *A List of All the Officers of the Army* [1781], 11; Johnson, *Traditions and Reminiscences,* 362.

21. Copies of two letters (A.M. and P.M.) of Charles Fraser to Isaac Hayne, July 26, 1781, PCC, NA microfilm series M247, roll 175 (vol. 2), 351.

22. Urban, *Fusiliers,* 266–67; Lord Moira (Francis Rawdon) to Henry Lee, June 24, 1813, in Lee, *Memoirs of the War in the Southern Department,* 617 (quoted).

23. Memorandum, June 29, 1781, and copy of Isaac Hayne to Nesbit Balfour and Francis Rawdon, July 29, 1781, PCC, NA microfilm series M247, roll 175 (vol. 2), 351–53; Hayne, "The Execution of Colonel Isaac Hayne," 91–92n*.

24. The exact identity of Major McKenzie is yet to be determined though he may have been Andrew McKenzie who was subject to the Confiscation Act of 1782. McCrady, *Revolution 1780,* 390n1.

25. Garden, *Anecdotes,* 1:251–52 (quoted); McCrady, *Revolution 1780,* 390n1.

26. Copy of Charles Fraser to Isaac Hayne, July 29, 1781, PCC, NA microfilm series M247, roll 175 (vol. 2), 351–52.

27. Copy of Isaac Hayne to Nesbit Balfour and Francis Rawdon, July 29, 1781, PCC, NA microfilm series M247, roll 175 (vol. 2), 353–54.

28. Ibid. 354–55 (quoted); Salley, "Capt. John Colcock and Some of His Descendants," 218–19.

29. Legal brief, in Colcock, "Case of Colonel Hayne, 1781," SCHS.

30. Ibid.

31. "Lord Rawdon's & the Commandant's Answer," July 30, 1781, in Colcock, "Case of Colonel Hayne, 1781," SCHS.

Chapter 6: "The imminent and shocking doom of the most unfortunate Mr. Hayne"

1. Other petitioners purportedly included Maj. Thomas Fraser, who was present at Hayne's capture, and deputy adjutant general Maj. Harry Barry. Simms, *Katharine Walton,* 521n465.26.

2. "Tuesday, July 31— One o'clock A.M.," in Colcock, "Case of Colonel Hayne, 1781," SCHS; Bull, *Oligarchs in Colonial and Revolutionary Charleston,* 297–98; "Outline," *Charleston Evening Gazette,* October 27, 1785.

3. Greene, *Papers of General Nathanael Greene,* 9:123n1. Hyrne had returned to the American camp by July 28. Nathanael Greene to the Marquis de Lafayette, July 28, 1781, *Papers of General Nathanael Greene,* 9:96; Johnson, *Sketches of the Life and Correspondence of Nathanael Greene,* 2:200–1.

4. It was of Egerton Leigh that Alexander Garden wrote that "the character of Sir E. Leigh, is so well known in Carolina, that it is sufficient to establish the infamy of a Court, to say that he presided at it." Garden, *Anecdotes,* 1:225.

5. Levett, "Loyalism in Charleston, 1761–1784," 10; Lord Moira (Francis Rawdon) to Henry Lee, June 24, 1813, in Lee, *Memoirs of the War in the Southern Department,* 617; Sabine, *Biographical Sketches of Loyalists,* 2:9 (first quote); Thompson and Lumpkin , *Journals of the House of Representatives, 1783–1784,* 35; Ramsay, *History of the Revolution of South Carolina,* 2:282; Garden, *Anecdotes,* 1:252 (second quote); Calhoon and Weir, "The Scandalous History of Sir Egerton Leigh," 49, 71.

6. Hayne, "The Execution of Colonel Isaac Hayne," 71; Lord Moira (Francis Rawdon) to Henry Lee, June 24, 1813, in Lee, *Memoirs of the War in the Southern Department,* 617 (first

quote); Harrison, *Charleston Album,* 49; Bull, *Oligarchs in Colonial and Revolutionary Charleston,* 298; Garden, *Anecdotes,* 2:187 (second quote).

7. "Ladies Petition for Colonel Hayne [n.d.]," in Gibbes, *Documentary History of the American Revolution* (1853), 112–13.

8. Ibid., 113–14 (quoted); Garden, *Anecdotes,* 1:235–37.

9. Harrison, *Charleston Album,* 49 (quoted); Nathanael Greene to Henry Lee, August 12, 1781, *Papers of General Nathanael Greene,* 9:171; Wigg, *Brief Memoir,* 15–16.

10. The North East Room was named by William Edward Hayne in an 1835 letter. A later source calls the room the Surveyor's Apartment. William Edward Hayne to Jeremiah A. Yates, December 23, 1835, William Edward Hayne Manuscript, South Caroliniana Library; South Carolina Institute, *Catalogue of Articles on Exhibition at the Second Annual Fair of the South-Carolina Institute,* 12.

11. Michael Coker to C. L. Bragg, April 21, 2014; Miller and Andrus, *Charleston's Old Exchange Building,* 34–35; Ramsay, *History of the Revolution of South Carolina,* 2:282 (quoted).

12. Hutson, "The Hutson Family of South Carolina," 127–28; Garden, *Anecdotes,* 2:55; William Edward Hayne to Jeremiah A. Yates, December 23, 1835, William Edward Hayne (1776–1843), Mss P, 2340, South Caroliniana Library; Lee, *Memoirs of the War in the Southern Department,* 455–56 (quoted); John Rutledge to John Dickinson (n.d.), Letters relating to Colonel Hayne, box 5, folder 7, John Dickinson Papers, Library Company of Philadelphia; Barnwell, "Dr. Henry Woodward," 38, 38n21.

13. Notation for August 31, 1781, at 3 o'clock A.M., "Memorandum, Friday Evening, 3d August 1781 (first quote)," and Hayne last request [August 3, 1781, after 11 o'clock P.M.] (second quote), in Colcock, "Case of Colonel Hayne, 1781," SCHS.

14. William Edward Hayne to Jeremiah A. Yates, December 23, 1835, William Edward Hayne (1776–1843), Mss P, 2340, South Caroliniana Library; Ramsay, *History of the Revolution of South Carolina,* 2:282; Miller and Andrus, *Charleston's Old Exchange Building,* 34–35; Simms, "Hayne: A Dirge," 247n*.

15. Garden, *Anecdotes,* 2:55.

16. Ramsay, *History of the Revolution of South Carolina,* 2:283; Fenhagen, "John Edwards and Some of His Descendants," 18; John Rutledge to John Dickinson (n.d.), Letters relating to Colonel Hayne, box 5, folder 7, John Dickinson Papers, Library Company of Philadelphia; Henry Laurens to George Appleby, February 15, 1774, *Papers of Henry Laurens,* 9:279, 279n3.

17. As town major Fraser likely commanded the detachment, but this is not verified.

18. Ramsay, *History of the Revolution of South Carolina,* 2:283; Simms, "Hayne: A Dirge," 247n*, 248n‡; Affidavit of Isaac Neufville, August 30, 1781, *Journals of the Continental Congress,* 21:927. The number and composition of the accompanying detachment are not substantiated.

19. "Charlestown, July 7," *Royal Georgia Gazette,* July 26, 1781; Williams, *Early Ministers at St. Michael's,* 21; Simms, *Katharine Walton,* 3, 521–22n469.20; Richard Hutson to Isaac Hayne, January 15, 1766 [typescript], Richard Hutson letter book, 1765–1777 (34/559), SCHS; Richard Hutson to the Senate committee to consider the petition of John Webb, February 4, 1783, "Transcription of three letters in support of the petition of the petition of John Webb to be removed from the amercement list," [March 6 and October 1, 1783,] South Carolina General Assembly, General Assembly and Other Miscellaneous Records, 1774–1910, Series 390008, Year: 1791, item 8, South Carolina Department of Archives and History (quoted). John Webb was among those who took protection to secure his property after the surrender of Charleston. Consequently, after the war he found himself on the amercement list. He applied for relief from amercement on the basis of his claim that he had rendered every assistance to his distressed countrymen who were

prisoners in town, a claim supported by statements from Richard Hutson, John McQueen, and Henry Pendleton. While awaiting execution, Isaac Hayne named Webb executor of his last will and testament. His real sentiments toward the British must have become known after Hayne's death, for he was expelled from Charleston in April 1762. "Persons whose Estates are Amerced in a Fine of 12 per Cent. Ad. Valorem," "Josiah Smith's Diary," 199; Thompson and Lumpkin, *Journals of the House of Representatives, 1783–1784,* 72–73; "List of persons ordered out of Charles Town April 28, 1782," in Barnwell, "Letters to General Greene and Others (Continued)," 8, 10n28.

20. Fenhagen, "John Edwards and Some of His Descendants," 22n53; South Carolina Institute, "The Martyrdom of Col. Hayne," *Catalogue of Articles on Exhibition at the Second Annual Fair of the South-Carolina Institute,* 12; Hutson, "The Hutson Family of South Carolina," 127–28; Shaffer, *To Be an American,* 60; "Rep. No. 176," *Reports of Committees of the [U.S.] House of Representatives,* 3; Wigg, *Brief Memoir,* 16–18, 37–38; Kirby, *Wigg Family,* 125 (quoted). James Fisher was subsequently banished from Charleston in December 1781. A list of expatriate Charleston families and individuals exiled to Philadelphia in 1781 may be found in "Josiah Smith's Diary," 79.

21. The route taken is subject to speculation; the procession could have easily turned on Meeting Street, but that route does not take into consideration the "town gates." According to Fraser, the "town gates" were located on King Street between George and Liberty. McCrady located the place of execution near the junction of Pitt and Vanderhorst Streets. The Charleston Orphan House was built on the block bordered by Boundary (Calhoun), King, Vanderhorst, and St. Phillip's Streets. Fraser, *Reminiscences,* 22; McCrady, *Revolution 1780,* 398; Murray, *Charleston Orphan House,* 16.

22. Ramsay, *History of the Revolution of South Carolina,* 2:283 (quoted); Simms, "Hayne: A Dirge," 248n‡; Affidavit of Isaac Neufville, August 30, 1781, *Journals of the Continental Congress,* 21:927.

23. Simms, "Hayne: A Dirge," 247n† (first quote), 248n‡; Ramsay, *History of the Revolution of South Carolina,* 2:283–84 (second and third quotes); McCrady, Revolution 1780' 398. The number and composition of the accompanying detachment are not substantiated.

24. "Col. Hayne Cruelly and Unjustly Hanged by British, Descendent [*sic*] Says," *Charleston Evening Post,* November 23, 1929.

25. Narrative thought to be in the handwriting of John Colcock, "Case of Colonel Hayne, 1781," SCHS (quoted); Salley, "Capt. John Colcock and Some of His Descendants," 220.

26. Kronenwetter, *Capital Punishment,* 115, 200.

27. South Carolina Institute, "The Martyrdom of Col. Hayne," *Catalogue of Articles on Exhibition at the Second Annual Fair of the South-Carolina Institute,* 12; South Carolina Historical Society, "Records Kept by Colonel Isaac Hayne," 15; Jarvis, "An American's Experience in the British Army," 728.

28. McCrady, *Revolution 1780,* 402 (second quote), 412 (first quote).

29. "Charlestown, August 8," *Royal Gazette* (Charleston), August 4–8, 1781 (first quote); Wells, *Two Essays,* xlii–xliv (second quote).

30. Garden, *Anecdotes,* 1:254n.

31. "Charlestown, August 18," *Royal Gazette* (Charleston, S.C.), August 15–18, 1781 (quoted); Nelson, *Francis Rawdon-Hastings,* 104; "Charlestown, August 22," *Royal Gazette* (Charleston, S.C.), August 18–22, 1781; Shea, *Operations of the French Fleet,* 64, 64n1; Entry for October 31, 1781, "Josiah Smith's Diary," 72, 77.

32. Nisbet Balfour to Henry Clinton, October 2, 1781, Nisbet Balfour to George Germain, October 12, 1781, Letter book of Lt. Col. Nisbet Balfour, MSS L2001F617, Society of the Cincinnati (quoted); Charles Cornwallis to Comte de Grasse, September 15, 1781, *Cornwallis Papers,* 6:66–68.

33. Stevens, "The Allies at Yorktown," 13–14; "New-York, September 12," *Royal Gazette* (New York), September 12, 1781 (quoted); Marquis de Lafayette to Nathanael Greene, September 2, 1781, *Papers of General Nathanael Greene,* 9:280.

34. William Washington to Nathanael Greene, September 8, 1781, Nathanael Greene to Thomas McKean, September 11, 1781, Nathanael Greene to James Mountflorence, September 17, 1781, *Papers of General Nathanael Greene,* 9:306, 306n2, 331, 365, 365n2; McCrady, *Revolution 1780,* 388, 465–66; Entry for October 16, 1781, in Baurmeister, *Revolution in America,* 468–69; Bowden, *Execution of Isaac Hayne,* 53 (the idea that Washington had placed his own life at hazard); Officers of the Southern army to Nathanael Greene, August 20, 1781, in Moultrie, *Memoirs,* 2:414–16 (quoted).

35. Nelson, *Francis Rawdon-Hastings,* 104–5; Marquis de Lafayette to Nathanael Greene, September 2, 1781, *Papers of General Nathanael Greene,* 9:280.

36. Lord Moira (Francis Rawdon) to Henry Lee, June 24, 1813, in Lee, *Memoirs of the War in the Southern Department,* 617; "Lord Huntingdon has received letters from Lord Rawdon," *Royal Gazette* (New York), March 13, 1782 (quoted). The 1782 *Parliamentary Register* (8:87–88) reported Huntingdon's claim that he had been misinformed about the papers containing an account of Hayne's execution being captured by the French. In Corbitt's 1814 *Parliamentary History* (966) Lord Huntingdon explained that the dispatches had been thrown overboard before the packet was captured.

37. Christopher Gadsden to the Delegates of the State of South Carolina, September 17, 1781, *Writings of Christopher Gadsden,* 176–77.

38. Nelson, *Francis Rawdon-Hastings,* 104–5; Bowden, *Execution of Isaac Hayne,* 53, 63n26; Jones, *History of New York During the Revolutionary War,* 2:213–16; "New-York, November 1," *Royal American Gazette,* November 1, 1781; Johnston, *Observations on Judge Jones' Loyalist History,* 84.

39. Nelson, *Francis Rawdon-Hastings,* 106; George Washington to Comte de Rochambeau, January 14 and February 9, 1782, *Writings of George Washington* (Fitzpatrick, ed.), 23:446, 494; George Washington to Comte de Rochambeau, February 21, 1782, *Writings of George Washington* (Fitzpatrick, ed.), 24:17–18; Henry Clinton to Nesbit Balfour, May 24, 1781, Comte de Rochambeau to Henry Clinton, January 23, 1782, Henry Clinton to Comte de Rochambeau, February 21, 1782, Comte de Rochambeau to Guy Carleton, June 29, 1782, in Stevens and Brown, *Report on American Manuscripts,* 2:283, 385, 402, 547.

Chapter 7: "We seriously lament the necessity of such a severe expedient"

1. Billias, *George Washington's Generals and Opponents,* 1:109–20; Gardiner, *Discovery of the Remains of Major-General Nathanael Greene,* 4–5.

2. Billias, *George Washington's Generals and Opponents,* 1:120–32.

3. Nathanael Greene to Francis Marion, August 10, 1781, *Papers of General Nathanael Greene,* 9:159; Johnson, *Sketches of the Life and Correspondence of Nathanael Greene,* 2:189.

4. Francis Marion to Nathanael Greene, September 3, 1781, *Papers of General Nathanael Greene,* 9:288–92; There are discrepancies among sources as to the actual date of the engagement at Parker's Ferry. The battle occurred on August 30 or 31, 1781. An August 13 date likely represents a transcription error.

5. Nathanael Greene to Francis Marion, August 10, 1781, *Papers of General Nathanael Greene,* 9:159 (quoted); Shaffer, *To Be an American,* 60.

6. Nathanael Greene to William Henderson, August 12, 1781, Nathanael Greene to Henry Lee, August 12, 1781, *Papers of General Nathanael Greene,* 9:169 (quoted), 171.

7. Nathanael Greene to William Henderson, August 16, 1781, Richard Campbell to Nathanael Greene, August 17, 1781, Henry Lee to Nathanael Greene, August 20, 1781, William

Washington to Nathanael Greene, August 23, 1781, *Papers of General Nathanael Greene,* 9:189, 195, 215, 226 (quoted).

8. Officers of the Southern army to Nathanael Greene, August 20, 1781, in Moultrie, *Memoirs,* 2:414–16. Older sources state that Greene's officers came together on their own and issued this memorial in response to their perception of hesitation on his part. See Nathanael Greene to William Henderson, August 16, 1781, Richard Campbell to Nathanael Greene, August 17, 1781, *Papers of General Nathanael Greene,* 9:189, 195; Johnson, *Sketches of the Life and Correspondence of Nathanael Greene,* 2:192.

9. Moultrie, *Memoirs,* 2:414–16 (first quote); Nathanael Greene to Nathan Brownson, August 28, 1781, *Papers of General Nathanael Greene,* 9:265 (second quote).

10. Nathaniel Greene to Thomas McKean, August 25, 1781, *Papers of General Nathanael Greene,* 9:242.

11. Nathanael Greene to the Marquis de Lafayette, August 26, 1781, Nathaniel Greene to Thomas McKean, October 25, 1781, *Papers of General Nathanael Greene,* 9:255 (first quote), 482 (second quote).

12. Nathanael Greene to the Marquis de Lafayette, August 26, 1781, *Papers of General Nathanael Greene,* 9:255; Nathanael Greene to George Washington, August 26, 1781, *Papers of General Nathanael Greene,* 9:257–58 (quoted).

13. Nathanael Greene to Nisbet Balfour, August 26, 1781, *Papers of General Nathanael Greene,* 9:249–51.

14. Ibid., 250–51.

15. Ibid., 251 (first quote); "A Proclamation," *Salem* (Mass.) *Gazette,* October 25, 1781 (second quote).

16. "A Proclamation," *Salem* (Mass.) *Gazette,* October 25, 1781.

17. Ibid.

18. Nathanael Greene to Charles Cornwallis, August 26, 1781, Nathanael Greene to the Marquis de Lafayette, August 26, 1781, *Papers of General Nathanael Greene,* 9:253, 255 (first quote); Nathanael Greene to Charles Cornwallis, December 17, 1780, *Papers of General Nathanael Greene,* 6:591–93 (second quote).

19. *Journals of the Continental Congress,* 21:917, 927, 941; Webber, "Moore of St. Thomas' Parish," 163; Ramsay, *History of the Revolution of South Carolina,* 2:161, 458n22; "Charlestown, 25th June, 1781," *Royal Gazette* (Charleston, S.C.), June 27–30, 1781; A list of persons embarking from St Augustine in July 1781, "Josiah Smith's Diary," 31; A list of expatriate Charleston families and individuals exiled to Philadelphia in 1781, "Josiah Smith's Diary," 78–84; McCrady, *Revolution 1780,* 375–76.

20. Affidavit of Isaac Neufville, August 30, 1781, *Journals of the Continental Congress,* 21:927.

21. Ibid.

22. Ibid., 917–18.

23. Ibid., 926–28.

24. Nisbet Balfour to Nathanael Greene, September 3, 1781, *Papers of General Nathanael Greene,* 9:284.

25. Nisbet Balfour to Henry Clinton, May 6, 1781, in Cornwallis, *An Answer,* 97–98 of appendix part 6 (first quote); Lord Moira (Francis Rawdon) to Henry Lee, June 24, 1813, in Lee, *Memoirs of the War in the Southern Department,* 617–18; Charles Cornwallis to John Harris Cruger, August 18, 1780, in Ross, *Correspondence of Charles, First Marquis Cornwallis,* 1:56–57; James, *Sketch of the Life of Brig. Gen. Francis Marion,* 130 (second quote).

26. Nisbet Balfour to Nathanael Greene, September 3, 1781, *Papers of General Nathanael*

Greene, 9:284–85(quoted), 285n5; Piecuch, *Three Peoples, One King,* 275; "Colonel Isaac Hayne," in Chesney, *Journal of Alexander Chesney,* 94–95.

27. Nathaniel Greene to Nisbet Balfour, September 19, 1781, *Papers of General Nathanael Greene,* 9:372.

28. Ibid. (first quote); Nathanael Greene to Thomas McKean, October 25, 1781, *Papers of General Nathanael Greene,* 9:482 (second quote).

29. Charles Cornwallis to Nathanael Greene, September 15, 1781, *Papers of General Nathanael Greene,* 9:348 (quoted); Nisbet Balfour to Henry Clinton, July 21, 1781, Letter book of Lt. Col. Nisbet Balfour, MSS L2001F617, Society of the Cincinnati.

30. Hayne's speech to his regiment urging them not to plunder does not seem to have been among the papers transmitted. A copy was not published in the newspapers and does not appear to be extant.

31. John Rutledge to Francis Marion, August 13, 1781, in Gibbes, *Documentary History of the American Revolution* (1853), 127; John Rutledge to John Dawson, September 18, 1781, "Letters of John Rutledge (Continued)," 155–57; John Rutledge to John Dickinson, July [n.d.], 1782, in Smith, *Letters of Delegates to Congress, 18:701;* Papers relating to Isaac Hayne forwarded to Philadelphia by Gen. Nathanael Greene, PCC, NA microfilm series M247, roll 175 (vol. 2), 349–60; "To the Printer," *Pennsylvania Packet* (Philadelphia, Pa.), September 6, 1781; "The following are authentic copies of Sundry papers . . . ," *Freeman's Journal* (Philadelphia, Pa.), September 19, 1781; Bowden, *Execution of Isaac Hayne,* 49.

32. Tench Tilghman to George Washington, October 27, 1781, in Sparks, *Correspondence of the American Revolution,* 3:434–35 (first quote); *Journals of the Continental Congress,* 21:1071, 1073–74 (second quote).

33. Boudinot, *Journal or Historical Recollections,* 59.

34. Clinton, *American Rebellion,* 354; Alexander Leslie to Henry Clinton, March 30 and March [n.d.], 1782, in Stevens and Brown, *Report on American Manuscripts,* 2:435–36 (first quote), 438 (second quote).

35. Johnson, *Sketches of the Life and Correspondence of Nathanael Greene,* 2:193–94; Lee, *Memoirs of the War in the Southern Department,* 459; Lord Moira (Francis Rawdon) to Henry Lee, June 24, 1813, in Lee, *Memoirs of the War in the Southern Department,* 619 (quoted).

36. Henry Clinton to Alexander Leslie, April 15 and May 2, 1782, Alexander Leslie to Guy Carleton, June 27, 1782, in Stevens and Brown, *Report on American Manuscripts,* 2:452, 478, 543.

37. Alexander Leslie to Guy Carleton, June 27, 1782, in Stevens and Brown, *Report on American Manuscripts,* 2:543 (quoted); Clinton, *American Rebellion,* 362; McCowen, *British Occupation of Charleston,* 144; "To Nisbet Balfour, Esq.," *Royal Gazette* (Charleston), July 20–24, 1782; Alexander Leslie to Guy Carleton, July 19, 1782, in Stevens and Brown, *Report on American Manuscripts,* 3:14–15, 29.

Chapter 8: Rawdon's Fantastic Shipboard Recollections

1. James M. Varnum to Nathanael Greene, September 17, 1781, John Mathewes to Nathanael Greene, September 29 and October 22, 1781, Nathanael Greene to George Washington, November 21, 1781, *Papers of General Nathanael Greene,* 9:366, 417, 465, 605 (quoted); *Journals of the Continental Congress,* 21:972–73; Nathanael Greene to Thomas McKean, December 9, 1781, *Papers of General Nathanael Greene,* 10:18–19.

2. George Washington to Nathanael Greene, December 15, 1781, *Papers of General Nathanael Greene,* 10:61–62 (first quote); Nathanael Greene to Alexander Leslie, February 1, 1782, *Papers of General Nathanael Greene,* 10:295 (second quote).

3. Bowden, *Execution of Isaac Hayne,* 58; Greene, *Papers of General Nathanael Greene,* 9:252n3, 252–53n2; John Rutledge to John Dawson, September 18, 1781, "Letters of John Rutledge (Continued)," 156–57 (quoted).

4. Lord Moira (Francis Rawdon) to Henry Lee, June 24, 1813, Lee, *Memoirs of the War in the Southern Department,* 619.

5. Nathanael Greene to Francis Marion, January 28, 1782, Nathanael Greene to John Laurens, February 19, 1782, *Papers of General Nathanael Greene,* 10:275, 384–85; Borick, *Relieve Us of This Burthen,* 107–12; Bull, *Oligarchs in Colonial and Revolutionary Charleston,* 298 (quoted).

6. Stephen and Lee, *Dictionary of National Biography,* 9:117; Nelson, *Francis Rawdon-Hastings,* 106–7.

7. *Parliamentary Register,* 8:81–82 (quoted); Nelson, *Francis Rawdon-Hastings,* 107; McCrady, *Revolution 1780,* 402–3, 408–9; Bowden, *Execution of Isaac Hayne,* 57, 65n40; Garden, *Anecdotes,* 1:253n*.

8. Henry Laurens to Charles Lennox, Duke of Richmond, January 31, 1782, Henry P. Kendell Collection of the Papers of Henry Laurens, South Caroliniana Library, South Caroliniana Library; Laurens, *Papers of Henry Laurens,* 398n143. Henry Laurens's daughter Martha married Isaac Hayne's close friend Dr. David Ramsay in 1787.

9. Eleven South Carolina loyalists vehemently denied Richmond's characterization of their conduct. Thomas Fletchall et al. to George III, April 19, 1782, CO5/82, folios 294–300, South Carolina Department of Archives and History, series B800124, microfilm roll RW3180.

10. *Parliamentary Register,* 8:81–82 (quoted), 89–91; Nelson, *Francis Rawdon-Hastings,* 107–8.

11. *Parliamentary Register,* 8:86 (second quote), 91–92 (first quote); Nelson, *Francis Rawdon-Hastings,* 107–8; McCrady, *Revolution 1780,* 405–6.

12. *Parliamentary Register,* 8:87–88, 99–100 (quoted); Nelson, *Francis Rawdon-Hastings,* 108; Hayne, "The Execution of Colonel Isaac Hayne," 71. The vote in the House of Lords on February 4, 1782, was twenty-five votes for the enquiry and seventy-three votes against the enquiry.

13. Nelson, *Francis Rawdon-Hastings,* 107–8; Francis Rawdon to Charles Lennox, Duke of Richmond, 12 P.M., February 21, 1782, in Dawson, "Lord Rawdon and the Duke of Richmond," 269–70 (quoted).

14. Charles Lennox, Duke of Richmond, to Francis Rawdon (via John Ligonier), 9 o'clock p.m., February 21, 1782, in Dawson, "Lord Rawdon and the Duke of Richmond," 270.

15. Francis Rawdon to Charles Lennox, Duke of Richmond, 10 o'clock P.M., February 21, 1782 (first quote), Charles Lennox, Duke of Richmond, to Francis Rawdon, 12 P.M., February 22, 1782 (second quote), in Dawson, "Lord Rawdon and the Duke of Richmond," 270–71.

16. Francis Rawdon to Charles Lenox, Duke of Richmond, 3 o'clock P.M., February 22, 1782 (quoted), "Memorandum of the Result," 2 o'clock P.M., February 23, 1782, in Dawson, "Lord Rawdon and the Duke of Richmond," 271.

17. Stephen and Lee, *Dictionary of National Biography,* 11:923–27; Dawson, "Lord Rawdon and the Duke of Richmond," 272. Interestingly, it appears that there is no mention of the Duke of Richmond submitting this "excuse" in the *Parliamentary Register* of that period or in the *London Morning Herald* on the day the letters were leaked to the press. But according to Nelson, Richmond "later made his speech in the House of Lords, with Lord Huntingdon listening. When he had finished, Huntingdon later complimented His Grace, assuring the lords that Richmond had not omitted a single word of Rawdon's required statement." Nelson, *Francis Rawdon-Hastings,* 109; "A late correspondence," *London Morning Herald,* June 6, 1782. See also William Petty, Lord Shelburne, to George III, June 12, 1782, *Correspondence of King George the Third,* 7:58.

18. Chesney, *Journal of Alexander Chesney,* 24 (quoted); Mackenzie, *Strictures on Lt. Col. Tar-leton's History of the Campaigns of 1780 and 1781,* 140n*; Lord Moira (Francis Rawdon) to Henry Lee, June 24, 1813, in Lee, *Memoirs of the War in the Southern Department,* 613; Stephen and Lee, *Dictionary of National Biography,* 9:117–22.

19. Lord Moira (Francis Rawdon) to Henry Lee, June 24, 1813, in Lee, *Memoirs of the War in the Southern Department,* 613–14, first published in Lee, *Campaign of 1781 in the Carolinas,* appendix xxxii–xliii.

20. In 1785 the opposite view would be proposed to the Royal Commission on the Losses and Services of American Loyalists by a group of South Carolina loyalists who maintained that "al-though the Subject takes an Oath of Allegiance to any foreign Power, that allegiance is only *local and temporary* . . . [and] always *pre-supposes Protection.*" Chesney, *Journal of Alexander Chesney,* 145–49.

21. Ibid., 614.

22. Ibid., 614–15.

23. Ibid., 617.

24. Ibid., 616.

25. Ibid. (quoted); Garden, *Anecdotes,* 1:23; "Ladies Petition for Colonel Hayne [n.d.]," in Gibbes, *Documentary History of the American Revolution* (1853), 112–13.

26. Lord Moira (Francis Rawdon) to Henry Lee, June 24, 1813, in Lee, *Memoirs of the War in the Southern Department,* 616–17.

27. Ibid., 617.

28. Ibid., 617–18.

29. Ibid., 615–16.

30. Ibid., 619.

31. Ibid.

32. Ibid., 616; "Tuesday, July 31— One o'clock A.M.," in Colcock, "Case of Colonel Hayne, 1781," SCHS; McCrady, *Revolution 1780,* 386, 397.

33. Jervey, "The Hayne Family," 171–73; Hayne, "The Execution of Colonel Isaac Hayne," 88 (quoted).

34. Memorandum, June 29, 1781, PCC, NA microfilm series M247, roll 175 (vol. 2), 351–52; Hayne, "The Execution of Colonel Isaac Hayne," 88, 89–90, 91–92, 95; Nisbet Balfour to Na-thanael Greene, August 18, 1781, *Papers of General Nathanael Greene,* 9:284; "Lord Rawdon's & the Commandant's Answer," July 30, 1781, in Colcock, "Case of Colonel Hayne, 1781," SCHS (quoted).

35. "Ladies Petition for Colonel Hayne [n.d.]," in Gibbes, *Documentary History of the American Revolution* (1853), 112 (first quote); "Lord Rawdon's & the Commandant's Answer," July 30, 1781, in Colcock, "Case of Colonel Hayne, 1781," SCHS (second quote); McCrady, *Revolution 1780,* 385–86; Nathanael Greene to the Marquis de Lafayette, August 26, 1781, Nathanael Greene to Thomas McKean, October 25, 1781, *Papers of General Nathanael Greene,* 9:255, 482; Hayne, "The Execution of Colonel Isaac Hayne," 101–5; Garden, *Anecdotes,* 2:187.

36. Lord Moira (Francis Rawdon) to Henry Lee, June 24, 1813, in Lee, *Campaign of 1781 in the Carolinas,* appendix xxxii–xliii; Hayne, "The Execution of Colonel Isaac Hayne," 102 (quoted).

37. Hayne, "The Execution of Colonel Isaac Hayne," 100; Lord Moira (Francis Rawdon) to Henry Lee, June 24, 1813, in Lee, *Campaign of 1781 in the Carolinas,* appendix xxxii.

Chapter 9: "In South Carolina no one even knows where he is buried"

1. McCrady, *Revolution 1780,* 402.

2. Ibid., 409 (first quote), 410–11 (second quote); Draper, *King's Mountain and Its Heroes,*

352–53; Gordon, *The History of the Rise, Progress, and Establishment of the Independence of the United States of America*, 3:466–67.

3. See ch. 8, note 20, above.

4. McCrady, *Revolution 1780*, 409.

5. Stephen and Lee, *Dictionary of National Biography*, 9:118; *A List of the Officers of the Army* [1784], 8; Entry for March 25, 1783, *Journals of the House of Lords* 36:624; Nelson, *Francis Rawdon-Hastings*, 11, 20, 109, 116, 118–22, 130–32.

6. Stephen and Lee, *Dictionary of National Biography*, 9:118–20; "Whitehall, December 6, 1816," *London Gazette*, December 7, 1816; "An interesting Letter from Earl Moira to Col. Mc-Mahon, on a Change of his Majesty's Ministries," Urban [Cave], *Gentleman's Magazine* 67, pt. 1:225–26; Nelson, *Francis Rawdon-Hastings*, 126–47.

7. Stephen and Lee, *Dictionary of National Biography*, 9:119–21; Nelson, *Francis Rawdon-Hastings*, 18–19, 147–69, 176–82, 188–89.

8. Stephen and Lee, *Dictionary of National Biography*, 9:121; Nelson, *Francis Rawdon-Hastings*, 19, 134, 145, 187, 188–93.

9. Stephen and Lee, *Dictionary of National Biography*, 1:976–77; "London, Oct. 24," *Salem* (Mass.) *Gazette*, February 20, 1783; "Foreign Intelligence," *Pennsylvania Packet, or, the General Advertiser* (Philadelphia, Pa.), April 8, 1783; *A List of the Officers of the Army* [1784], 7, 81.

10. Willcox, *Portrait of a General*, 38, 60, 69, 174, 198–99, 447–48, 451–54, 466–91. Wyatt and Willcox, "Sir Henry Clinton: A Psychological Exploration in History," 4; Stephen and Lee, *Dictionary of National Biography*, 4:550; Clinton, *Narrative of Lieutenant-General Sir Henry Clinton*, passim; Clinton, *Observations*, passim.

11. Billias, *George Washington's Generals and Opponents*, 2:215–25; Wickwire and Wickwire, *Cornwallis: The Imperial Years*, 3–6; Cornwallis, *An Answer*, passim.

12. Stephen and Lee, *Dictionary of National Biography*, 4:1161–66.

13. Billias, *George Washington's Generals and Opponents*, 1:110, 133; Gardiner, *Discovery of the Remains of Major-General Nathanael Greene*, 6–7; Gage, "Woman as Inventor," 482–83.

14. Jervey, "The Hayne Family," 180–81; Richard Hutson to Benjamin Rush, February 27 and July 8, 1782, Letters to Benjamin Rush possibly regarding politics/nation building, etc., 1753–1812. Benjamin Rush Papers [Yi2 7260], vol. 43, 7260.F p69, 71 (first quote); Gibson, "Benjamin Rush's Apprenticed Students," 129, 132; Richard Hutson to Nathanael Greene, August 19, 1783, *Papers of General Nathanael Greene*, 13:104–5 (second quote).

15. Edwards, *Journals of the Privy Council, 1783–1789*, 204–5; Legislative notice, *City Gazette*, Monday, February 15, 1790; Will of Isaac Hayne (n.d.) [typescript], Biographical and genealogical research on Isaac Hayne (30-4 Hayne), SCHS, "It is with great regret," *South-Carolina State-Gazette* (Charleston, S.C.), April 8, 1802; Farmer, "Col. Isaac Haynes [*sic*]," *Collections, Historical and Miscellaneous* 3 (May 1824): 152–53 (quoted); "An Anecdote of War," in *Supplement to the Connecticut Courant* 4, no. 32 (May 9, 1836): 255–56.

16. Jervey, "The Hayne Family," 181–84; Legislative notice, *City Gazette*, Monday, February 15, 1790; Hayne, "Colonel Isaac Hayne," 77; Stevens, *Journals of the House of Representatives, 1792–1794*, 392–93; Cowan, "William Hill and the Aera Ironworks," 15, 1824, 27n8; Lander, "The Iron Industry in Ante-Bellum South Carolina," 339, 352.

17. Jervey, "The Hayne Family," 170, 177, 181–84; Salley, *Marriage Notices*, 83.

18. Jervey, "The Hayne Family," 181; William Edward Hayne to Jeremiah A. Yates, December 23, 1835, William Edward Hayne (1776–1843), Mss P, 2340, South Caroliniana Library.

19. Jervey, "The Hayne Family," 181; William Edward Hayne to Jeremiah A. Yates, December 23, 1835, William Edward Hayne (1776–1843), Mss P, 2340, South Caroliniana Library; Hayne, "Colonel Isaac Hayne," 77.

20. Salley, "Capt. John Colcock and Some of His Descendants," 218–24.

21. "Historical Notes," *South Carolina Historical and Genealogical Magazine* 6, no. 4 (1905): 177; John Lewis Gervais to Henry Laurens, September 27, 1782, *Papers of Henry Laurens,* 16:31, 31n13; Nathanael Greene to John Mathews, December 22, 1782, *Papers of Nathanael Greene,* 12:331–32 (quoted); Thompson and Lumpkin, *Journals of the House of Representatives, 1783–1784,* 33, 42, 553, 569–70; *Columbian Herald* (Charleston, S.C.), March 23, 1786.

22. Johnson, *Traditions and Reminiscences,* 68–69, 362 (quoted).

23. Hayne, "The Execution of Colonel Isaac Hayne," 77; Bragg, *Crescent Moon over Carolina,* 281.

24. Jervey, "The Hayne Family," 168n*a;* Franklin B. Hayne to Theodore D. Jervey, June 3, 1905, Isaac Hayne (1745–1781), Mss P, 3000, South Caroliniana Library (quoted).

25. Franklin B. Hayne to Theodore D. Jervey, June 3, 1905, Isaac Hayne (1745–1781), Mss P, 3000, South Caroliniana Library (quoted); McCrady, *Revolution 1780,* 130–36, 149–50, 318–21, 330, 364, 381–412; Franklin B. Hayne to Edward Terry Hendrie Shaffer, March 12, 1926, Isaac Hayne (1745–1781), Mss P, 3000, South Caroliniana Library.

26. N. Vaman Bailey (Mrs. Joseph H. Bailey) to Franklin B. Hayne, May 12, 1926, Isaac Hayne (1745–1781), Mss P, 3000, South Caroliniana Library; Franklin B. Hayne to N. Vaman Bailey (Mrs. Joseph H. Bailey), May 22, 1926, Isaac Hayne (1745–1781), Mss P, 3000, South Caroliniana Library (quoted); Bowden, *Execution of Isaac Hayne,* 72, 76n17; Franklin B. Hayne to Edward Terry Hendrie Shaffer, March 12, 1926, Isaac Hayne (1745–1781), Mss P, 3000, South Caroliniana Library.

27. "Service in Memory of Martyred Hayne at Grave on Plantation in Colleton Led by Descendant of Hayne's Sister," *The State* (Columbia, S.C.), August 7, 1934; "Col. Isaac Hayne Cruelly and Unjustly Hanged by British, Descendent [*sic*] Says," *Charleston Evening Post,* November 23, 1929; "[. . .] Unveil Monument to Isaac Hayne," *The State* (Columbia, S.C.), [n.d.: November 19, 1929], clipping, Newspaper Article, Manuscript, and Church History Database, York County Library, Rock Hill, S.C.; "Isaac Hayne Burial Site" pamphlet [n.d], Historic Cemetery Series, South Carolina State Park Service, Columbia, S.C.

Chapter 10: A Survey of the Story of Isaac Hayne in Art and Literature

1. Cobbett, *Parliamentary History of England,* 963–84; Mackenzie, *Strictures on Lt. Col. Tarleton's History of the Campaigns of 1780 and 1781,* 140n*.

2. *Capture of Hayne and death of M'Laughlin,* woodcut illustration from Moore, *Life and Times of Gen. Francis Marion,* 141.

3. Turner, *"John Blake White,"* 1; Simms, *Letters of William Gilmore Simms,* 194n74.

4. Partridge, "John Blake White," 215–27; Kloss and Skvarla, *United States Senate Catalogue of Fine Art,* 32–33, 202–3, 268–71, 290–293; Clement and Hutton, *Artists of the Nineteenth Century and Their Works,* 347–48. The titles of White's paintings have varied slightly over time; the most modern titles are used in this work.

5. "Senate Accepts Pictures," *Charleston News and Courier,* February 24, 1899; "Paintings for the Fair," *Charleston Courier,* November 16, 1850 (quoted); Partridge, "John Blake White," 201.

6. Jack Ketch was an infamous English executioner of the 1680s.

7. South Carolina Institute, "The Martyrdom of Col. Hayne," *Catalogue of Articles on Exhibition at the Second Annual Fair of the South-Carolina Institute,* 12.

8. "The Society," *South Carolina Historical Magazine* 75, no. 1 (1974): 61; Advertisement for the sale of prints of *Colonel Isaac Hayne Being Led to His Execution, South Carolina Historical Magazine* 76, no. 4 (1975): 268; Alexander Moore, personal communication with the author. The South Carolina Historical Society also titled the painting *Colonel Isaac Hayne Being Led to His Execution* and later *The Execution of Isaac Hayne.*

9. Miller and Andrus, *Charleston's Old Exchange Building,* 35.

10. Barnard, *New, Comprehensive and Complete History of England,* 694; Pamphlet, Isaac Hayne Burial Site [2005], South Carolina Department of Parks, Recreation and Tourism; *Daniel J. Bell, historic resource coordinator* of the South Carolina State Park Service, telephone conversation with the author, December 18, 2014.

11. *The Lady's Book* (later *Godey's Lady's Book*) was the most widely circulated magazine before the Civil War.

12. Hale, *Ormond Grosvenor, a Tragedy, Lady's Book* 16: 33–40, 33n* (quoted), 49–53, 145–52; Richards and Nathans, *Oxford Handbook of American Drama,* 118; Baym, *Feminism and American Literary History,* 172–73.

13. Shook, *Dictionary of Early American Philosophers,* 1:490–93.

14. Hale, *Ormond Grosvenor, a Tragedy, Lady's Book* 16: 33–40, 49–53, 145–52.

15. Lippard, *Legends of the American Revolution,* dedication (first quote), 270–76 (second quote).

16. Poe and Butterfield. "George Lippard and His Secret Brotherhood," 285–309.

17. Lippard, "The Entranced," 13–14 .

18. Perry and Weaks-Baxter, *History of Southern Women's Literature,* 64–69; Gilman, "Isaac Hayne, or, The Patriot Martyr of South Carolina," 107–23.

19. Shook, *Dictionary of Early American Philosophers,* 2:1061–66; Upham, *American Cottage Life,* title page (first quote); Upham, "Death of Colonel Hayne," 51–58 (second quote); Hale, *Ormond Grosvenor, a Tragedy, Lady's Book* 16:53, 152; Upham, "Influence of War on Domestic Life," 57 (third quote).

20. Simms, "Hayne—Let the Death-Bell Toll," 26–28 (quoted); Simms, "Hayne: A Dirge," 247–48; Guilds, *Simms: A Literary Life,* 185–86.

21. Simms, *The Partisan,* 120, passim; Hopkins, "Carolina Epic," 1.

22. Simms, *The Partisan,* vi (second quote), 152 (first quote), 529–31; Guilds, *Simms,* 64–67.

23. "Mr. Simms's Katherine Walton," *Literary World* 9, no. 243 (1851): 244–45; William Gilmore Simms to Marcus Claudius Marcellus Hammond, October 11, 1851, *Letters of William Gilmore Simms,* 3:145n201; "New Publications," *Charleston Courier,* September 11, 1851; Okker, "Gender and Secession," 17–31; Trent, *Simms,* 192–93; Guilds, *Simms: A Literary Life,* 198; Watson, *From Nationalism to Secessionism,* 88–93.

24. Hale, *Ormond Grosvenor, a Tragedy, Lady's Book* 16: 33–40, 49–53, 145–52; Simms, *Katharine Walton,* 339–40, 412–14, 419–25, 468–74 (quoted); Guilds, *Simms: A Literary Life,* 57.

25. Simms, *History of South Carolina,* 246–53; Simms, *Katharine Walton,* 3, 521–22n469.20; Simms, "Hayne—Let the Death-Bell Toll," 26–28; Simms, "Hayne: A Dirge," 247–48.

26. Trent, *Simms,* 135; Simms, *Katharine Walton,* title page, 33, 190, 234, 238, 308, 313, 315, 317, 324, 335, 350, 486n33.4, 501n190.24, 506n234.28, 506n238.38, 512n308.22, 512n313.7, 513n315.15, 513n317.11, 513n317.12, 514n324.11, 515n335.1, 515n350.25.

27. Shakespeare, *Measure for Measure,* 165, 176, and passim; Gillespie, *Shakespeare's Books,* 115–18. The concept of Simms's use of Shakespeare's play as a model for a subplot in *Katharine Walton* originated with my editor, Alexander Moore, and formed the basis for this chapter.

28. Faulkner, *Faulkner's History of the Revolution in the Southern States,* 49–51.

29. Ibid.

30. Bowden, *Execution of Isaac Hayne,* 83–85; Allstorm, "Death of Isaac Hayne," Isaac Hayne Manuscripts, South Caroliniana Library (clipping; n.p., n.d.).

31. Elson, "'Liberty Tree' Offers Drama and History," *News and Courier* (Charleston, S.C.), August 11, 1969; "Hanging of Isaac Hayne," *News and Courier,* August 7, 1970.

32. Stokes, *Letters for Catherine,* 129–35; Wigg, *Brief Memoir of the Life,* 15–18.

33. Ravenel, *Charleston,* 319.

34. Harrison, *Charleston Album,* 50–51; Martin, *Charleston Ghosts,* 33–34; Zepke, *Ghosts and Legends*

of the Carolina Coasts, 142–43; Pickens, *Charleston Mysteries,* 54–55; Barefoot, *Spirits of '76,* 295–96.

Appendix B: The Correspondence between Col. Isaac Hayne and His British Captors

1. To the author's best knowledge, the wording of the presented correspondence is rendered more accurately than in any other published source. Original spellings and capitalizations have been retained; punctuation has been lightly edited for clarity. Nos. 1–4 are transcribed from the copy of the narrative that originated with Hayne and was transmitted to the Continental Congress via Maj. Gen. Nathanael Greene. Nos. 5–9 seem to have been written by Hayne's own hand and are included with John Colcock's legal brief in the collections of the South Carolina Historical Society.

2. Copy of Charles Fraser to Isaac Hayne (A.M.), July 26, 1781, PCC, NA microfilm series M247, roll 175 (vol. 2), 351.

3. Copy of Charles Fraser to Isaac Hayne (P.M.), July 26, 1781, PCC, NA microfilm series M247, roll 175 (vol. 2), 351.

4. Memorandum, June 29, 1781, PCC, NA microfilm series M247, roll 175 (vol. 2), 351–52.

5. The exact identity of Mr. Jarvis has not been established.

6. Copy of Isaac Hayne to Nesbit Balfour and Francis Rawdon, July 29, 1781, PCC, NA microfilm series M247, roll 175 (vol. 2), 351–53.

7. "Lord Rawdon's & the Commandant's Answer," July 30, 1781, in Colcock, "Case of Colonel Hayne, 1781," SCHS; Clark, *Loyalists in the Southern Campaign of the Revolutionary War,* 1:179.

8. "Tuesday, July 31— One o'clock A.M.," in Colcock, "Case of Colonel Hayne, 1781," SCHS.

9. Notation for August 31, 1781, at 3 o'clock A.M., in Colcock, "Case of Colonel Hayne, 1781," SCHS.

10. "Memorandum, Friday Evening, 3d August 1781," in Colcock, "Case of Colonel Hayne, 1781," SCHS.

11. Hayne last request [August 3, 1781, after 11 o'clock P.M.], in Colcock, "Case of Colonel Hayne, 1781," SCHS.

Bibliography

Primary Sources

Manuscripts and Original Documents

Allstorm, Oliver. "Death of Isaac Hayne." Isaac Hayne Manuscripts. South Caroliniana Library, University of South Carolina, Columbia, S.C.

Balfour, Nisbet (1743–1823). Correspondence, 1780–1781. Library of Congress, Washington, D.C.

Balfour, Nisbet (1743–1823). Will, proved December 3, 1823. PROB 11/1678/109. National Archives [United Kingdom], Richmond, Surrey, UK.

Brown, Anne S. K. Military Collection. John Hay Library, Brown University, Providence, R.I.

Bush, Joshua Danforth, Jr. Collection. Society of the Cincinnati, Washington, D.C.

Colcock, John (1744–1782). "Case of Colonel Hayne, 1781." Call no. 43/0083. South Carolina Historical Society, Charleston, S.C.

Continental Congress. Papers of the Continental Congress, 1774–1789. Record Group 360: Records of the Continental and Confederation Congresses and the Constitutional Convention, 1765–1821. Microfilm series M247, roll 175. National Archives and Records Administration, Washington, D.C.

Dickinson, John (1732–1808). John Dickinson Papers, 1676–1885. Library Company of Philadelphia, Philadelphia, Pa.

Emmet, Thomas Addis. Collection of Illustrations Relating to the American Revolution and Early United States History. Miriam and Ira D. Wallach Division of Art, Prints, and Photographs, New York Public Library, New York, N.Y.

Hayne, Isaac (1745–1781). Biographical and genealogical research on Isaac Hayne. Letters (30-4 Hayne). South Carolina Historical Society, Charleston, S.C.

Hayne, Isaac (1745–1781). Isaac Hayne ledger, 1765-1781 (34/561). South Carolina Historical Society, Charleston, S.C.

Hayne, Isaac (1745–1781). Manuscripts P, accession no. 3000. South Caroliniana Library, University of South Carolina, Columbia, S.C.

Hayne, William Edward (1776–1843). Manuscripts P, accession no. 2340. South Caroliniana Library, University of South Carolina, Columbia, S.C.

Hutson, Richard (1747–1795). Richard Hutson letter book, 1765–1777 (34/559). South Carolina Historical Society, Charleston, S.C.

Kendall, Henry P. Collection of the Papers of Henry Laurens. South Caroliniana Library, University of South Carolina, Columbia, S.C.

Letter book of Lt. Col. Nisbet Balfour (1743–1823), British Commandant of Charleston, S.C.: Charleston, S.C., 1 Jan.–1 Dec. 1781. MSS L2001F617. Robert Charles Lawrence Fergusson Collection. Archives and Library Collections of the Society of the Cincinnati at Anderson House, Washington, D.C.

Newspaper Article, Manuscript, and Church History Database. York County Library, Rock Hill, S.C.

Photographs Depicting "Life in the United States," compiled 1942–1946, documenting the period 1881–1946. Record Group 208. Records of the Office of War Information, 1926–1951. National Archives and Records Administration, Washington, D.C.

Public Records of Great Britain: Indian Affairs, 1760–1784 (CO5/82). Series B800124, reel RW3180. South Carolina Department of Archives and History, Columbia, S.C.

Rush, Benjamin (1746–1813). Rush Family Papers, 1748–1876. Series I, Benjamin Rush Papers. Library Company of Philadelphia, Philadelphia, Pa.

South Carolina General Assembly. General Assembly and Other Miscellaneous Records, 1774–1910. Series 390008. South Carolina Department of Archives and History, Columbia, S.C.

Published Sources and Personal Accounts

Advertisement for the sale of prints of *Colonel Isaac Hayne Being Led to His Execution*. *South Carolina Historical Magazine* 76, no. 4 (1975): 268.

The Annual Register or a View of the History, Politics, and Literature, for the Year 1780. London: J. Dodsley, 1782.

Barnwell, Joseph W., ed. "Letters to General Greene and Others (Continued)." *South Carolina Historical and Genealogical Magazine* 17, no. 1 (1916): 3–13.

Baurmeister, Carl Leopold. *Revolution in America: Confidential Letters and Journals 1776–1784 of Adjutant General Major Baurmeister of the Hessian Forces*. Edited and annotated by Hernhard A. Uhlendorf. New Brunswick, N.J.: Rutgers University Press, 1957.

Boswell, James, ed. *Scots Magazine*. Vol. 43. Edinburgh: A. Murray and J. Cochran, 1781.

Boudinot, Elias. *Journal or Historical Recollections of American Events during the Revolutionary War*. Philadelphia: Frederick Bourquin, 1894.

Bowden, David K. *The Execution of Isaac Hayne*. Lexington, S.C.: The Sandlapper Store, 1977.

Chesney, Alexander. *The Journal of Alexander Chesney, a South Carolina Loyalist in the Revolution and After*. Edited by E. Alfred Jones, with an introduction by Wilbur Henry Siebert. *Ohio State University Bulletin* 26, no. 4 (1921).

Clark, Murtie June. *Loyalists in the Southern Campaign of the Revolutionary War*. Vol. 1. Baltimore: Genealogical Publishing Company, 1981.

Clinton, Henry. *The American Rebellion: Sir Henry Clinton's Narrative of His Campaigns, 1775–1782, with an Appendix of Original Documents*. Edited by William B. Willcox. New Haven: Yale University Press, 1954.

Clinton, Henry. *The Narrative of Lieutenant-General Sir Henry Clinton, K.B. Relative to His Conduct during Part of His Command of the King's Troops in North America; Particularly to That Which Respects the Unfortunate Issue of the Campaign in 1781. With an Appendix, Containing Copies an Extracts of Those Parts of His Correspondence with Lord George Germain, Earl Cornwallis, Rear Admiral Graves, &C. Which Are Referred to Therein*. London: J. Debrett, 1783.

Clinton, Henry. *Observations on Some Parts of the Answer of Earl Cornwallis to Sir Henry Clinton's Narrative Containing Extracts of Letters and Other Papers, to Which Reference Is Necessary*. London: J. Debrett, 1783.

Clinton, Henry. "Sir Henry Clinton's 'Journal of the Siege of Charleston, 1780.'" Edited by William T. Bulger. *South Carolina Historical Magazine* 66, no. 3 (1965): 147–174.

Coleman, Charles Washington, Jr., comp. "Southern Campaign of General Greene 1781–2, Letters of Major William Pierce to St. George Tucker." *Magazine of American History* 7, no. 6 (1881): 431–45.

Cooper, Thomas, ed. *The Statutes at Large of South Carolina*. Vol. 4. Columbia, S.C.: A. S. Johnson, 1838.

Cornwallis, Charles Earl. *An Answer to That Part of the Narrative of Lieutenant-General Sir Henry Clinton, K.B.: Which Relates to the Conduct of Lieutenant-General Earl Cornwallis during the Campaign in North-America in in the Year 1781.* London: J. Debrett, 1783.

Cornwallis, Charles Earl. *The Cornwallis Papers: The Campaigns of 1780 and 1781 in the Southern Theatre of the American Revolutionary War.* 6 vols. Edited by Ian Saberton. East Sussex: Naval & Military Press, 2010.

Davies, K. G. *Documents of the American Revolution, 1770–1783.* 21 vols. Shannon, Ireland: Irish University Press, 1972–81.

Edwards, Adele Stanton, ed. *Journals of the Privy Council, 1783–1789.* Columbia: University of South Carolina Press, 1971.

Faden, William. *A Map of South Carolina and a Part of Georgia.* London: 1780. Geography and Map Division, Library of Congress, Washington, D.C.

Gadsden, Christopher. *The Writings of Christopher Gadsden, 1746–1805.* Edited by Richard Walsh. Columbia: University of South Carolina Press, 1966.

George III. *The Correspondence of King George the Third from 1760 to December 1783.* Vol. 7. Edited by John W. Fortescue. London: Macmillan, 1928.

George IV. *The Correspondence of George, Prince of Wales, 1770–1812.* Vol. 4. Edited by A. Aspinall. New York: Oxford University Press, 1967.

Gibbes, Robert Wilson, ed. *Documentary History of the American Revolution, Consisting of Letters and Papers Relating to the Contest for Liberty, Chiefly in South Carolina, in 1781 and 1782.* Columbia, S.C.: Banner Steam-Power Press, 1853.

Force, Peter, ed. and comp. *American Archives.* Series 4, vol. 2. Washington: M. St. Clair Clark and Peter Force, 1839.

Gilman, Caroline Howard. "Isaac Hayne, or, The Patriot Martyr of South Carolina." In *Verses of a Life Time.* Boston and Cambridge, Mass.: James Munroe and Company, 1849.

Greene, Nathanael. *The Papers of General Nathanael Greene.* 13 vols. Edited by Richard K. Showman et. al. Chapel Hill: University of North Carolina Press, 1976–2005.

Hale, Sarah Josepha Buell. *Ormond Grosvenor, a Tragedy. The Lady's Book* 16 (January 1838): 33–40; 16 (February 1838): 49–53; and 16 (April 1838): 145–52.

Hemphill, William Edwin, and Wylma Anne Wates, eds. *Extracts from the Journals of the Provincial Congresses of South Carolina, 1775–1776.* Columbia: South Carolina Archives Department, 1960.

Hill, William. *Col. William Hill's Memoirs of the Revolution.* Edited by A. S. Salley. Columbia, S.C.: The State Company, 1921.

Howe, William. *General Sir William Howe's Orderly Book at Charlestown, Boston and Halifax, June 17, 1775 to 1776, 26 May.* Edited by Benjamin Franklin Stevens. London: Benjamin Franklin Stevens, 1890.

Jarvis, Stephen. "An American's Experience in the British Army." *Journal of American History* 1, no. 4 (1907): 727–40.

Journals of the Continental Congress, 1774–1789. Vol. 21. Edited by Galliard Hunt. Washington, D.C.: Government Printing Office, 1912.

Journals of the House of Lords. Vol. 36: 1779–1783. London: H.M.S.O., [1783].

Kemble, Stephen. *Journals of Lieut. Col. Stephen Kemble, 1773–1789; And British Army Orders: Gen. Sir William Howe, 1775–1778; Gen. Sir Henry Clinton, 1778; and Gen. Daniel Jones, 1778.* 1884. Reprint, Boston: Gregg Press, 1972.

Kolb, Wade S., III, and Robert M. Weir, eds. *Captured at Kings Mountain: The Journal of Uzal Johnson, a Loyalist Surgeon.* Columbia: University of South Carolina Press, 2011.

Lamb, Roger. *Memoir of His Own Life*. Dublin: J. Jones, 1811.

Laurens, Henry. *The Papers of Henry Laurens*. 16 vols. Edited by David R. Chestnut et al. Columbia: University of South Carolina Press, 1968–2002.

Lee, Henry, III. *Memoirs of the War in the Southern Department of the United States*. 3rd ed. Edited, with a biography of the author by Robert E. Lee. Vol. 2. New York: University Publishing Company, 1869.

Lippard, George. "The Entranced; or the Wanderer of Eighteen Centuries (continued)," *Univercœlum and Spiritual Philosopher* 4, no. 1 (1849): 13–14.

A List of All the Officers of the Army: Viz. the General and Field Officers; The Officers of the Several Troops, Regiments, Independent Companies, and Garrisons: with an Alphabetical Index to the Whole. London: War-Office, 1781.

A List of the Officers of the Army: (with an Alphabetical Index) of the Officers of the Royal Artillery, the Engineers, the Marine Forces: and of the Officers on Half-Pay: and a Succession of Colonels. London: War-Office, 1784.

A List of the General and Field Officers, As They Rank in the Army: Of the Officers in the Several Regiments of Horse, Dragoons, and Foot, on the British and Irish Establishments. London: J. Millan, 1778.

Mackenzie, Roderick. *Strictures on Lt. Col. Tarleton's History of the Campaigns of 1780 and 1781, in the Southern Provinces of North America*. London: R. Jameson, R. Faulder, T. and J. Egerton, and T. Sewell, 1787.

Mills, Robert. *Atlas of the State of South Carolina, Prefaced with a Geographical, Statistical and Historical Map of the State*. Baltimore: F. Lucas Jr.,1825.

Morton, Robert. "The Diary of Robert Morton." *Pennsylvania Magazine of History and Biography* 1, no. 1 (1877): 1–39.

Moultrie, William. *Memoirs of the American Revolution so far as it Related to the States of North and South-Carolina, and Georgia*. 2 vols. 1802. Reprint, North Stratford, N.H.: Ayer Company, 2004.

The Parliamentary Register; or, History of the Proceedings and Debates of the House of Lords. Fifteenth Parliament, Second Session, vol. 8. London: J. Debrett, 1782.

Piecuch, Jim. *The Battle of Camden: A Documentary History*. Charleston: History Press, 2006.

Reports of Committees of the [U.S.]House of Representatives, Made during the First Session of the Thirty-Second Congress. Washington, D.C.: A. Boyd Hamilton, 1852.

Ross, Charles, ed. *Correspondence of Charles, First Marquis Cornwallis*. Vol. 1. London: John Murray, 1859.

Rutledge, John. "Letters of John Rutledge (Continued)." Edited by Joseph W. Barnwell. *South Carolina Historical and Genealogical Magazine* 18, no. 4 (1917): 155–67.

Salley, Alexander S., Jr., ed. *Journal of the House of Representatives of South Carolina. January 8, 1782–February 26, 1782*. Columbia, S.C.: The State Company, 1916.

Salley, Alexander S., Jr., ed. *Marriage Notices in the South-Carolina Gazette Its Successors (1732–1801)*. Albany, N.Y.: Joel Munsell's Sons, 1902.

Salley, Alexander S., Jr., ed. "Papers of the First Council of Safety of the Revolutionary Party in South Carolina, June–November, 1775 (Continued)." *South Carolina Historical and Genealogical Magazine* 2, no. 1 (1901): 3–26.

Shakespeare, William. *Measure for Measure*. Evans Shakespeare Edition. Edited by John Klause. Boston: Wadsworth Cengage Learning, 2011.

Shea, John Gilmary, ed. *The Operations of the French Fleet under the Count De Grasse in 1781–1782, as Described in Two Contemporaneous Journals*. 1864. Reprint, New York: Da Capo Press, 1971.

Simcoe, John Graves. *Simcoe's Military Journal: A History of the Operations of a Partisan Corps, Called the Queen's Rangers, Commanded by Lieut. Col. J. G. Simcoe, during the War of the American Revolution.* New York: Bartlett & Welford, 1844.

Simms, William Gilmore. "Hayne: A Dirge." *Russell's Magazine* 4, no. 3 (1858): 247–48.

Simms, William Gilmore. "Hayne—Let the Death-Bell Toll." In *Areytos, or, Songs and Ballads of the South: With Other Poems.* Charleston, S.C.: Russell & Jones, 1860.

Simms, William Gilmore. *Letters of William Gilmore Simms.* Vols. 1 and 3. Edited by Mary C. Simms Oliphant, Alfred Taylor Odell, and T. C. Duncan Eaves. Columbia: University of South Carolina Press, 1951–52.

Simms, William Gilmore. *Katharine Walton by William Gilmore Simms; with Introduction and Explanatory Notes.* Edited by James B. Meriwether and Stephen Meats. *Revolutionary War Novels 4.* Published for the Southern Studies Program, University of South Carolina. 1854. Reprint, Spartanburg, S.C.: The Reprint Company, 1976.

Simms, William Gilmore. *The Partisan by William Gilmore Simms; With Introduction and Explanatory Notes.* Edited by James B. Meriwether and Stephen Meats. *Revolutionary War Novels 2.* Published for the Southern Studies Program, University of South Carolina. 1854. Reprint, Spartanburg, S.C.: The Reprint Company, 1976.

Smith, Josiah. "Josiah Smith's Diary, 1780–1781 (Continued)." Annotated by Mabel L. Webber. *South Carolina Historical and Genealogical Magazine* 34, nos. 1, 2, and 4 (1933): 31–39, 67–84, 194–210.

Smith, Paul H., et al., eds. *Letters of Delegates to Congress, 1774–1789.* Vol. 18. Washington, D.C.: Library of Congress, 1991).

South Carolina Historical Society. "Journal of the Second Council of Safety, Appointed by the Provisional Congress, November, 1775." *Collections of the South-Carolina Historical Society* 3 (1859): 35–271.

South Carolina Historical Society. "Records Kept by Colonel Isaac Hayne (Continued)." *South Carolina Historical and Genealogical Magazine* 12, no. 1 (1911): 14–23.

Sparks, Jared. *Correspondence of the American Revolution: Being Letters of Eminent Men to George Washington, from the Time of His Taking Command of the Army to the End of His Presidency.* Vol. 3. Boston: Little, Brown, 1853.

Stevens, Benjamin Franklin, ed. *The Campaign in Virginia, 1781: An Exact Reprint of Six Rare Pamphlets on the Clinton-Cornwallis Controversy.* Vol. 1. London: [s.n.], 1888.

Stevens, Benjamin Franklin, and Henry J. Brown, eds. *Report on American Manuscripts in the Royal Institution of Great Britain.* Vols. 2 and 3. Dublin: John Falconer, 1906, 1907.

Stevens, Michael E., and Christine M. Allen, eds. *Journals of the House of Representatives, 1791.* Columbia, S.C.: University of South Carolina Press, 1985.

Stevens, Michael E., ed. *Journals of the House of Representatives, 1792-1794.* Columbia, S.C.: University of South Carolina Press, 1988.

Tarleton, Banastre. *A History of the Campaigns of 1780 and 1781, in the Southern Provinces of North America.* Dublin, Ireland: Colles, Exshaw, White, H. Whitestone, Burton, Byrne, Moore, Jones, and Dornin, 1787.

Thompson, Theodora J., and Rosa S. Lumpkin, eds. *Journals of the House of Representatives, 1783-1784.* Columbia, S.C.: University of South Carolina Press, 1977.

Upham, Thomas C. "Death of Colonel Hayne." In *American Cottage Life.* 2nd ed. Brunswick, Me.: Joseph Griffin, 1850–51.

Urban, Sylvanus [Edward Cave, pseud.], ed. *Gentleman's Magazine: and Historical Chronicle. For the Year 1798.* Vol. 67, pt. 1. London: John Nichols, 1798.

Washington, George. *The Writings of George Washington: Being His Correspondence, Addresses, Messages, and Other Papers, Official and Private*. Vol. 7. Edited by Jared Sparks. Boston: Ferdinand Andrews, 1838.

Washington, George. *The Writings of George Washington from the Original Manuscript Sources, 1745–1799*. Edited by John Clement Fitzpatrick. 39 vols. Washington, D.C.: Government Printing Office, 1931.

Newspapers

Charleston Courier, 1850–51.

Charleston Evening Gazette, 1785.

Charleston Evening Post, 1929.

City Gazette, or Daily Advertiser (Charleston, S.C.), 1790.

Columbian Herald, or the Independent Courier of North-America (Charleston, S.C.), 1786.

Freeman's Journal (Philadelphia, Pa.), 1781.

Gazette of the State of South Carolina (Charleston, S.C.), 1779.

London Gazette, 1816.

London Morning Herald, and Daily Advertiser, 1782.

News and Courier (Charleston, S.C.), 1899, 1969–70.

Pennsylvania Packet, or, the General Advertiser (Philadelphia, Pa.), 1781–83.

Royal American Gazette (New York), 1781.

Royal Gazette (Charleston, S.C.), 1780–82.

Royal Gazette (New York), April 3, 1779–81.

Royal Georgia Gazette (Savannah, Ga.), 1781.

Salem (Mass.) *Gazette*, October 25, 1781–83.

South-Carolina Gazette and Country Journal (Charleston, S.C.), 1770.

South-Carolina State-Gazette, and Timothy's Daily Advertiser (Charleston, SC), 1802.

The State (Columbia, S.C.), 1929–34.

Secondary Sources

Books and Pamphlets

Adams, W. H. Davenport. *Famous Regiments of the British Army: Their Origin and Service*. London: Cassell, Petter, and Galpin, 1868.

Barefoot, Daniel W. *Spirits of '76: Ghost Stories of the American Revolution*. Winston-Salem, N.C.: John F. Blair, 2009.

Barnard, Edward. *The New, Comprehensive and Complete History of England*. London: Alexander Hoag, 1783.

Barnwell, Stephen B. *The Story of an American Family*. Marquette, Mich.: Privately printed, 1969.

Baym, Nina. *Feminism and American Literary History: Essays*. New Brunswick, N.J.: Rutgers University Press, 1992.

Billias, George Athan, ed. *George Washington's Generals and Opponents: Their Exploits and Leadership*. 2 vols. New York: Da Capo Press, 1994.

Borick, Carl P. *Relieve Us of This Burthen: American Prisoners of War in the Revolutionary South, 1780–1782*. Charleston: University of South Carolina Press, 2012.

Bowden, David K. *The Execution of Isaac Hayne*. Lexington, S.C.: The Sandlapper Store, 1977.

Bragg, C. L. *Crescent Moon over Carolina: William Moultrie and American Liberty*. Columbia: University of South Carolina Press, 2013.

Buchanan, John. *The Road to Guilford Courthouse: The American Revolution in the Carolinas.* New York: John Wiley and Sons, 1997.

Bull, Kinloch. *The Oligarchs in Colonial and Revolutionary Charleston: Lieutenant Governor William Bull II and His Family.* Columbia: University of South Carolina Press, 1991.

Busick, Sean R. *A Sober Desire for History: William Gilmore Simms as Historian.* Columbia: University of South Carolina Press, 2005.

Cannon. Richard, comp. *Historical Record of the Fifth Regiment of Foot, or Northumberland Fusiliers Containing an Account of the Formation of the Regiment in the Year 1674, and of Its Subsequent Services to 1837.* London: W. Clowes and Sons, 1838.

Cary, Arthur Deering Lucius, and Stouppe McCance. *Regimental Records of the Royal Welch Fusiliers (Late the 23rd Foot).* Vol. 1: 1689–1815. London: Forster Groom, 1921.

Clement, Clara Erskine, and Laurence Hutton. *Artists of the Nineteenth Century and Their Works.* Boston: Houghton, Osgood, 1879.

Cobbett, William, ed. *The Parliamentary History of England, from the Earliest Period to the Year 1803.* London: Thomas C. Hasnard, 1814.

Commager, Henry Steele, and Richard B. Morris, eds. *The Spirit of Seventy-Six: The Story of the American Revolution as Told by the Participants.* 1975. Reprint, New York: Da Capo Press, 1995.

Cowper, L. I. *The King's Own: The Story of a Royal Regiment.* Vol. 1: 1680–1814. Oxford: University Press, 1939.

Draper, Lyman C. *King's Mountain and Its Heroes: History of the Battle of King's Mountain, October 7th, 1780, and the Events Which Led to It.* Cincinnati: Peter G. Thomson, 1881.

Drayton, John. *A View of South-Carolina as Respects Her Natural and Civil Concerns.* Charleston: W. P. Young, 1802.

Dull, Jonathan R. *A Diplomatic History of the American Revolution.* New Haven, Conn: Yale University Press, 1987.

Edgar, Walter B. *Partisans and Redcoats: The Southern Conflict That Turned the Tide of the American Revolution.* New York: Morrow, 2001.

Edgar, Walter B., and N. Louise Bailey. *Biographical Directory of the South Carolina House of Representatives, Vol. II: The Commons House of Assembly, 1692–1775.* Columbia: University of South Carolina Press, 1977.

Faulkner, Thomas C. *Faulkner's History of the Revolution in the Southern States Including the Special Messages of President Buchanan: The Ordinance of Secession of the Six Withdrawing States and Etc.* New York: John F. Trow, 1861.

Fraser, Charles. *Reminiscences of Charleston.* Charleston: John Russell, 1854.

Frothingham, Richard. *The Centennial: Battle of Bunker Hill.* Boston: Little, Brown, 1875.

Garden, Alexander. *Anecdotes of the Revolutionary War in America: With Sketches of Character of Persons the Most Distinguished, in the Southern States, for Civil and Military Services.* First Series. Charleston: A. E. Miller, 1822.

Garden, Alexander. *Anecdotes of the American Revolution Illustrative of the Talents and Virtues of the Heroes and Patriots, Who Acted the Most Conspicuous Parts Therein.* Second Series. Charleston: A. E. Miller, 1828.

Gardiner, Asa Bird. *The Discovery of the Remains of Major-General Nathanael Greene, First President of the Rhode Island Cincinnati.* New York: Blumenberg Press, 1901.

Gillespie, Stuart. *Shakespeare's Books: A Dictionary of Shakespeare Sources.* London: Athlone Press, 2001.

Glover, Beulah. *Narratives of Colleton County, South Carolina.* 1984. Reprint, Spartanburg: Reprint Company, 2009.

Glover, James Bolan V. *Colonel Joseph Glover (1719–1783) and His Descendants: Thirteen Generations of the Glover Family.* Marietta, Ga.: Glover Family Association, 1996.

Glover, Lorri. *All Our Relations: Blood Ties and Emotional Bonds among the Early South Carolina Gentry.* Baltimore: Johns Hopkins University Press, 2000.

Gordon, John W. *South Carolina and the American Revolution: A Battlefield History.* Columbia: University of South Carolina Press, 2003.

Gordon, William. *The History of the Rise, Progress, and Establishment of the Independence of the United States of America.* Vol. 3. London: Printed for the author, 1788.

Gottschalk, Louis Reichenthal. *Lafayette Comes to America.* Chicago: University of Chicago Press, 1935.

Guilds, John Caldwell. *Simms: A Literary Life.* Fayetteville: University of Arkansas Press, 1992.

Harrison, Margaret Hayne. *A Charleston Album.* Rindge, N.H.: Richard R. Smith, 1953.

Hopkins, Konrad H. V. "Carolina Epic: A Critical Study of William Gilmore Simms's Romances of the Revolution." M.A. thesis, Florida State University, Tallahassee, 1955.

Howe, George. *History of the Presbyterian Church in South Carolina.* Vol. 1. Columbia, S.C.: Duffie and Chapman, 1870.

"Isaac Hayne Burial Site." Pamphlet. Historic Cemetery Series. South Carolina State Park Service, Columbia, 2005.

James, William Dobein. *A Sketch of the Life of Brig. Gen. Francis Marion and a History of His Brigade from Its Rise in June 1780 until Disbanded in December, 1782.* Marietta, Ga.: Continental Book Company, 1948.

Johnson, Joseph. *Traditions and Reminiscences, Chiefly of the American Revolution in the South: Including Biographical Sketches, Incidents, and Anecdotes, Few of Which Have Been Published, Particularly of Residents in the Upper Country.* Charleston: Walker and James, 1851.

Johnson, William. *Sketches of the Life and Correspondence of Nathanael Greene, Major General of the Armies of the United States, in the War of the Revolution.* Vol. 2. Charleston: A. E. Miller, 1822.

Johnston, Henry Phelps. *Observations on Judge Jones' Loyalist History of the American Revolution: How Far Is It an Authority.* New York: D. Appleton, 1880.

Jones, Thomas. *History of New York during the Revolutionary War.* Vol. 2. Edited by Edward F. De Lancey. New York: New York Historical Society, 1879.

Kirby, Lewis. *The Wigg Family.* Chichester, Sussex, England: Phillimore, 1989.

Kloss, William, and Diane K. Skvarla. *United States Senate Catalogue of Fine Art* [Senate Document 107–11]. Edited by Jane R. McGoldrick. Washington, D.C.: Senate Commission on Art, 2002.

Kronenwetter, Michael. *Capital Punishment: A Reference Handbook.* Santa Barbara, Calif.: ABC-CLIO, 1993.

Lambert, Robert Stansbury. *South Carolina Loyalists in the American Revolution.* Columbia: University of South Carolina Press, 1987.

Lee, Henry, IV. *The Campaign of 1781 in the Carolinas; With Remarks, Historical and Critical, on Johnson's Life of Greene. To Which Is Added an Appendix of Original Documents, Relating to the History of the Revolution.* Philadelphia: E. Littell, 1824.

Lippard, George. *Legends of the American Revolution: Or, Washington and His Generals.* Philadelphia: T. B. Peterson, 1847.

Martin, Margaret Rhett. *Charleston Ghosts.* Columbia: University of South Carolina Press, 1963.

McCowen, George Smith. *The British Occupation of Charleston, 1780–82.* Columbia: University of South Carolina Press, 1972.

McCrady, Edward. *The History of South Carolina in the Revolution, 1775–1780.* New York: Macmillan, 1901.

McCrady, Edward. *The History of South Carolina in the Revolution, 1780–1783.* New York: Macmillan, 1902.

Miller, Ruth M., and Ann Taylor Andrus. *Charleston's Old Exchange Building: A Witness to American History.* Charleston: History Press, 2005.

Moore, Horatio Newton. *The Life and Times of Gen. Francis Marion.* Philadelphia: Leary, Getz, 1845.

Moss, Bobby Gilmer. *Roster of South Carolina Patriots in the American Revolution.* Baltimore: Genealogical Publishing Company, 1983.

Murray, John. *The English Review; or, an Abstract of English and Foreign Literature.* Vol. 10. London: J. Murray, 1787.

Murray, John E. *The Charleston Orphan House: Children's Lives in the First Public Orphanage in America.* Chicago: University of Chicago Press, 2013.

Nadelhaft, Jerome J. *The Disorders of War: The Revolution in South Carolina.* Orono: University of Maine at Orono Press, 1981.

Nelson, Paul David. *Francis Rawdon-Hastings, Marquess of Hastings: Soldier, Peer of the Realm, Governor-General of India.* Madison, N.J.: Fairleigh Dickinson University Press, 2005.

Neuffer, Claude Henry, ed. *Names in South Carolina, Vols. I–XII: 1954–1965.* Columbia, S.C.: The State Printing Company, 1967.

Partridge, Paul W. "John Blake White, Southern Romantic Painter and Playwright." Ph.D. dissertation, University of Pennsylvania, Philadelphia, 1951.

Pattillo, Edward. *Carolina Planters on the Alabama Frontier: The Spencer-Robeson-McKenzie Family Papers.* Montgomery: NewSouth Books, 2011.

Pickens, Cathy. *Charleston Mysteries: Ghostly Haunts in the Holy City.* Charleston: History Press, 2007.

Piecuch, James. *Three Peoples, One King: Loyalists, Indians, and Slaves in the Revolutionary South, 1775–1782.* Columbia: University of South Carolina Press, 2008.

Perry, Carolyn, and Mary Weaks-Baxter, eds. *The History of Southern Women's Literature.* Baton Rouge: Louisiana State University Press, 2002.Ramsay, David. *The History of the Revolution in South Carolina: From a British Province to an Independent State.* Vol. 2. Trenton: Isaac Collins, 1785.

Ramsay, David. *The History of the American Revolution.* Vol. 2. London: J. Stockdale, 1793.

Ravenel, Harriott Horry. *Charleston, the Place and the People.* New York: Macmillan, 1922.

Richards, Jeffrey H., and Heather S. Nathans. *The Oxford Handbook of American Drama.* New York: Oxford University Press, 2014.

Ripley, Warren. *Battleground, South Carolina in the Revolution.* Charleston, S.C.: *News and Courier,* 1983.

Ross-of-Bladensburg, John Foster George. *The Marquess of Hastings, K.G.* Oxford: Clarendon Press, 1893.

Sabine, Lorenzo. *Biographical Sketches of Loyalists of the American Revolution with an Historical Essay.* Vol. 2. 1864. Reprint, Port Washington, N.Y.: Kennikat Press, 1966.

Shaffer, Arthur H. *To Be an American: David Ramsay and the Making of the American Consciousness.* Columbia: University of South Carolina Press, 1991.

Shook, John R., ed., *The Dictionary of Early American Philosophers.* 2 vols. New York: Continuum International Publishing Group, 2012.

Simms, William Gilmore. *The History of South Carolina, from Its First European Discovery to Its Erection into a Republic: With a Supplementary Chronicle of Events to the Present Time.* Charleston: S. Babcock, 1840.

Simms, William Gilmore. *The Life of Francis Marion*. New York: G.F. Cooledge, 1844.

South Carolina Institute. *Catalogue of Articles on Exhibition at the Second Annual Fair of the South-Carolina Institute, at the Military Hall, November, 1850*. Charleston: Walker and James, 1850. Copy at the Charleston Library Society (Pamphlets; Willis Pm. 1843–51), Charleston, S.C.

Stedman, Charles. *The History of the Origin, Progress, and Termination of the American War*. Vol. 2. London: Stedman, 1794.

Stephen, Leslie, and Sidney Lee, eds. *Dictionary of National Biography*. 22 vols. New York: Macmillan, 1908–9.

Stokes, Gerald G., Jr. *Letters for Catherine*. Nashville, Tenn.: NorLightsPress, 2009.

Trent, William P. *William Gilmore Simms*. Boston: Houghton, Mifflin, 1892.

Trevelyan, Charles E. *The Purchase System in the British Army*. London: Longmans, Green, 1867.

Upham, Thomas C. *American Cottage Life*. 2nd ed. Brunswick, Me.: Joseph Griffin, 1850–51.

Urban, Mark. *Fusiliers: The Saga of a British Redcoat Regiment in the American Revolution*. New York: Walker, 2007.

Watson, Charles S. *From Nationalism to Secessionism: The Changing Fiction of William Gilmore Simms*. Westport, Conn: Greenwood Press, 1993.

Wells, William Charles. *Two Essays: One upon Single Vision with Two Eyes; the Other on Dew*. London: Archibald Constable, 1818.

Wickwire, Franklin B., and Mary Wickwire. *Cornwallis and the War of Independence*. London: Faber and Faber, 1971.

Wickwire, Franklin B., and Mary Wickwire. *Cornwallis, the Imperial Years*. Chapel Hill: University of North Carolina Press, 1980.

Wigg, William Hazzard, II. *A Brief Memoir of the Life, and Revolutionary Services, of Major William Hazzard Wigg, of South Carolina*. Washington: C. Alexander, 1860.

Willcox, William Bradford. *Portrait of a General: Sir Henry Clinton in the War of Independence*. New York: Knopf, 1964.

Williams, George W. *Early Ministers at St. Michael's, Charleston*. Charleston: Dalcho Historical Society, 1961.

Wilson, David K. *The Southern Strategy: Britain's Conquest of South Carolina and Georgia, 1775–1780*. Columbia: University of South Carolina Press, 2005.

Zepke, Terrance. *Ghosts and Legends of the Carolina Coasts*. Sarasota, Fla.: Pineapple Press, 2005.

Articles from Journals, Magazines, and Periodicals

"Anecdote of War." *Supplement to the Connecticut Courant* 4, no. 32 (May 9, 1836): 255–56.

Barnwell, Joseph W. "Dr. Henry Woodward, the First English Settler in South Carolina, and Some of His Descendants." *South Carolina Historical and Genealogical Magazine* 8, no. 1 (1907): 29–41.

Billias, George Athan. Review of *The Execution of Isaac Hayne*, by David K. Bowden. *Journal of American History* 65, no. 1 (1978): 139–40.

Borick, Carl P. Review of *The Cornwallis Papers: The Campaigns of 1780 and 1781 in the Southern Theatre of the American Revolutionary War* by Ian Saberton. *South Carolina Historical Magazine* 112, no. 1/2 (2011) : 88–90.

Calhoon, Robert M., and Robert M. Weir. "The Scandalous History of Sir Egerton Leigh." *William and Mary Quarterly*, 3rd ser., vol. 26, no. 1 (1969): 47–74.

"Col. Isaac Haynes." In John Farmer, ed., *Collections, Historical and Miscellaneous* 3 (May 1824): 152–53.

"Colonel Isaac Hayne." *Army and Navy Chronicle, and Scientific Repository* 2, no. 11 (1836): 161–62.

Conway, Stephen. "To Subdue America, British Army Officers and the Conduct of the Revolutionary War." *William and Mary Quarterly,* 3rd ser., vol. 43, no. 3 (1986): 381–407.

Cowan, Thomas. "William Hill and the Aera Ironworks." *Journal of Early Southern Decorative Arts* 13, no. 2 (1987): 1–31.

Crary, Catherine Snell. "The Tory and the Spy: The Double Life of James Rivington." *William and Mary Quarterly,* 3rd ser., vol. 16, no. 1 (1959): 61–72.

Daso, Dik Alan. "Colonel William Harden: The Unsung Partisan Commander." *Proceedings of the South Carolina Historical Association* (1995): 95–111.

Davis, Mary Katherine. "The Feather Bed Aristocracy: Abbeville District in the 1790s." *South Carolina Historical Magazine* 80, no. 2 (1979): 136–55.

Dawson, Henry B., ed. "Lord Rawdon and the Duke of Richmond, on the Execution of Colonel Isaac Hayne." *Historical Magazine,* 1st ser., vol. 10, no. 9 (1866): 269–72.

Fenhagen, Mary Pringle. "John Edwards and Some of His Descendants." *South Carolina Historical Magazine* 55, no. 1 (1954): 15–27.

"Fourth (or the King's Own) Regiment of Foot." *United Service Journal and Naval and Military Magazine.* 1830, part 2: 558–67.

Franklin, John Hope. "The North, the South, and the American Revolution." *Journal of American History* 62, no. 1 (1975): 5–23.

Gage, Matilda Jocelyn. "Woman as Inventor." *North American Review* 136, no. 318 (1883): 478–89.

Gibson, James E. "Benjamin Rush's Apprenticed Students." *Transactions and Studies of the College of Physicians of Philadelphia,* 4th series, vol. 14, no. 3 (1946): 127–32.

Hayne, Isaac W. "Colonel Isaac Hayne." *Historical Magazine,* 2nd ser., vol. 2, no. 2 (1867): 76–78.

Hayne, Robert Young. "The Execution of Colonel Isaac Hayne." *Southern Review* 1 (February and May 1828): 70–106.

Higginbotham, Don. Review of *The Execution of Isaac Hayne,* by David K. Bowden. *South Carolina Historical Magazine* 79, no. 2 (1978): 151.

"Historical Notes." *South Carolina Historical and Genealogical Magazine* 6, no. 4 (1905): 1770–81.

Hutson, William Maine. "The Hutson Family of South Carolina." *South Carolina Historical and Genealogical Magazine* 9, no. 3 (1908): 127–40.

Jervey, Theodore D. "The Hayne Family." *South Carolina Historical and Genealogical Magazine* 5, no. 3 (1904): 168–88.

Knight, Betsy. "Prisoner Exchange and Parole in the American Revolution." *William and Mary Quarterly,* 3rd ser., vol. 48, no. 2 (1991): 201–22.

Lander, Ernest M., Jr. "The Iron Industry in Ante-Bellum South Carolina." *Journal of Southern History* 20, no. 3 (1954): 337–55.

Levett, Ella Pettit. "Loyalism in Charleston, 1761–1784." *Proceedings of the South Carolina Historical Association* 6 (1936): 3–17.

"Mr. Simms's Katherine Walton." *Literary World* 9, no. 243 (1851): 244–45.

Okker, Patricia. "Gender and Secession in Simms's *Katharine Walton.*" *Southern Literary Journal* 29, no. 2 (1997): 17–31.

Poe, Edgar A., and Roger Butterfield. "George Lippard and His Secret Brotherhood." *Pennsylvania Magazine of History and Biography* 79, no. 3 (1955): 285–309.

Ranlet, Philip. "In the Hands of the British: The Treatment of American POWs during the War of Independence." *Historian* 62, no. 4 (2000): 731–58.

Salley, Alexander S., Jr. "Capt. John Colcock and Some of His Descendants." *South Carolina Historical and Genealogical Magazine* 3, no. 4 (1902): 216–41.

Simms, William Gilmore. "Battle of Fort Moultrie." *The Southern Literary Gazette* 1, no. 6 (1829): 137–43.

Simms, William Gilmore. Review of *Women of the American Revolution,* by Elizabeth F. Ellet. *Southern Quarterly Review,* 2nd ser., vol. 1, no. 2 (1850): 314–54.

Simms, William Gilmore. "Hayne: A Dirge." *Russell's Magazine* 4, no. 3 (1858): 247–48.

"The Society." *South Carolina Historical Magazine* 75, no. 1 (1974): 61–63.

Stevens, John Austin. "The Allies at Yorktown, with Appendix." *Magazine of American History: With Notes and Queries* 6, no. 1 (1881): 1–53.

Turner, Mary Ellen. "John Blake White: An Introduction." *Journal of Early Southern Decorative Arts* 16, no. 1 (1990): iv–17.

Upham, Thomas C. "Influence of War on Domestic Life." *Advocate of Peace* 1, no. 2 (1934): 57–64.

Webber, Mabel L. "Moore of St. Thomas' Parish." *South Carolina Historical and Genealogical Magazine* 27, no. 3 (1926): 156–69.

Wyatt, Frederick, and William Bradford Willcox. "Sir Henry Clinton: A Psychological Exploration in History." *William and Mary Quarterly,* 3rd ser., vol. 16, no. 1 (1959): 3–26.

Index

Page numbers in italic type indicate illustrations.